INDEX OF ORAL HISTORIES RELATING TO NAVAL RESEARCH AND DEVELOPMENT

CAROLE ELIZABETH NOWICKE
DAVID K. ALLISON
PETER S. BUCHANAN

NIMBLE BOOKS LLC: THE AI LAB FOR BOOK-LOVERS

Humans and AI making books richer, more diverse, and more surprising.

PUBLISHING INFORMATION

(c) 2023 Nimble Books LLC
ISBN: 9781934840931

AI-GENERATED KEYWORD PHRASES

Oral histories; U.S. Navy research and development;
Interviewees;
Indices;
Contact points;
First edition;
Updated version;
Historian of Navy Laboratories; D.K. Allison;
Guide improvement suggestions;
Navy research and development;
Institutions and cities;
Wide range of topics;
Three indices;
Contact information;
Material repositories;

ABOUT THE AI LAB FOR BOOK-LOVERS

This annotated edition illustrates the capabilities of the AI Lab for Book-Lovers to add context and ease-of-use to manuscripts. It includes five types of abstracts, building from simplest to more complex: TLDR (one word), ELI5, TLDR (vanilla), Scientific Style, and Action Items; four essays to increase viewpoint diversity: Grounds for Dissent; Red Team Critique; and MAGA Perspective.

It should be understood that this selection of annotations is experimental, and the results vary in quality. As time moves forward, new features will be added, others dropped, and all will be improved. Feedback is very welcome to wfz@nimblebooks.com.

PUBLISHER'S NOTE

This publication is dedicated to my grandfather and namesake, William Zimmerman III, who worked as a research scientist for the Naval Research Laboratory for many years. His 1947 publication for NRL, *The Determination of Some Common Alloying Elements in Aluminum and Its Alloys,* is included as Appendix A.

FRONT AND BACK MATTER

ABSTRACTS

TL;DR (ONE WORD)

Oral histories.

EXPLAIN IT TO ME LIKE I'M FIVE YEARS OLD

This document is like a special book that tells us about the history of the U.S. Navy and how they made new things. It has interviews with people who were a part of the Navy's research and development. It also has a list of important people who were interviewed, three lists that help us find information easily, and a list of places where we can find more of these interviews. The book is the first edition, which means it's the first version, and there might be more versions coming.

TL;DR (VANILLA)

This document is a guide to oral histories related to U.S. Navy research and development. It includes interviews, indices, and contact information for repositories holding the material. It covers various topics and may be updated in the future.

SCIENTIFIC STYLE

This document serves as a guide to oral histories related to U.S. Navy research and development. It includes a list of interviewees, three indices, and contact information for repositories holding the material. The guide is a first edition and may be updated in the future. It provides a comprehensive overview of the topics covered, including interviews with individuals involved in Navy research and development, discussions about institutions and cities, and other subjects. The document aims to facilitate access to the oral histories and serve as a resource for researchers interested in this field.

ACTION ITEMS

Read the message from the Historian of Navy Laboratories, D.K. Allison, to gain a better understanding of the purpose and importance of the oral histories.

Review the list of interviewees to identify individuals of interest or relevance to your research or project.

Explore the three indices to locate specific topics or subjects that you are interested in.

Take note of the contact points at repositories holding the material, as they may be valuable resources for accessing the oral histories.

Consider the suggestions for improving the guide and provide feedback if applicable.

VIEWPOINTS

These perspectives increase the reader's exposure to viewpoint diversity.

GROUNDS FOR DISSENT

Lack of Inclusion: One possible reason for dissent from this report could be the belief that the guide is not inclusive enough in terms of the interviewees and topics covered. The dissenter may argue that by only including interviews related to Navy research and development, other important perspectives and voices are being excluded. They might believe that a more comprehensive approach would provide a more holistic understanding of the historical context.

Limited Scope: Another reason for dissent could be the perception that the guide has a limited scope. The dissenter might argue that by focusing solely on oral histories related to U.S. Navy research and development, other significant aspects of naval history are being overlooked. They may advocate for a broader range of topics and themes to be incorporated into the guide, such as discussions on social impact, environmental concerns, or cultural perspectives.

Biased Perspective: A dissenting view could also arise from concerns about bias within the guide. The dissenter might argue that the guide only presents a particular perspective on Navy research and development, potentially neglecting alternative viewpoints or critical analysis. They may believe that a more balanced approach, highlighting both successes and failures, would provide a more accurate representation of the subject matter.

Incomplete Representation: Another substantive reason for dissent could be the perception that the guide does not adequately represent the diversity of experiences within Navy research and development. The dissenter might argue that certain marginalized groups or individuals are underrepresented or overlooked in the interviews included. They may advocate for a more inclusive approach that ensures a broader range of voices are heard and represented in the guide.

Lack of Transparency: Lastly, a dissenter could raise concerns about the lack of transparency or accountability in the creation of the guide. They might question the selection process for interviewees, the criteria used for inclusion or exclusion, and the potential biases of the individuals responsible for compiling the guide. They may believe that without greater transparency, the guide cannot be considered a reliable or comprehensive resource.

Overall, these hypothetical reasons for dissent highlight the importance of considering diverse perspectives, inclusivity, and transparency when creating historical documents. By addressing these concerns, the organization responsible for the report can ensure a more comprehensive and accurate representation of the subject matter at hand.

RED TEAM CRITIQUE

The overall structure and organization of the document are commendable. The inclusion of a list of interviewees and contact points at repositories holding the material is valuable for researchers looking to access the oral histories related to Navy research and development. The three indices provide a helpful way to navigate through the document and find specific information easily.

However, there are a few areas in which the guide could be improved. Firstly, the message from the Historian of Navy Laboratories, D.K. Allison, could be more concise and focused. While it is important to provide an introduction from a reputable source, the message should be clear and succinct, highlighting the significance and relevance of the oral histories for Navy research and development.

Additionally, the list of suggestions for improving the guide could be expanded upon. While it is helpful to acknowledge that the guide may be updated in the future, there should be specific recommendations for how the guide could be enhanced. This could include suggestions such as adding additional interviews or expanding the range of topics covered.

Furthermore, the guide could benefit from a more detailed overview of the topics covered in the oral histories. While it is mentioned that the interviews encompass a wide range of subjects, providing a brief summary or categorization of these topics would help users understand the breadth of information available.

Another area that could be improved is the presentation of the contact information for repositories holding the material. It would be helpful to provide more context or additional guidance on how to access the material at these repositories, especially for researchers who may be unfamiliar with the process.

Lastly, the document should provide a clear indication of how often and when the guide will be updated in the future. This will ensure that researchers are aware of potential updates and can access the most current version of the guide.

Overall, the guide provides valuable information for accessing oral histories related to Navy research and development. With some improvements to the message from the Historian, suggestions for improvement, overview of topics covered, presentation of contact information, and clarification on future updates, the guide would be even more effective in serving its intended purpose.

MAGA PERSPECTIVE

This document is just another example of the deep state's attempt to rewrite history and push its liberal agenda. The fact that it includes a message from the Historian of Navy Laboratories, D.K. Allison, shows that this guide is nothing more than a tool for indoctrination. We all know that government historians are biased and only interested in promoting their own narrative.

Furthermore, why should we trust a first edition that may be updated in the future? [1] It's clear that they can't even get their facts straight and need constant revisions. This just goes to show that this document is not based on solid evidence or research, but rather on the whims of whoever is in charge at the moment.

The guide's coverage of a wide range of topics is nothing more than an attempt to distract and confuse readers. Instead of focusing on important issues like national security and American exceptionalism, it wastes time

---

[1] An innovative argument from the AI.—Ed.

on interviews about institutions and cities. Who cares about these trivial matters when there are real threats facing our country?

And let's not forget the bias in the indices. I'm sure they cherry-picked interviewees who align with their liberal agenda, leaving out any voices that might challenge their narrative. This is just another example of how the left controls the narrative and silences anyone who dares to speak out against them. We must reject their attempts to rewrite history and instead focus on making America great again!

DAVID W. TAYLOR NAVAL SHIP
RESEARCH AND DEVELOPMENT CENTER

Bethesda, Maryland 20084-5000

INDEX OF ORAL HISTORIES RELATING TO

NAVAL RESEARCH AND DEVELOPMENT

by

Carole Elizabeth Nowicke
David K. Allison
Peter S. Buchanan

APPROVED FOR PUBLIC RELEASE· DISTRIBUTION UNLIMITED

SUPPORT AND ADMINISTRATIVE SERVICES DEPARTMENT
NAVAL MATERIAL COMMAND HISTORICAL REPORT

DTIC
SELECTED
JUN 1 3 1985

January 1985

DTNSRDC-85/CT02

85 5 24 140

MAJOR DTNSRDC ORGANIZATIONAL COMPONENTS

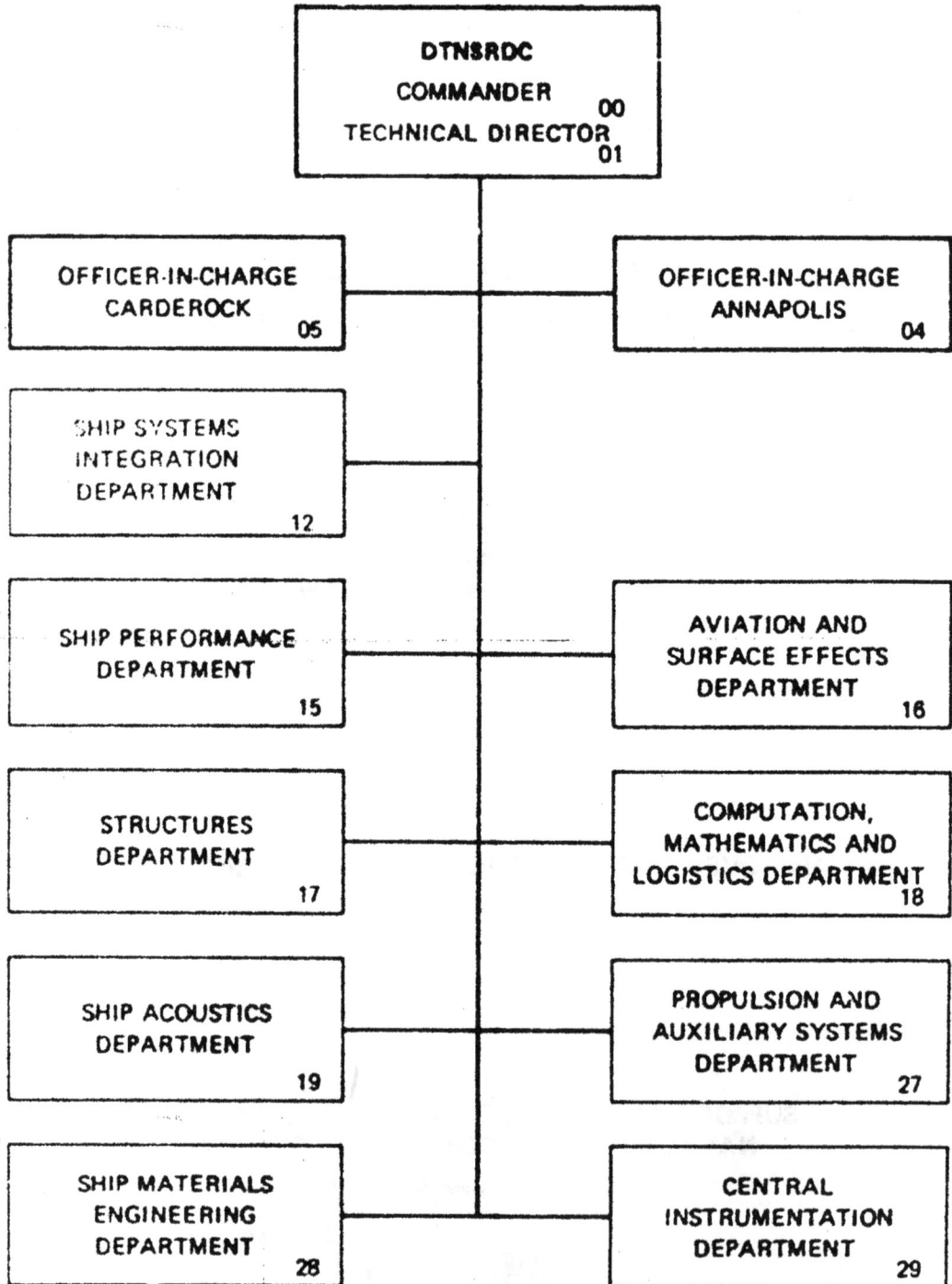

```
                    ┌─────────────────────────┐
                    │        DTNSRDC          │
                    │       COMMANDER      00 │
                    │  TECHNICAL DIRECTOR  01 │
                    └─────────────────────────┘
                                 │
   ┌─────────────────────────┐   │   ┌─────────────────────────┐
   │   OFFICER-IN-CHARGE      │   │   │   OFFICER-IN-CHARGE      │
   │      CARDEROCK       05  │───┤   │      ANNAPOLIS       04  │
   └─────────────────────────┘   │   └─────────────────────────┘
                                 │
   ┌─────────────────────────┐   │
   │     SHIP SYSTEMS        │   │
   │     INTEGRATION         │───┤
   │    DEPARTMENT       12   │   │
   └─────────────────────────┘   │
                                 │
   ┌─────────────────────────┐   │   ┌─────────────────────────┐
   │   SHIP PERFORMANCE      │   │   │     AVIATION AND         │
   │    DEPARTMENT       15  │───┼───│   SURFACE EFFECTS        │
   └─────────────────────────┘   │   │   DEPARTMENT         16  │
                                 │   └─────────────────────────┘
   ┌─────────────────────────┐   │   ┌─────────────────────────┐
   │     STRUCTURES          │   │   │    COMPUTATION,          │
   │     DEPARTMENT      17  │───┼───│  MATHEMATICS AND         │
   └─────────────────────────┘   │   │ LOGISTICS DEPARTMENT 18  │
                                 │   └─────────────────────────┘
   ┌─────────────────────────┐   │   ┌─────────────────────────┐
   │   SHIP ACOUSTICS        │   │   │   PROPULSION AND         │
   │    DEPARTMENT       19  │───┼───│  AUXILIARY SYSTEMS       │
   └─────────────────────────┘   │   │   DEPARTMENT         27  │
                                 │   └─────────────────────────┘
   ┌─────────────────────────┐   │   ┌─────────────────────────┐
   │   SHIP MATERIALS        │   │   │     CENTRAL              │
   │   ENGINEERING           │───┴───│  INSTRUMENTATION         │
   │   DEPARTMENT       28   │       │   DEPARTMENT         29  │
   └─────────────────────────┘       └─────────────────────────┘
```

REPORT DOCUMENTATION PAGE		READ INSTRUCTIONS BEFORE COMPLETING FORM
1. REPORT NUMBER DTNSRDC-85/CT02	2. GOVT ACCESSION NO. AD-A154980	3. RECIPIENT'S CATALOG NUMBER
4. TITLE (and Subtitle) INDEX OF ORAL HISTORIES RELATING TO NAVAL RESEARCH AND DEVELOPMENT		5. TYPE OF REPORT & PERIOD COVERED Final
		6. PERFORMING ORG. REPORT NUMBER
7. AUTHOR(s) Carole Elizabeth Nowicke David K. Allison Peter S. Buchanan		8. CONTRACT OR GRANT NUMBER(s)
9. PERFORMING ORGANIZATION NAME AND ADDRESS David W. Taylor Naval Ship Research and Development Center Bethesda, Maryland 20084-5000		10. PROGRAM ELEMENT, PROJECT, TASK AREA & WORK UNIT NUMBERS Program Element 65681N Task Area Z0832
11. CONTROLLING OFFICE NAME AND ADDRESS Director of Navy Laboratories Naval Material Command Washington, D.C. 20360		12. REPORT DATE January 1985
		13. NUMBER OF PAGES 290
14. MONITORING AGENCY NAME & ADDRESS(If different from Controlling Office)		15. SECURITY CLASS. (of this report) UNCLASSIFIED
		15a. DECLASSIFICATION/DOWNGRADING SCHEDULE

16. DISTRIBUTION STATEMENT (of this Report)

APPROVED FOR PUBLIC RELEASE: DISTRIBUTION UNLIMITED

17. DISTRIBUTION STATEMENT (of the abstract entered in Block 20, if different from Report)

18. SUPPLEMENTARY NOTES

19. KEY WORDS (Continue on reverse side if necessary and identify by block number)

Military History,   Naval Research and Development,
Naval History,   Oral History
Naval Research Laboratories,
Naval Laboratory Management,

20. ABSTRACT (Continue on reverse side if necessary and identify by block number)

This report is a comprehensive index and guide to oral histories on naval research and development. Tapes and transcripts of the interviews, prepared during the past twenty years, are held in Navy, Federal Government, and nongovernmental respositories. Abstracts and indices by name and subject have been prepared for each interview. The report includes contact points at repositories holding the materials, and an acronym and abbreviation list.

cont keywords include:

DD FORM 1473 EDITION OF 1 NOV 68 IS OBSOLETE
1 JAN 73
S/N 0102-LF-014-6601

INDEX OF ORAL HISTORIES RELATED TO

NAVY RESEARCH AND DEVELOPMENT

TABLE OF CONTENTS

INTRODUCTION

This guide resulted from an attempt to locate and describe all oral history interviews related to U. S. Navy research and development that are available in major U. S. repositories. In a sense, it is a companion to the broader U. S. Naval History Sources in the United States (Washington: U. S. Naval History Division, 1979), which primarily covers written documentation in all areas of Naval history, not just research and development.

The listing of an interview in this guide does not guarantee that it will be available to all researchers. Access restrictions vary from repository to repository, and they change over time. The guide indicates only the existence of oral histories. Provisions for access must be determined by contacting the repositories that hold the material.

Oral history has proven an attractive and useful tool for recording the history of Navy research and development. Of the many reasons for this, the most important is that the engineers, scientists, managers, and naval officers who have shaped the field over the years have generally considered technical reports and articles as the principal permanent records of their enterprise. For this material, there are reasonably reliable systems for access and preservation. Papers published in technical journals are indexed and may be identified through the use of abstracting services or on-line searches. The Defense Technical Information Center provides access to most post World War II technical reports written in the defense establishment. And most Navy R&D institutions maintain complete, indexed archival collections of the documentation that they have produced. However, the technical "result" literature, as this is sometimes called, gives a skewed, if not inaccurate picture of how naval research and development has actually evolved. The reason is that technical literature is not designed to give an accurate historical account of how things happened, but rather a logically reconstructed account of why results are valid.

The care that those involved in naval research and development have devoted to preserving their technical publications has not generally extended to preserving good historical records that explain why work was done, how it was supported, how it progressed over time, the false starts encountered, the interpersonal relations that shaped research activities, and so on. One reason is that complete documentation is frequently not generated as programs advance. Throughout history, few technically minded people have felt compelled to maintain accurate diaries, and the routine practice of writing memoranda to file, keeping personal reflections or notes on meetings, or writing detailed, descriptive correspondence to their colleagues has

- v -

largely disappeared. Indeed it is a sad irony that
increasingly less historically valuable documentation is
generated even as the quantity of administrative paperwork
scientists and engineers prepare about their work has
increased. A second, more troubling reason for inadquate
historical documentation is that research and development
institutions have not made serious, professional attempts to
ensure that the records that are prepared are subsequently
identified, catalogued, and preserved so that they remain
available and easily accessible.

Oral history is a valuable, if imperfect, means for
filling some of the consequent gaps in the primary
historical documentation. It is an effective way for
capturing memories individuals have of key events,
reflections on their own actions and motivations and also
those of others, and judgments about the relative
significance of policies, decisions, and interpersonal
relationships. These retrospective views obviously lack the
immediacy and authenticity of primary sources and cannot
replace them. However recollection is far better than
speculation, and used in conjunction with primary source
material, can greatly enrich understanding of the past.

It is for these reasons that oral history has been used
by historians, policy analysts, and management consultants
who have needed, for a variety of different reasons, to
understand aspects of the evolution of Navy research and
development over the past several decades. The interviews
they have conducted vary widely in depth and quality, but
collectively, they are an extremely valuable resource that
should be available to all who need to understand the
subject. Meeting that need is the purpose of this guide.

The index entries should largely be self explanatory.
Each begins with the name of the person or persons
interviewed. A "title" follows, which gives the name of the
interviewer. The remainder of each entry provides
information about the interview, including its date,
documentation, repositories holding it, and, when we were
able to analyze the interview, an abstract and content
analysis. You should note that the index is arranged
alphabetically by name of the individual interviewed. When
multiple interviewees were involved in a single interview,
however, the full citation appears only once in the body.
The text is supplemented by three indices. The first, which
appears at the beginning of the work, is a complete list of
all interviewees. In a sense, it is a table of contents.
The other two indices, which appear at the rear of the
volume, are a name index and a subject index. The name
index includes both the names of interviewees and the names
of individuals who were discussed to a significant degree in
the interviews (the "individuals mentioned" entries in the

body). An * in this index indicates the that the person was actually interviewed, and the page on which the description of the interview begins. The subject index subsumes what, in the body, are broken into the subcategories of subject, institutions, cities, and other added entries. We thought the subcategorization in the body would be helpful to the user, but that multiple indices would be distracting. Finally, the volume includes a list of contact points at the repositories whose collections the guide covers.

This index is a first edition. As oral histories related to Navy research and development continue to be conducted, we hope to prepare revised versions of the guide. If you have suggestions about ways to improve it, or know about oral histories that it does not include but should, please let us know so that we can make subsequent issues better research tools.

D. K. Allison
HISTORIAN OF NAVY LABORATORIES

November 1984

LIST OF INTERVIEWEES

ORAL HISTORY INDEX

Abrams, Robert

Interview of Robert Abrams, conducted by Dr. David K. Allison

Date of Interview: 8210705

Documentation: 2 Tapes, Index 8 pp.

Abstract: Mr. Abrams reviews the history of the Office of the Director of Navy Laboratories, the creation of the office, the first personnel, selection of DNLs, and changes in the office over the past 17 years.

Repositories: DTNSRDC

Individuals mentioned: Kleback, Thomas
Volmut, Rosemary
Gralla, VADM Arthur R.
Towle, CAPT Bernard
Langille, CAPT John
Hughes, David
Johnson, Dr. Gerald
Teller, Dr. Edward
Frosch, Dr. Robert A.
Andrews, CAPT Albert
Smith, Howard
Huang, Theodore S.
Crook, Mary Charlotte
Parrish, CAPT David

Institutions: Bureau of Weapons
Navy Science Assistance Program
Bureau of Ordnance
Bureau of Ships
Naval Material Command
Director of Navy Laboratories
Deputy Chief of Naval Material (**Laboratories**)

Other added entries: Laboratory Management
Dillon Study
Hermann Study
Reduction in Force
Laboratory Consolidations

Adams, A. J.
Baldwin, Dr. Ralph B.
Burke, ADM Arleigh A.
Clement, Lewis M.
Ford, Curry
Hafstad, Dr. Lawrence R.
Hussey, VADM George F.
Minter, Jerry
Offenhauser, William
Pearce, John
Schwede, Harold
Sprague, Robert C.
Trotter, Dr. Herbert

Transcript of Meeting on VT (Proximity) Fuze

Date of Interview: 781117

Documentation: Transcript, 100 pp.

Abstract: This is a transcript of the Annual Conference of the Radio Club of America. The participants reminisce about their roles and the roles of their agencies in the development of the proximity fuze. The manufacturing process was highly compartmentalized, thus many interviews deal with components of the fuze - the batteries and capacitators, and differences in assembly line procedures at plants. ADM Burke discusses the actual use of the fuzes, Dr. Ralph B. Baldwin describes the effect of the fuze on the German war machine, several interviews are about testing at the Naval Proving Ground.

Repositories: NHC, DTNSRDC

Individuals mentioned: Robinson, Dr. Preston
Tuve, Dr. Merle
Parsons, RADM William S.
Brooks, Dr. Lester
Currie, Dr. Lauchlin M.
McPherson, Dr. Herbert G.

Institutions: Applied Physics Laboratory
U. S. Army
Eastman Kodak Company
Naval Proving Ground
Hoover Company
Baldwin Piano Company
McQuay-Norris Corporation
Johns Hopkins University
Office of Scientific Research and Development
Crosley Corporation
Bureau of Ordnance
Department of Terrestrial Magnetism

Subjects: Ordnance
Artillery

Cities: Pearl Harbor, HI.

Other added entries: Proximity Fuze

Adkins, Dr. John

Interview of Dr. John Adkins, conducted by Vincent Ponko, Jr.

Date of Interview: 810409

Documentation: 2 Tapes, Index, Transcript 48 pp.

Interview number: NL-T35

Abstract: Dr. Adkins talks about his first R&D appointment as head of Geophysics at the Office of Naval Research, his promotion to Assistant Chief Scientist of ONR, and studies of R&D during the McNamara Era. He discusses the work of the Naval Research Advisory Committee, the unilinear Navy, and Dr. Chalmers Sherwin and the Sherwin Plan for reorganizing the laboratories of the Department of Defense. Adkins also comments on the role of in-house laboratories in the Navy, the Mansfield Amendment, and the Blue Ribbon Defense Panel. He describes Navy Industrial Funding and Project REFLEX, ONR's relationship with other agencies and military-civilian relationships in the Navy. Adkins explains the impact of the creation of the National Science Foundation on the Office of Naval Research and the effect of centralized management on Navy Research and Development.

Repositories: DTNSRDC

Individuals mentioned: Kennedy, PRES John F.
Sherwin, Dr. Chalmers

Institutions: Office of Naval Research
Naval Research Advisory Committee
National Science Foundation

Other added entries: Glass Report
Unilinear Navy
Blue Ribbon Defense Panel
Mansfield Amendment
Sherwin Plan
Project REFLEX
Navy Industrial Fund

Agnew, Harold

Interview of Mr. Harold Agnew, conducted by Albert B. Christman

Date of Interview: 670100

Documentation: Index, transcript 22 pp.

Interview number: NOTS-75201-S26

Abstract: This interview was originally conducted as background for a biography of RADM William S. Parsons. Mr. Agnew discusses Parsons and Dr. Norman Ramsey at Tinian and the test flights from there. He also reflects on the uses of small nuclear weapons and the communication problems involved.

Repositories: NWC, DTNSRDC, NHC

Individuals mentioned: Parsons, RADM William S.
Ramsey, Dr. Norman

Cities: Los Alamos, NM.
Tinian

Other added entries: Manhattan Project

Alpers, Frederick C.
Fletcher, Dr. Robert C.

Interview of Frederick C. Alpers and Dr. Robert C. Fletcher, conducted by Leroy L. Doig, III.

Date of Interview: 810127

Documentation: Index, transcribed, 89 pp.

Interview number: S-118

Abstract: Mr. Alpers details early missile work on the Bat and Pelican missiles at the National Bureau of Standards. He talks about German contributions to missile research, wartime supply problems, and postwar developments of Bat II and Corvus. Alpers discusses the search for nuclear weapons and the shift in missile research to the Naval Ordnance Laboratory at Corona, California. He mentions the later move of NOL-Corona to the Naval Weapons Center-China Lake and the work on Walleye II and Puma missiles. In addition,

Alpers explains the current trends in R&D and his contributions to the Naval Weapons Center.

Repositories: NWC, DTNSRDC, NHC

Individuals mentioned: McLean, Dr. William B.
Riggs, Leroy

Institutions: Naval Ordnance Laboratory
National Bureau of Standards
Naval Weapons Center

Subjects: Missile Research

Other added entries: Bat II Missile
Corvus Missile
Puma Missile Project
Walleye II Missile Project

Alvarez, Dr. Luis W.

Interview of Dr. Luis W. Alvarez, conducted by Albert B. Christman

Date of Interview: 670300

Documentation: Transcript 32 pp.

Interview number: NOTS-75201-S35

Abstract: This interview was originally conducted as background for a biography of RADM William S. Parsons. Dr. Alvarez assesses Parsons' role in the Manhattan Project, as well as his own. He describes Parsons' missions on the Enola Gay and Parsons' promotion from Captain to Commodore to Rear Admiral. Alvarez also explains the role of the Los Alamos laboratory in atomic research and development.

Repositories: DTNSRDC, NWC, NHC

Individuals mentioned: Parsons, RADM William S.
Oppenheimer, Dr. Robert
Tibbets, COL Paul
Lauritsen, Dr. Charles C.

Institutions: Naval Ordnance Test Station

Cities: Los Alamos, NM.

Other added entries: Manhattan Project

Amlie, Dr. Thomas S.

Interview of Dr. Thomas S. Amlie, conducted by Michelle Ballinger

Date of Interview: 760824

Documentation: Transcript, Index

Interview number: S-109

Abstract: Amlie comments on the qualities the technical director of a laboratory should have, his education, and his military service. He reflects on his career at NWC, first working on the Sidewinder missile and then as technical director. Amlie discusses problems with the Condor and Harpoon missile programs and SARAH, a radar guided version of Sidewinder. He describes his job as Technical Director, his work with the FAA, and his hobbies, including old cars and a penchant for Shakespeare.

Repositories: NWC, DTNSRDC, NHC

Individuals mentioned: Amlie, Dr. June
McLean, Dr. William B.
Wilson, Dr. Haskell G.

Institutions: Naval Weapons Center
Federal Aviation Administration

Subjects: Missile Research

Cities: China Lake, CA.

Other addey entries: Sidewinder Missile Project
Harpoon Missile Project
Condor Missile
SARAH Missile Project
Technical Director

Amlie, Dr. Thomas S.
Cartwright, Dr. Frank W.
Crawford, Jack A.
Donaldson, Earl J.
Schreiber, J. Raymond
Smith, Charles P.
Ward, Dr. Newton E.
Wilson, Dr. Haskell G.
Wilcox, Dr. Howard A.

Group Interview, conducted by William F. Wright and Budd Gott.

Date of Interview: 800314

Documentation: Index, Transcript 101 pp.

Interview number: S-112

Abstract: This is a group discussion on the occasion of the reunion of the Air Ordnance Department at NOTS. The goals of weapon design, Sidewinder from its start to its finished product, and Dr. William B. McLean as Technical Director are discussed. They describe NOTS role in the Korean War, Dr. L. T. E. Thompson's management style, and NOTS' relations with Washington. Also included are sections on the 1967 reorganization of the Navy, R&D at NOTS, Dr. Amlie as Technical Director, and changes in the NOTS-NWC management philosophy.

Repositories: NWC, DTNSRDC, NHC

Individuals mentioned: Amlie, Dr. Thomas S.
LaBerge, Dr. Walter
McLean, Dr. William B.
Parsons, RADM William S.
Smith, Chuck
Thompson, Dr. Louis T. E.
Wilcox, Dr. Howard A.
Wilson, Dr. Haskell G.

Institutions: Naval Ordnance Test Station
Naval Weapons Center

Cities: China Lake, CA.

Other added entries: Sidewinder Missile Project
Korean War
Technical Director

Anderson, Evan

Interview of Mr. Evan Anderson, conducted by Dr. Vincent Ponko, Jr.

Date of Interview: 801104

Documentation: 2 Tapes, Index, Transcript 29 pp.

Interview number: DNL-T29

Abstract: Mr. Anderson describes his work with the government before 1962 at the Franklin Arsenal, Diamond Ordnance Fuze Laboratory, and the Special Assistant to the Chief of Ordnance. He recalls his selection as a staff member in the Office of the Secretary of Defense and his work in the Base Utilization Division. Anderson talks about his transfer to the office of Director of Defense Research and Engineering (DDR&E) in 1966 and his relationships with Dr. Chalmers Sherwin and Dr. Edward Glass. He discusses studies and reports done at DDR&E, his associations with DNL/DLP and ASN (R&D), and military-civilian relationships in R&D. Anderson comments on Navy R&D efforts and opportunities in the McNamara and Laird eras, Congress' role in R&D, and his duties at the National Science Foundation.

Repositories: DTNSRDC

Individuals mentioned: Glass, Dr. Edward
Johnson, Dr. Gerald
Sherwin, Dr. Chalmers

Institutions: National Science Foundation
Director of Navy Laboratories
Director of Laboratory Programs
Assistant Secretary of the Navy (R&D)
Director of Defense Research and Engineering
Franklin Arsenal

Other added entries: Sherwin Plan

Andrews, RADM B. F.

Date of Interview: 740912

Documentation: 2 Tapes

Interview number: BA-22

Repositories: NHC, DTNSRDC

Andrews, Dr. Dan

Interview of Dr. Dan Andrews, conducted by Albert B. Christman

Date of Interview: 780300

Documentation: Transcript 18 pp.

Interview number: DNL-T8-78

Abstract: Dr. Andrews discusses his work at NOTS and NOSC during World War II and after, the differences between wartime and peacetime funding, and bureaucratic problems created by Navy reorganizations. He talks about doing contract work for industry; in particular, compartmentalization and the resulting loss in quality. He mentions profit as industry's motivating factor.

Repositories: DTNSRDC

Institutions: Naval Ocean Systems Center
Naval Ordnance Test Station

Ashworth, VADM Frederick L.

Interview of VADM Frederick L. Ashworth, conducted by Albert B. Christman

Date of Interview: 690410

Documentation: Index, Transcript 98 pp.

Interview number: NWC-75201-S61

Other interview date: 690409

Abstract: This interview was conducted partly as background for a biography of RADM William S. Parsons and partly for inclusion in a history of Navy Research and Development. Ashworth talks about his initial contacts with Parsons, Parsons role in the Manhattan Project, and Parsons' flight to Hiroshima on the Enola Gay. He discusses Parsons' administrative talent and general disposition. Ashworth also comments on industry and the Navy and weapons R&D, the effect of officers' short tours on R&D, and the military-industrial complex. Also included are segments on NWC and Navy R&D, in general.

Repositories: NWC, DTNSRDC, NHC

Individuals mentioned: Blandy, ADM George
Farrell, GEN
Groves, GEN Leslie
Hayward, ADM John T.
McLean, Dr. William B.
McNamara, SECDEF Robert S.
Oppenheimer, Dr. Robert
Parsons, RADM William S.
Ramsey, Dr. Norman
Rivero, ADM Horacio
Sweeney, MAJ Charles W.
Thompson, Dr. Louis T. E.
Tibbets, COL Paul

Institutions: Naval Ordnance Test Station
Naval Weapons Center

Cities: Hiroshima, Japan
Nagasaki, Japan
Tinian
Los Alamos, NM.
China Lake, CA.
Inyokern, CA.

Other added entries: Manhattan Project

Ashworth, VADM Frederick L.

"Nagasaki", conducted by John Burnett

Date of Interview: 560000

Documentation: Transcript 62 pp.

Interview number: S-92

Abstract: VADM Ashworth describes the preparation behind the dropping of the atom bombs on Hiroshima and Nagasaki. He comments on the Hiroshima flight; in particular, the perfect

timing of the run. Ashworth then details the Nagasaki flight
- his role as weaponeer, CAPT Beahan's role as bombardier,
the no drop situation at Krokura, and the flight from there
to Nagasaki. In addition, Ashworth recalls the weather
conditions at Nagasaki, plans to drop the bomb by radar if
necessary, the fuel situation on the plane, and the
emergency landing on Okinawa. Also included are comments on
the roles of GEN Doolittle and GEN Groves and accuracy of
the bomb drop.

Repositories: NWC, DTNSRDC, NHC

Individuals mentioned: Beahan, CAPT
Groves, GEN Leslie
Doolittle, GEN James H.
Parsons, RADM William S.
Sweeney, MAJ Charles W.

Cities: Okinawa, Japan
Nagasaki, Japan
Hiroshima, Japan
Krokura, Japan
Los Alamos, NM.
Potsdam, East Germany

Other added entries: Manhattan Project
Enola Gay

Bainbridge, Dr. Kenneth Tompkins

   Interview of Dr. Kenneth Tompkins Bainbridge

Date of Interview: 600000

Documentation: Transcript 150 pp.

Abstract: Dr. Bainbridge talks of his education and early
research at MIT, the creation of the NDRC Radiation
Laboratory at MIT in 1940, the 1941 technical mission to
England on radar development, and testing the first atom
bomb.

Repositories: COL

Individuals mentioned: Szilard, Dr. Leo
Compton, Karl
Oppenheimer, Dr. Robert
Smyth, Henry D.

Institutions: National Defense Research Committee
Radiation Laboratory

Massachusetts Institute of Technology

Cities: Los Alamos, NM.

Other added entries: Manhattan Project
Radar Research

Baker, Walter L.

Interview of Walter L. Baker, conducted by Richard D. Glasow

Date of Interview: 800818

Documentation: 2 Tapes, Transcript

Abstract: Mr. Baker discusses his career at the Applied Research Laboratory of Pennsylvania State University.

Repositories: ARL

Institutions: Applied Research Laboratory
Ordnance Research Laboratory
Pennsylvania State University

Other added entries: Acoustics Research

Ballentine, ADM John Jennings

Interview of ADM John Jennings Ballentine

Date of Interview: 640000

Documentation: Transcript 758 pp.

Abstract: Of interest in this interview are ADM Ballentine's experiences in testing and development, his work at the Naval Proving Ground and his involvement in the development of the Norden bombsight.

Repositories: COL, NHC

Individuals mentioned: King, FADM Ernest

Institutions: Naval Proving Ground

Cities: Dahlgren, VA.
Pensacola, FL.

Barnaby, CAPT Ralph

   Interview of CAPT Ralph Barnaby, conducted by Albert B.
Christman

Date of Interview: 780400

Documentation: Tape, Transcript 32 pp.

Interview number: DNL-T19-78

Abstract: CAPT Barnaby talks about his background in
aviation, his early days in the Navy, and his duties during
World War I. He discusses inter-war Naval aviation research
and the design and evaluation of aircraft. Barnaby
describes aviation work during World War II and his tenure
as CO of NADC.

Repositories: DTNSRDC

Institutions: Boeing Airplane Company
Naval Aviation Development Center

Other added entries: Commanding Officer

Baum, Dr. William A.

   Interview of Dr. William A. Baum, conducted Dr. David
H. DeVorkin

Date of Interview: 820112

Documentation: Tapes, 1.5 hours, Transcript 26 pp.

Abstract: Dr. Baum discusses his family background and
training, World War II involvement with the Caltech rocket
project, and his career at the Naval Research Laboratory.
At NRL he first worked in fire control, then on constructing
the ultra-violet solar spectrograph for V-2 rocket flights.
He describes technical difficulties with the solar
spectrograph, his contact with von Braun and other German
rocket scientists, V-2 firings at White Sands in 1946, co-
workers, his doctoral thesis, and accepting a position at
Mount Wilson observatory.

Repositories: NASM

Tousey, Dr. Richard
Braun, Wernher von
Strong, John
Wood, R. W.
Lyman, Theodore

Institutions: Naval Research Laboratory
California Institute of Technology

Subjects: Astrophysics

Cities: White Sands, NM.

Other added entries: V-2 Rocket
Ultra-Violet Solar Spectrograph
Fire Control

Bastedo, George

   Interview of George Bastedo, conducted by Mickey Strang

Date of Interview: 750416

Documentation: Index, Transcript 13 pp.

Interview number: S-98

Abstract: Mr. Bastedo discusses his work on various missile projects, including Bat, Dove, Petrel, Terrier, and Sidewinder. He describes his work at the Bureau of Standards, the establishment of the Naval Ordnance Laboratory at Corona, CA, and his transfer to the Naval Weapons Center.

Repositories: NWC, DTNSRDC, NHC

Individuals mentioned: Sams, Gerald R.

Institutions: Naval Weapons Center
Bureau of Standards
Bureau of Ordnance
Bureau of Aeronautics

Other added entries: Bat Missile
Dove Missile Project
Sidewinder Missile Project
Petrel Missile
Terrier Missile

Beach, Dr. Eugene H.

Interview of Dr. Eugene H. Beach, conducted by Albert
B. Christman

Date of Interview: 780321

Documentation: Transcript 17 pp.

Interview number: DNL-T12-78

Abstract: Dr. Beach comments on NOL's move to the Navy Yard
in 1941; in particular, on the leadership of Dr. Duncan and
Dr. McLean, on wartime research and development, and on the
commitment of the scientists involved. He talks about the
turnover in personnel after the war and the reduction in
workload in peacetime. Beach discusses the mission of NSWC
and the effort to further define it. He also mentions
duplication in the labs. and describes the consolidation of
NOL and NWL into NSWC in 1974 and subsequent reorganizations. He explains the role of commanding officers
in recent times.

Repositories: DTNSRDC

Individuals mentioned: Bennett, Dr. Ralph
Hartmann, Dr. Gregory
McLean, Dr. William B.
Duncan, Dr.

Institutions: Naval Ordnance Laboratory
Naval Weapons Laboratory
Naval Surface Weapons Center
Washington Navy Yard

Cities: White Oak, MD.
Dahlgren, VA.

Beach, CAPT Edward Latimer

Interview of CAPT Edward Latimer Beach

Date of Interview: 670000

Documentation: Transcript 470 pp.

Abstract: CAPT Beach recalls his World War II submarine service, and the development of atomic submarines.

Repositories: COL, NHC

Individuals mentioned: Rickover, ADM Hyman

Other added entries: Atomic Submarines

Beckmann, CAPT Alcorn G.

Interview of CAPT Alcorn G. Beckmann, conducted by Albert B. Christman

Date of Interview: 680500

Documentation: Index, Transcribed 38 pp.

Interview number: NWC-75201-S53

Abstract: CAPT Beckmann discusses his time at NOTS from June 1946 to June 1947, including comments on the CO, CAPT James Sykes, the effectiveness of the laboratory workforce, and technical/scientific staff. He also describes his pre-NOTS career.

Repositories: NWC, DTNSRDC, NHC

Individuals mentioned: Brode, Dr. Wallace C.
Bush, Dr. Vannevar
Hussey, VADM George F.
Richmond, CDR John
Sage, Dr. Bruce
Sykes, RADM James B.
Thompson, Dr. Louis T. E.
Warner, Dr. Arthur H.

Institutions: Naval Ordnance Test Station

Cities: China Lake, CA.

Bergstralh, Thor

Interview of Thor Bergstralh, conducted by Dr. David H. DeVorkin

Date of Interview: 8300801

Documentation: Tapes, 3.5 hours, Transcript, 70 pp.

Abstract: This interview contains descriptions of Bergstralh's background and schooling, radar school at MIT and Bowdin, his recruitment by NRL after World War II, and interest in upper atmosphere research. He discusses his work on the V-2, procedures at White Sands, co-workers, the Viking and Aerobee projects, rocket impact point prediction systems, cosmic ray research, and the NRL nuclear reactor. He describes his later position at Ford Aeronautics, and Ford's involvement with lunar and planetary exploration.

Repositories: NASM

Individuals mentioned: Rosen, Milton
Alter, Dr. Dinsmore
Blifford, I. H.
Havens, Dr. Ralph J.
Tombaugh, Clyde
Krause, Dr. Ernst H.
Tousey, Dr. Richard

Institutions: Naval Research Laboratory
Massachusetts Institute of Technology
Bowdin
University of Minnesota
Ford Aeronautics

Subjects: Physics
Navigation
Rocketry
Nuclear Reactors
Telemetry

Cities: White Sands, NM.

Other added entries: Ranger Hard Lander
Solar Spectrograph
Lunar Research
Starfish
Cosmic Ray Research
Aerobee Rocket
Viking Rocket
V-2 Rocket
NAVSTAR

Berman, Dr. Alan

Interview of Dr. Alan Berman, conducted by Dr. Vincent
Ponko, Jr.

Date of Interview: 800922

Documentation: 2 Tapes, Index, Transcript 30 pp.

Interview number: DNL-T27

Abstract: Dr. Berman talks about his motivation for
accepting the position as Director of Research, NRL, his
background at Hudson Laboratories, Columbia University, and
the efficiency and productivity of the Navy R&D effort. He
comments on placing Navy labs under the CNM, the
establishment of the DNL/DLP, and military-civilian
relationships in the labs. Berman evaluates the Civil
Service Commission's policies on R&D, compares NRL with
other labs, and describes his personal research and his
management philosophy. He talks about the possible effects
of putting NRL under the DNL, why it wasn't placed there in
1966, and the impact of visiting committees, reviews, and
studies on NRL. He discusses technical guidance from the
higher levels, coordination with other labs, and the use of
colleges and universities. Berman compares the U. S. and
Soviet R&D efforts, describes the Advanced Research Projects
Agency, and suggests changes in the Navy's R&D
organizational approach.

Repositories: DTNSRDC

Individuals mentioned: Probus, Dr. James H.
Lawson, Dr. Joel
Morse, Dr. Robert W.
Smith, Howard

Institutions: Advanced Research Projects Agency
Chief of Naval Material
Director of Navy Laboratories
Director of Laboratory Programs
Naval Research Laboratory
Office of Naval Research

Dr. Alan A. Berman (left) former Technical Director, and Captain Edward E. Henifin, former Commanding Officer of the Naval Research Laboratory.

Berman, Dr. Alan

   Interview of Dr. Alan Berman, conducted by Dr. John A.
S. Pitts, and Dr. David K. Allison

Date of Interview: 821118

Other interview dates: 820603, 820610, and 820619

Documentation: 9 Tapes, 12 Sides, Transcript 140 pp.

Interview number: NRL 1

Abstract: Dr. Berman gives his perspective on Naval R&D
policy making, R&D management initiatives at Hudson
Laboratories and NRL, and Navy R&D requirements from 1952 to
1982. He also discusses the main thrusts of Hudson Labs' and
NRL's research programs.

Repositories: DTNSRDC, NRL

Institutions: Naval Research Laboratory
Hudson Laboratories

Beshany, VADM Philip A.

   Interview of VADM Philip A. Beshany, conducted by Paul
Stillwell

Date of Interview: 771200

Other interview date: 790100

Documentation: Index, Transcript 504 pp, Vol. 2

Abstract: VADM Beshany discusses his command of Submarine
Squadron 4 in the early 1960's during the transition from
diesel to nuclear powered submarines, THRESHER, ground work
involved in setting up bases for Polaris submarines in Rota,
Spain. Director of Submarine Warfare during the development
phases of the the LOS ANGELES class attack submarine, first
Deputy Chief of Naval Operations (Submarine Warfare).

Repositories: USNI, USNA, NWCM, NHC

Individuals mentioned: Zumwalt, ADM Elmo
Rickover, ADM Hyman

Institutions: Deputy Chief of Naval Operations (Submarine Warfare)

Subjects: Nuclear Propulsion

Nuclear Submarines

Other added entries: USS THRESHER
USS LOS ANGELES
Polaris Submarines

Birch, Dr. A. Francis

    Interview of Dr. A. Francis Birch, conducted by Albert
B. Christman

Date of Interview: 710217

Documentation: Index, Transcript 31 pp.

Interview number: NOTS-75201-S79

Abstract: This interview was originally conducted as
background for a biography of RADM William S. Parsons. Dr.
Birch describes his association with Parsons as Head of
Group 01 in the Manhattan Project, an Ordnance liaison. He
discusses Parsons' role as administrator and gunnery expert.
Birch talks about the tests at Muroc and Tinian and the
Hiroshima flight. He comments on his contacts with Parsons
after the war.

Repositories: NWC, DTNSRDC, NHC

Individuals mentioned: Bainbridge, Dr. Kenneth
Parsons, RADM William S.

Cities: Los Alamos, NM.
Tinian
Hiroshima, Japan
Muroc, CA.

Other added entries: Manhattan Project

Black, CAPT Robert G.

Interview of CAPT Robert G. Black, conducted by Roger Kempler

Date of Interview: 820621

Documentation: Index, Transcript 24 pp.

Interview number: NPRDC-4

Abstract: CAPT Black talks about his initial exposure to Naval research, his assignment as Director of the Personnel Research Division of BUPERS, and the organization of Navy personnel research. He examines the research emphasis at NPRDC, Navy attitudes toward personnel research, and CAPT Black's philosophy on the subject. Black describes his major contributions to the Navy Personnel Research Program, changing the physical location of Pers-A3, and officer-civilian reslationships in BUPERS.

Repositories: DTNSRDC, NPRDC

Individuals mentioned: Sjoholm, Dr. Allan A.
Price, D. George

Institutions: Bureau of Naval Personnel
Personnel Research Division
Naval Research Advisory Committee
Navy Personnel Research and Development Center

Other added entries: Personnel Research

Blood, Dr. Howard

Interview of Dr. Howard Blood, conducted by Albert B. Christman

Date of Interview: 780310

Documentation: Transcript 16 pp.

Interview number: DNL-T2-78

Abstract: Dr. Blood talks about the merger which created the Naval Ocean Systems Center and the management problems involved. He discusses the purpose of NOSC and evaluates the products produced.

Repositories: NHC, DTNSRDC

Institutions: Naval Ocean Systems Center
Naval Undersea Center

Other added entries: Laboratory Consolidations

Bodenburg, John

   Interview of John Bodenburg, conducted by Elizabeth Babcock

Date of Interview: 801230

Documentation: Index, Transcript 67 pp.

Interview number: S-115

Abstract: Mr. Bodenburg describes his background, his early work at NWC, and discusses the danger of bureaucratization at a Navy lab. He comments on NWC top management's concern for communication, morale, and productivity and the relationship between the CO and the Technical Director. Bodenburg notes a decline in the amount of innovative research and talks about the advantages of having a Rear Admiral as commander of NWC. He also states that the research end of RDT&E is a low cost, high yield field. Bodenburg explains the changing nature of Naval warfare and the political nature of weapons development. He comments on problems with the new SES system in high management, NWC's relations with Washington, and the spirit of cooperation among the labs.

Repositories: NWC, DTNSRDC, NHC

Individuals mentioned: Freeman, ADM Rowland G.
Harris, ADM William L.
Hillyer, Robert
White, ADM Alfred J., Jr.

Institutions: Naval Weapons Center

Other added entries: Senior Executive Service
Laboratory Management
Weapons Development

Bolt, Dr. Richard Henry

Interview of Dr. Richard Henry Bolt, conducted by Richard D. Glasow

Date of Interview: 800821

Documentation: Tapes, Transcript

Abstract: Dr. Bolt describes his background and education, his work with the OSRD and his research in acoustics.

Repositories: ARL

Individuals mentioned: Knudson, Dr. Vern
Meyer, Irwin

Institutions: Office of Scientific Research and Development
National Defense Research Committee
University of California

Cities: Berkeley, CA.

Other added entries: Acoustics Research

Bowen, Dr. Edward G.

Interview of Dr. Edward G. Bowen, conducted by Dr. David K. Allison

Date of Interview: 790316

Documentation: 4 Tapes (7 Sides), Index, 7 pp.

Interview number: NRL 2

Abstract: Dr. Bowen discusses radar development in England in the 1930's, radar as a source of cooperation and conflict between the United States and England, the development of radar, and radar technology during World War II.

Repositories: NRL

Subjects: Radar Research

Other added entries: Tizard Mission

Bowen, VADM Harold G.

Interview of VADM Harold G. Bowen, conducted by Dr.
Peter Burton and CAPT Robert L. Hansen

Date of Interview: 740000

Documentation: Index, Transcript 45 pp.

Interview number: BA-8

Abstract: VADM Bowen talks about the Navy planning system
for R&D from 1945 through 1958, the DCNO (Dev)'s
responsibilities, and the Development Characteristics
instituted in 1953. In the post-1958 era, Bowen discusses
the DCNO (Dev)'s evaluation of the TDP, OPNAV's size and
consequent inefficiency, and ASN (R&D)'s responsibility for
RDT&E appropriations. He describes DDR&E interference in
some programs, the DCNO (Dev)'s relationship with
Congressional Armed Services Committees, and the Navy's
exclusion from the space program. Bowen notes that creation
of the DNL was seen as an additional act of centralization
and that labs want more independent R&D authority. He also
talks about the difficulty of recruiting good personnel
because of competition from industry.

Repositories: NHC, DTNSRDC

Individuals mentioned: Frosch, Dr. Robert A.
Martell, VADM Charles B.
McNamara, SECDEF Robert S.

Institutions: Deputy Chief of Naval Operations (Development)
Assistant Secretary of the Navy (R&D)
Director of Navy Laboratories
Secretary of Defense
Director of Defense Research and Engineering

Subjects: Research, Development, Test, and Evaluation

Bowen, Harold G., Jr.

Interview of Harold G. Bowen, Jr., conducted by Dr. David K. Allison

Date of Interview: 790423

Documentation: 1 Tape (2 Sides), Index on four 5 x 8 cards.

Interview number: NRL 3

Abstract: This interview concerns the career and activities of VADM Harold G. Bowen, Sr.

Repositories: NRL

Individuals mentioned: Bowen, VADM Harold G.

Bowen, Dr. Ira S.

Interview of Dr. Ira S. Bowen, conducted by Albert B. Christman

Date of Interview: 701005

Documentation: Index, Transcript 33 pp.

Interview number: NWC-75201-S72

Abstract: Dr. Bowen describes his involvement in the rocket program at CalTech, the choice of China Lake, CA., for NOTS, and the first tests at NOTS. He talks about Dr. Charles C. Lauritsen, Dr. Emory Ellis, and Dr. Robert A. Millikan, and comments on his own involvement in the war effort. Bowen details his military contacts at China Lake and recalls the accidents at Eaton Canyon and Kellogg. He also mentions the tests at Goldstone Lake.

Repositories: NWC, DTNSRDC, NHC

Individuals mentioned: Ellis, Dr. Emory L.
Fowler, Dr. William
Lauritsen, Dr. Charles C.
Millikan, Dr. Robert A.

Institutions: Naval Ordnance Test Station

Cities: China Lake, CA.
Goldstone Lake, CA.
Eaton Canyon, CA.

Bowyer, Dr. C. Stewart

Interview of Dr. C. Stewart Bowyer, conducted by
Richard F. Hirsch

Date of Interview: 780728

Documentation: 2 Tapes (4 Sides), Typed notes, 11 pp.

Interview number: NRL 22

Abstract: Dr. Bowyer, an NRL space scientist was
interviewed by Richard Hirsh as part of his research for his
doctoral dissertation on the beginnings of x-ray astronomy.
These tapes were prepared in conjunction with the National
Air and Space Museum (NASM) and the American Institute of
Physics (AIP).

Repositories: NRL, NASM

Institutions: Naval Research Laboratory
National Aeronautics and Space Administration
Lawrence Livermore Laboratory
Lockheed Corporation
National Air and Space Museum
American Institute of Physics

Subjects: Astronomy
X-Ray Astronomy

Other added entries: Neutron Stars
Black Holes

Bradbury, Dr. Norris E.

Notes on Unrecorded Interview of Dr. Norris E.
Bradbury, conducted by Albert B. Christman

Date of Interview: 670123

Documentation: Index, not taped 9 pp.

Interview number: NOTS-75201-S23

Abstract: This interview was originally conducted as
background for a biography of RADM William S. Parsons. Dr.
Bradbury recalls that at NPG-Dahlgren, Parsons stimulated
people in their work and was able to work well with people
of various backgrounds. At the Manhattan Project-Los Alamos,
Parsons contributed "common sense" and was probably second
on command. He and Oppenheimer were natural compliments.

Bradbury also comments on Parsons after the war and, in a general way, on NOTS and the Salt Wells Pilot Plant.

Repositories: NWC, DTNSRDC, NHC

Individuals mentioned: Parsons, RADM William S. Oppenheimer, Dr. Robert

Institutions: Naval Proving Ground

Cities: Los Alamos, NM.
Dahlgren, VA.

Other added entries: Manhattan Project
Salt Wells Pilot Plant

Bramble, Dr. Charles C.

"Dahlgren's First Director of Research: Dr. Charles C. Bramble", conducted by Cynthia Rouse

Date of Interview: 770131

Documentation: Transcript 6 pp.

Note: This interview is Chapter VI of Dahlgren, edited by Kenneth G. McCollum.

Abstract: Dr. Bramble relates his first experiences at Dahlgren, in 1924 when as an instructor at the Naval Postgraduate School he would travel to Dahlgren to observe ordnance testing, his work at Dahlgren in World War II, Dr. L. T. E. Thompson, Nils Riffolt, the Aiken Relay Calculator, NORC, and the MARK I through MARK III calculators.

Repositories: NSWC, DTNSRDC

Individuals mentioned: Thompson, Dr. Louis T. E.
Riffolt, Nils

Institutions: Naval Postgraduate School
Naval Proving Ground

Subjects: Computers
Fire Control Computers
Ordnance

Cities: Dahlgren, VA.

Other added entries: Aiken Relay Calculator
Naval Ordnance Research Calculator

Braun, RADM Boynton L.

"Early Work in Aviation: RADM Boynton L. Braun",
conducted by Jack Brooks, Jr.

Date of Interview: 750509

Documentation: Transcript 23 pp.

Note: This interview is Chapter III in <u>Dahlgren</u>, edited by
Kenneth G. McCollum

Abstract: RADM Braun describes his education and his early
experiences in bombing and fire control, aerial bombing, the
Norden bombsight, Dahlgren in the 1920s and 1930s, and
testing procedures.

Repositories: NSWC, DTNSRDC

Individuals mentioned: Thompson, Dr. Louis T. E.
King, FADM Ernest
Leary, VADM Herbert F.
Schuyler, RADM Garret Lansing
Furlong, RADM William Rea

Institutions: Naval Proving Ground

Subjects: Naval Aviation
Ordnance

Cities: Dahlgren, VA.

Other added entries: Norden Bombsight
Aerial Bombing

Breslow, Arthur

Interview of Arthur Breslow, conducted by Albert B.
Christman

Date of Interview: 661000

Documentation: Index, Transcript 68 pp.

Interview number: NOTS-75201-S17

Abstract: This interview was originally conducted as
background for a biography of RADM William S. Parsons. Mr.
Breslow describes the B-29 tests at Muroc, including

problems with the types of bombs to be loaded and training the crews. He also describes his work on the Manhattan Project; in particular, the day-to-day operations of the base at Los Alamos and the atom bomb test Trinity.

Repositories: NWC, DTNSRDC, NHC

Individuals mentioned: Kistiakowsky, Dr. George B.
Parsons, RADM William S.
Ramsey, Dr. Norman
Thompson, Dr. Louis T. E.

Institutions: Naval Ordnance Test Station

Cities: Muroc, CA.
Los Alamos, NM.

Other added entries: Manhattan Project
B-29 Bomber
Fat Man Bomb
Thin Man Bomb
Trinity Test

Brode, Dr. Wallace C.

   Interview of Dr. Wallace C. Brode, conducted by Albert B. Christman

Date of Interview: 690500

Documentation: Index, Transcript 35 pp.

Interview number: NWC-75201-S66

Abstract: Dr. Brode discusses military-civilian relationships at Navy labs, how he came to NOTS, and his job there. He comments on discrimination problems between officers and civilians, the need for scientists to have a voice in the Navy, and the lack of contact with other scientists outside the labs. Brode also details Forrestal's visit to NOTS, his philosophy toward operating a lab, and the operation of NOTS.

Repositories: NWC, DTNSRDC, NHC

Individuals mentioned: Bush, Dr. Vannevar
Forrestal, SECNAV James
Hussey, VADM George F.
Sykes, RADM James B.
Thompson, Dr. Louis T. E.

Institutions: Naval Ordnance Test Station

Cities: Inyokern, CA.

Brooks, Dr. Harvey

    Interview of Dr. Harvey Brooks, conducted by Richard D. Glasow

Date of Interview: 800820

Documentation: Tapes, Transcript

Abstract: Dr. Brooks describes his background and education, and his work with the Harvard Underwater Sound Laboratory.

Repositories: ARL

Individuals mentioned: Hunt, Prof. Ted
Hickman, Roger

Institutions: National Defense Research Committee
Harvard University
Underwater Sound Laboratory

Cities: Cambridge, MA.

Subjects: Sonar
Solid State Physics

Other added entries: Acoustics Research
Ordnance Research

Bryan, Dr. Glenn L.

    Interview of Dr. Glenn L. Bryan, conducted by Roger Kempler

Date of Interview: 820729

Documentation: Transcript, 26 pp.

Abstract: Dr. Bryan discusses the background of Navy personnel research, personnel research in the 1960s, the relationship of Navy R&D to Navy Objectives, the CO/TD organizational relationship, the Psychological Sciences Division ONR, the "Center of Excellence" as a concept, the NRAC Life Sciences Committee, the establishment of NPRDC, NPRDC becoming a NAVMAT laboratory, Human Factors R&D and

NPRDC, its impact on the fleet, and achievements in its ten years of existence.

Repositories: NPRDC, DTNSRDC

Individuals mentioned: Rigney, Dr. Joseph
Dudek, Dr. Edward
Fields, Dr. Victor
Sjoholm, Dr. Allan A.
Collins, Dr. John J.
Wallace, Dr. Raines
Price, D. George

Institutions: Navy Personnel Research and Development Center
Naval Research Advisory Committee
Office of Naval Research

Other added entries: Personnel Research
Center of Excellence

Burke, ADM Arleigh A.

   Interview of ADM Arleigh A. Burke

Date of Interview: 720900

Documentation: Transcript 36 pp.

Abstract: ADM Burke served as Chief of Naval Operations during the development of the Polaris weapons system. This is one part of a series of seven interviews on concept and development of Polaris program conducted by the U. S. Naval Institute.

Repositories: NHC, NWCM, USNA, USNI

Institutions: Chief of Naval Operations

Subjects: Submarine Launched Ballistic Missiles
Ballistic Missile Submarines
Nuclear Powered Fleet Ballistic Missile Submarines
Fleet Ballistic Missiles
Nuclear Missiles
Weapons Systems

Other added entries: Polaris Program

Burns, Dr. Robert O.

Interview of Dr. Robert O. Burns

Date of Interview: 741111

Documentation: 2 Tapes

Interview number: BA-21

Repositories: DTNSRDC

Burroughs, Kay (Mrs. Sherman E.)

Interview of Mrs. Kay Burroughs, conducted by John D. Gerrard-Gough

Date of Interview: 721101

Documentation: Index, Transcript 19 pp.

Interview number: NWC-75103-S83

Abstract: Mrs. Burroughs explains how she met her husband, the future ADM Burroughs, She comments on the early days of NOTS, social life there, and the men who worked around her husband. She comments on CAPT Duncan, Emory Ellis, and CDR John Richmond.

Repositories: NWC, DTNSRDC, NHC

Individuals mentioned: Duncan, CAPT James
Ellis, Dr. Emory L.
Richmond, CDR John
Burroughs, Kay (Mrs. Sherman E.)
Burroughs, ADM Sherman E.

Institutions: Naval Ordnance Test Station

Burroughs, Mrs. Robert (former Mrs. William S. Parsons)

Interview of Mrs. Robert Burroughs, conducted by Albert B. Christman

Date of Interview: 660421

Documentation: Index, Transcribed 154 pp.

Interview number: NOTS-75201-S10

Abstract: This interview was originally conducted as background for a biography of RADM William S. Parsons. Mrs. Burroughs discusses Parsons' family life, personal characteristics, and decision to enter the Navy. She describes the rapport between Parsons and Dr. L. T. E. Thompson when both were at NPG and Parsons' peculiar ability (for a Navy man) to understand and communicate with scientists. Other sections cover Parsons' work with radar, the proximity fuze, and the atomic bomb, and his relationship with Dr. Robert Oppenheimer. Mrs. Burroughs also relays Parsons' opinion on postwar R&D.

Repositories: NWC, DTNSRDC, NHC

Individuals mentioned: Ashworth, VADM Frederick L.
Fuller, Clarissa Parsons
Parsons, Mrs. William S.
Groves, GEN Leslie
Oppenheimer, Dr. Robert
Parsons, RADM William S.
Thompson, Dr. Louis T. E.

Institutions: Naval Ordnance Test Station
Naval Research Laboratory

Subjects: Radar Research
Atomic Research

Cities: Los Alamos, NM.
Dahlgren, VA.

Other added entries: Manhattan Project
Sidewinder Missile Project
Proximity Fuze

Burroughs, RADM Sherman E.

Interview of RADM Sherman E. Burroughs, conducted by
Albert B. Christman

Date of Interview: 660400

Documentation: Index, Transcript 22 pp.

Interview number: NOTS-75201-S2

Abstract: This interview was originally conducted as
background f r a biography of RADM William S. Parsons. RADM
Burroughs discusses the origin of NOTS, its connections with
CalTech, and the choice of its location. He reminisces on
his work with Dr. L. T. E. Thompson and RADM Parsons and
talks about Parsons' work on the Manhattan Project and the
Proximity Fuze.

Repositories: NWC, DTNSRDC, NHC

Individuals mentioned: Hussey, VADM George F.
Lauritsen, Dr. Charles C.
Parsons, RADM William S.
Thompson, Dr. Louis T. E.

Institutions: Naval Ordnance Test Station
Naval Proving Ground
California Institute of Technology

Cities: Inyokern, CA.
Pasadena, CA.
Dahlgren, VA.

Other added entries: Proximity Fuze
Manhattan Project

Burroughs, RADM Sherman E.

Interview of RADM Sherman E. Burroughs, conducted by
Albert B. Christman

Date of Interview: 661104

Documentation: Index, Transcribed 51 pp.

Interview number: NOTS-75201-S20

Abstract: RADM Burroughs talks about his early career in
aviation ordnance, and his time as a member of VADM Hussey's
staff. Next, he discusses the idea of NOTS as a permanent

The Naval Ordnance Test Station - California Institute of Technology team.
Left to right: Commander John O. Richmond, Dr. Charles C. Lauritsen,
Captain Sherman E. Burroughs, Jr., Commander John T. Hayward,
Dr. William A. Fowler, and Dr. Emory L. Ellis.

R&D facility. He describes the relationship between military
men, engineers, and scientists at NOTS and profiles the
first group of officers stationed at NOTS.

Repositories: NWC, DTNSRDC, NHC

Individuals mentioned: Blandy, ADM George
Byrnes, CAPT James
Duncan, CAPT James
Halsey, ADM William F.
Hayward, ADM John T.
Lauritsen, Dr. Charles C.
Moses, William
Richmond, CDR John
Schoeffel, RADM Malcom F.

Institutions: Naval Ordnance Test Station

Cities: Inyokern, CA.
China Lake, CA.

Other added entries: Naval Aviation
Aviation Ordnance

Byrum, E. T.

Interview of E. T. Byrum, conducted by Richard Hirsh

Date of Interview: 760000

Documentation: Tapes

Repositories: AIP

Camp, Victor W.

Interview of Victor W. Camp, conducted by Roger Kempler

Date of Interview: 820707

Documentation: Index, Transcript 23 pp.

Interview number: NP-3

Abstract: Mr. Camp discusses the Navy's attitude toward
personnel research in the 1940's and 1950's, his association
with ADM Rickover's staff, and the Personnel Research
Division under the Assistant Chief for Personnel -- Plans
and Programs. He talks about R&D budgeting under Pers-A3,

relations between field activities and agencies in Washington, and the effect of personnel research on systems design. Camp describes the role of John J. Collins in the establishment of NPRDC, his own role in planning NPRDC, and his place in the NPRDC organization. He comments on the change in management from BUPERS to the CNM and the improved quality of Navy Personnel Research.

Repositories: NPRDC, DTNSRDC

Individuals mentioned: Price, D. George
Ramses, Dr. Eugene
Collins, Dr. John J.

Institutions: Navy Personnel Research and Development Center
Bureau of Naval Personnel
Chief of Naval Material

Cities: San Diego, CA.

Other added entries: Technical Director
Personnel Research

Carome, Dr. Edward F.

Interview of Dr. Edward F. Carome, conducted by Dr. David K. Allison

Date of Interview: 800805

Documentation: 2 Tapes, 3 sides, Index, 1 p.

Abstract: NRL pioneered in fiber optics research and has been the Navy's lead laboratory for the tri-service Fiber Optics Sensor System (FOSS) development program. Dr. Carome discusses early experiments at NRL's Schlieren laboratory, coworkers, and initial patents for a optical fiber hydrophone.

Repositories: NRL

Institutions: Naval Research Laboratory
Schlieren Laboratory
John Carroll University
Stanford University
Thompson Ramo-Wooldridge Corporation

Individuals mentioned: Davis, Dr. Charles M.
Berman, Dr. Alan

Subjects: Fiber Optics

Other added entries: Fiber Optics Sensor System
Acoustics Research
Fiber Optic Hydrophone
Hydrophones

Carstater, Dr. Eugene D.

Interview of Dr. Eugene D. Carstater, conducted by
Roger Kempler

Date of Interview: 820723

Documentation: Transcript 19 pp.

Interview number: NP-7

Abstract: Dr. Carstater discusses his entry into Navy
personnel research, and the leadership of the Navy personnel
research program. He talks about the organization of Pers-
15, its major accomplishments, and the military staffing
within Pers-15. Dr. Carstater discusses the expansion of
Navy personnel research programs in Washington and San Diego
in the 1960's.

Repositories: NPRDC, DTNSRDC

Individuals mentioned: Price, D. George
Brundage, Dr. Everett G.

Institutions: Navy Personnel Research and Development Center
Bureau of Naval Personnel
Personnel Research Division

Other added entries: Personnel Research

Christman, Albert B.

Interview of Albert B. Christman, conducted by Robert
J. Taormina

Date of Interview: 800108

Documentation: 2 Tapes, Transcript 59 pp.

Interview number: DNL-T-22

Abstract: Mr. Christman discusses pre-World War I R&D --

including the need for R&D work in the Navy, new developments in the Fleet, and means of attracting civilians to Navy research work, and obsolescence of weapons. He also comments on R&D during the two World Wars, particularly scientists' understanding of Fleet needs and the difficulty of getting new technologies introduced into the Fleet. Christman talks about the difficulties involved in R.. planning in the nuclear age, increasing bureaucracy in Navy R&D, and the reorganization of Navy R&D in the mid-1960's.

Repositories: DTNSRDC

Institutions: Systems Commands

Other added entries: Navy Research and Development Bureau System

---

Chubb, Dr. Talbot A.

   Interview of Dr. Talbot A. Chubb, conducted by Richard F. Hirsh

Date of Interview: 760000

Documentation: Tapes

Repositories: AIP

Institutions: Naval Research Laboratory

Subjects: Astronomy

Chubb, Dr. Talbot A.

   Interview of Dr. Talbot A. Chubb, conducted by Richard F. Hirsh

Date of Interview: 780000

Documentation: 2 Tapes (4 Sides), Notes, 17 pp.

Abstract: Dr. Chubb, an NRL space scientist was interviewed by Richard F. Hirsh as part of his research for his doctoral dissertation on the beginnings of x-ray astronomy. These tapes were produced in conjunction with the National Air and Space Museum (NASM) and the American Institute of Physics (AIP).

Repositories: NRL, NASM

Dr. Talbot A. Chubb (left) and Dr. Herbert Friedman shock testing a
Deacon rocket payload.

Institutions: Naval Research Laboratory
National Air and Space Museum
American Institute of Physics

Individuals mentioned: Bowyer, D.. C. Stewart

Subjects: X-Ray Astronomy
Nebulae

Other added entries: Aerobee Rocket
Neutron Stars
Nike-Dan Rockets
ASP Munition

Cleeton, Dr. Claud E.

Interview of Dr. Claud E. Cleeton, conducted by Dr. David K. Allison

Date of Interview: 790122

Documentation: 2 Tapes (4 Sides), list of questions on two 5 x 7 cards

Interview number: NRL-4

Abstract: Dr. Cleeton gives his perspective on Naval electronics research and applications from 1936-1972. Cleeton conducted pioneering research in microwave communications and digital electronic circuits, and directed NRL programs in radar identification, advanced radar development and applications, particularly in relation to the Space Surveillance System.

Repositories: NRL

Institutions: Naval Research Laboratory

Subjects: Radar
Space Surveillance System
Digital Systems
Electronic Equipment
Microwave Communications

Collins, Dr. John J.

    Interview of Dr. John J. Collins, conducted by Roger
Kempler

Date of Interview: 820727

Documentation: Index, Transcript 43 pp.

Interview number: NP-6

Abstract: Dr. Collins discusses key people in the Personnel
Research Division of BUPERS, the Personnel Research Field
Activity, and the attitude of BUPERS toward personnel
research. He talks about supervision of PRFA, differences
between the San Diego and Washington branches of PRFA, and
criticism of the existence of two personnel research units.
Collins talks about new developments in human factors
engineering, growth in personnel research in the 1960's, the
opposition to the formation of NPRDC. He describes his role
in NPRDC's formation, the work of others in its formation,
and his relationship with the Office of Naval Research.
Collins explains the major problems that NPRDC faced at its
inception, NPRDC as a CNM managed lab, and his views on the
possible merger of NPRDC with another lab.

Repositories: NPRDC, DTNSRDC

Individuals mentioned: Price, D. George
Frosch, Dr. Robert A.
Regan, Dr. James J.

Institutions: Navy Personnel Research and Development Center
Personnel Research Field Activity
Personnel Research Division
Bureau of Naval Personnel
Chief of Naval Material
Office of Naval Research

Cities: San Diego, CA.
Washington, DC.

Other added entries: Personnel Research
Human Factors Engineering

Dr. John J. Collins of the Navy Personnel Research and Development Center.

Colvard, Dr. James E.

    Interview of Dr. James E. Colvard, conducted by Dr.
Vincent Ponko, Jr.

Date of Interview: 801103

Documentation: 2 Tapes, Index, Transcript 40 pp.

Interview number: DNL-T28

Abstract: Dr. Colvard describes his first work assignments
at NOTS in the 1950's, his time at the Applied Physics
Laboratory, Johns Hopkins, working on satellite trackers for
nuclear subs, and his return to NOTS in 1962. He talks
about NOTS' relations with Washington, his association with
Exploratory Development projects at China Lake, and the
adverse effects on fire control systems of taking the lab
out of the Naval Ordnance Systems Command. Colvard comments
on CNM command of the labs, the establishment of the Office
of the Director of Navy Laboratories, his promotion to
division head at China Lake, and McLean at NOTS' Technical
Director. He describes his transfer to the Naval Weapons
Center at Dahlgren, VA., in 1969, his promotion to Technical
Director, and the combination of NWC and NOL-White Oak into
one center, the Naval Surface Weapons Center. He explains
the NSWC organization and comments on the problems he had at
NSWC. He talks generally about the Navy in-house laboratory
system as a whole, civilian-military relationships in the
Navy, and the current Navy R&D situation.

Repositories: DTNSRDC

Individuals mentioned: Amlie, Dr. Thomas S.
Gralla, VADM Arthur R.
McLean, Dr. William B.
Smith, Bernard

Institutions: Applied Physics Laboratory
Naval Ordnance Test Station
Director of Navy Laboratories
Naval Surface Weapons Center
Naval Weapons Center

Cities: China Lake, CA.
Dahlgren, VA.
White Oak, MD.

Other added entries: Technical Director
Laboratory Consolidations

Connolly, VADM Thomas

"25 Years of Value"

Date of Interview: 681108

Documentation: Index, transcript 16 pp.

Interview number: S57

Abstract: VADM Connolly makes a testimonial speech to the employees, former employees, and friends of the Naval Weapons Center.

Repositories: NWC, DTNSRDC, NHC

Institutions: Naval Ordnance Test Station
Naval Weapons Center

Cooper, Dr. Eugene P.

Interview of Dr. Eugene P. Cooper, conducted by J. D. Gerrard-Gough

Date of Interview: 751024

Documentation: Index, Transcript 18 pp.

Interview number: 5313 S-101

Abstract: Dr. Cooper remembers the controversy over the location of NOTS and discusses his background in theoretical and nuclear physics. He describes fire control problems with aircraft and tells why he left NOTS. Cooper comments on his time at the University of Oregon and his return to NOTS-Pasadena. He expostulates on underwater ordnance research, his time as Associate Head of the Underwater Ordnance Department, and his feelings about NOTS at China Lake and at Pasadena.

Repositories: NWC, DTNSRDC, NHC

Individuals mentioned: McLean, Dr. William B.
Saylor, William
Thompson, Dr. Louis T. E.

Institutions: Naval Ordnance Test Station

Cities: China Lake, CA.
Pasadena, CA.

Couperus, Pierce G.

Interview of Pierce G. Couperus, conducted by Richard D. Glasow

Date of Interview: 800823

Documentation: Tapes, Transcript

Abstract: Mr. Couperus describes his background and education, and his work with the Harvard Underwater Sound Laboratory.

Repositories: ARL

Individuals mentioned: Smith, Fred

Institutions: Harvard University
Underwater Sound Laboratory

Cities: Cambridge, MA.

Other added entries: Acoustics Research

Cozzens, Ernest G.

Interview of Ernest G. Cozzens, conducted by Leroy L. Doig, III

Date of Interview: 810625

Documentation: Index, Transcript 47 pp.

Interview number: S-126

Abstract: Mr. Cozzens explains his background, his involvement with Sidewinder, and comments on recent developments in air-to-air weaponry. He talks about relationships with contractors, quality control, and the cost and effectiveness of weapons. Cozzens discusses NWC's relationships with other labs and with the Naval hierarchy in Washington and reflects on Tom Amlie's tenure as Technical Director. He lists NOTS/NWC's contributions to the Navy.

Repositories: NWC, DTNSRDC, NHC

Individuals mentioned: Amlie, Dr. Thomas
McLean, Dr. William B.

Thompson, Dr. Louis T. E.

Institutions: Naval Weapons Center
Naval Ordnance Test Station

Other added entries: Sidewinder Missile Project

Crary, Dr. Albert P.

Interview of Dr. Albert P. Crary

Date of Interview: 620000

Documentation: Transcript 87 pp.

Abstract: Dr. Crary talks about his work in oceanography and geophysics, involvement with the IGY, early LORAN and SOFAR, air acoustics and balloons.

Repositories: COL

Institutions: International Geophysical Year

Subjects: Oceanography
Hyperbolic Navigation

Other added entries: Sound Fixing and Ranging
Long Range Navigation

Crosbie, Richard

Interview of Richard Crosbie, conducted by Tom Misa and Ed Todd

Date of Interview: 820703

Documentation: 2 Tapes, Index 4 pp.

Interview number: NADC-5,6

Abstract: Mr. Crosbie talks about the Human Centrifuge at NADC, the dynamic flight simulation of the X-15 Rocket Airplane, Boeing 707, and flight simulation training for the Project Mercury astronauts. He comments on the LBJ Space Center in Houston, Texas, and the development of the NADC in-house computer, Typhoon. Crosbie describes NADC's relations with the University of Pennsylvania, AMAL Projects, and Human Centrifuge projects, including the world's record of 31.25 G's for five seconds, set by R.

Richard Crosbie of the Naval Air Development Center.

Flanagan Gray. He discusses the Directorate Programs and the Systems Approach.

Repositories: NADC, DTNSRDC

Individuals mentioned: Gray, R. Flanagan
Poppin, CAPT Jack R.
Hardy, Dr. James D.

Institutions: Naval Air Development Center
Boeing Airplane Company
Johnson Space Center
American Medical Acceleration Laboratory
University of Pennsylvania
Bureau of Medicine and Surgery

Subjects: Centrifuges
Aerospace Medicine
Space Simulation Chambers
Computers

Other added entries: Systems Approach
Federal Contract Research Centers
Human Centrifuge
Typhoon Project

Cummins, Dr. William E.

   Interview of Dr. William E. Cummins, conducted by Albert B. Christman

Date of Interview: 780328

Documentation: 1 Tape

Repositories: DTNSRDC

Institutions: Naval Ship Research and Development Center

Cummins, Dr. William E.

   Interview of Dr. William E. Cummins, conducted by Dr.
David K. Allison

Date of Interview: 820802

Documentation: 7 Tapes, Index, Transcript 92 pp.

Abstract: Dr. Cummins relates his early training in naval
architecture, working conditions at the Experimental Model
Basin and the David Taylor Model Basin in the 1940's, and
his views on the engineering ability and management style of
CAPT Harold Saunders. He mentions the GUPPY program,
submarine hull design, seaworthiness studies for several
types of ships, describes testing procedures and the Polaris
program in detail, reorganizations during the 1960's and
relations between NAVSEA and DTNSRDC.

Repositories: DTNSRDC

Institutions: David Taylor Model Basin
David Taylor Naval Ship Research and Development Center
Experimental Model Basin
Naval Sea Systems Command
Naval Ship Research and Development Center
Society of Naval Architects
Webb Institute

Individuals mentioned: Ellsworth, William
Janes, Charlie
St. Denis, Manley
Hill, Johnny
Landweber, Dr. Louis
Saunders, CAPT Harold E.
Schoenherr, Dr. Karl E.

Subjects: Cavitation
Hull Design
Hydrodynamics
Hydromechanics
Torpedos
Submarines
Seaworthiness
Waveforms
Waveform Generators

Cities: Washington, DC.
Washington Navy Yard
Carderock, MD.

Other added entries: FIDO Torpedo
Model Basins

Model Testing
Greater Underwater Propulsive Power
Seakeeping
Polaris Program

Custer, CAPT Benjamin Scott

   Interview of CAPT Benjamin Scott Custer

Date of Interview: 650000

Documentation: Transcript, 1,022 pp.

Abstract: Of interest in this interview are CAPT Custer's recollections of his career in early Naval aviation, his flying boat squadron, command of the NORTON SOUND and involvement with the Manhattan project.

Repositories: COL, NHC

Other added entries: USS NORTON SOUND
Naval Aviation
Flying Boats
Manhattan Project

Davis, Dr. Charles M.

   Interview of Dr. Charles M. Davis, conducted by Dr. David K. Allison

Date of Interview: 820701

Documentation: 2 Tapes, Index, 1 p., Transcript of selections from interview "FOSS: A Glance at the Past", 28 pp.

Abstract: NRL pioneered in fiber optics research and has been the Navy's lead laboratory for the tri-service Fiber Optics Sensor System (FOSS) development program. Dr. Davis discusses early experimentation, cultivating support and trying to obtain funding from DARPA, NRL and NAVMAT, how the program was managed, co-workers, and the difficulty of recruiting qualified personnel.

Repositories: NRL

Institutions: Naval Research Laboratory
Defense Advanced Research Projects Agency
John Carroll University

Naval Material Command
Office of Naval Research
Thompson Ramo-Wooldridge Corporation

Individuals mentioned: Berman, Dr. Alan
Bucaro, Joe
Carome, Dr. Edward F.
Donovan, Jack
Giallorenzi, Dr. Thomas G.
Henifin, CAPT Edward E.
Probus, Dr. James H.
Shajenko, Peter
Windsor, Harry

Subjects: Fiber Optics
Hydrophones
Hydroacoustics

Other added entries: Systems Commands
Fiber Optics Sensor System
Fiber Optic Hydrophone

Diehl, CAPT Walter S.

Interview of CAPT Walter Stuart Diehl

Date of Interview: 650000

Documentation: Transcript 93 pp.

Abstract: CAPT Diehl recalls his work in aerodynamics and aeronautics, designing and testing Navy airplanes, his participation in World Wars I and II, and his work at the David Taylor Model Basin.

Repositories: COL, NHC

Institutions: Experimental Model Basin
David Taylor Model Basin

Subjects: Aerodynamics
Aeronautics

Cities: Pensacola, FL.

Other added entries: Aircraft Design
Naval Aviation

DiPol, C. John

   Interview of C. John DiPol, conducted by Leroy L. Doig
III

Date of Interview: 810209

Documentation: Index, Transcript 23 pp.

Interview number: S-119

Abstract: Mr. DiPol comments on his arrival at NWC, the
mission of the ranges, and range improvements. He mentions
changes in NWC work, trends for the future, and NWC
relationships with other agencies and labs. DiPol discusses
the contributions of NWC, his personal philosophy on the
RDT&E environment, and the people that make up China Lake
and its surrounding communities.

Repositories: NWC, DTNSRDC, NHC

Individuals mentioned: McLean, Dr. William B.

Institutions: Naval Weapons Center

Drummeter, Dr. Louis F.

   Interview of Dr. Louis F. Drummeter, conducted by Dr.
David K. Allison

Date of Interview: 791220

Other interview dates: 800114 and 800118

Documentation: 6 Tapes (7 Sides)

Abstract: Dr. Drummeter gives his perspective on NRL optic
tests and on organization and management of NRL research
programs. Drummeter played a key role in the development
of NRL's programs in optical science and technology, in
particular optical radiometry, quantum optics, and high-
energy lasers. The interviews are supplemented by a
collection of papers.

Repositories: NRL

Institutions: Naval Research Laboratory

Subjects: Optical Radar
Radiometry
High Energy Laser

Other added entries: Quantum Optics

Duncan, ADM Donald

Interview of ADM Donald Duncan

Date of Interview: 640000

Documentation: Transcript 981 pp.

Abstract: ADM Duncan reminisces about his education at the University of Michigan and the Naval Academy, his service in World War I and early Naval aviation, his experience in ordnance and communications, work in the BUAER Plans Division, his involvement in the Manhattan Project and NACA.

Repositories: COL, NHC

Institutions: National Advisory Committee on Aeronautics
Bureau of Aeronautics

Subjects: Missiles

Cities: Pensacola, FL.

Other added entries: Manhattan Project
Naval Aviation

Duncan, CAPT James

Interview of CAPT James Duncan, conducted by Albert B. Christman

Date of Interview: 660426

Documentation: Index, Transcript 61 pp., Appendix 7 pp.

Interview number: NOTS-75201-S9

Abstract: CAPT Duncan describes the building and equipping of NOTS in Inyokern, CA. He discusses how Prof. Michelson came to work there, Dr. Louis T. E. Thompson's influence, and CAPT Burroughs' tenure as commanding officer.

Repositories: NWC, DTNSRDC, NHC

Individuals mentioned: Burroughs, ADM Sherman E.
Byrnes, CAPT James
Hayward, ADM John T.

McLean, Dr. William B.
Thompson, Dr. Louis T. E.

Institutions: Naval Ordnance Test Station
Naval Proving Ground

Cities: Dahlgren, VA.
Inyokern, CA.

Dunlap, Jack

   Interview of Jack Dunlap

Date of Interview: 721000

Documentation: Transcript 32 pp.

Abstract: Mr. Dunlap was a member of the civilian steering committee for Polaris. This is one of a series of seven interviews on concept and development of Polaris program conducted by the U. S. Naval Institute Oral History Program.

Repositories: NHC, NWCM, USNA, USNI

Subjects: Submarine Launched Ballistic Missiles
Fleet Ballistic Missiles
Ballistic Missile Submarines
Nuclear Powered Fleet Ballistic Missile Submarines
Nuclear Missiles
Weapons Systems

Other added entries: Polaris Program

Ebaugh, Paul

   Interview of Paul Ebaugh, conducted by Richard D. Glasow

Date of Interview: 800715

Documentation: Tapes, Transcript

Abstract: Mr. Ebaugh describes his background and education, his work with the Harvard Underwater Sound Laboratory, and the Applied Research Laboratory.

Repositories: ARL

Institutions: Harvard University
Underwater Sound Laboratory

- 51 -

Ordnance Research Laboratory
Applied Research Laboratory
Pennsylvania State University

Other added entries: Acoustics Research
Ordnance Research

Ebbert, CAPT Edwin L.

   Interview of CAPT Edwin L. Ebbert, conducted by Dr.
John A. S. Pitts

Date of Interview: 820622

Documentation: 2 Tapes (4 Sides), Index 4 pp.

Abstract: CAPT Ebbert discusses NRL's Commanding Officers
and Technical Directors and reflects upon the problems
involved when translating Navy operational needs into R&D
programs.

Repositories: NRL

Institutions: Naval Research Laboratory

Ekas, RADM Claude P.

   Interview of RADM Claude P. Ekas, conducted by CAPT
Robert L. Hansen

Date of Interview: 750000

Documentation: 1 Tape, Index, Transcript 42 pp.

Interview number: BA-13

Abstract: RADM Ekas discusses the project history of the
Harpoon missile, NAVAIR-NAVORD cooperation on the project,
and communication between the Harpoon Program Managers and
the technical workers involved. He talks about the problems
of coordination between the SYSCOM commander, CNM, and CNO.
He also comments on major trends in Navy R&D, including
SARS, SYSCOM and CNM methods of program management, and
cradle-to-grave technical continuity.

Repositories: NHC, DTNSRDC

Individuals mentioned: McNamara, SECDEF Robert S.

Institutions: Chief of Naval Operations
Bureau of Aeronautics
Bureau of Ordnance

Other added entries: Harpoon Missile Project
Selected Acquisition Reporting System

Ellis, Dr. Emory L.

Interview of Dr. Emory L. Ellis, conducted by Albert B. Christman

Date of Interview: 680500

Documentation: Index, Transcript 43 pp.

Interview number: NWC-75201-S54

Abstract: Dr. Ellis describes his own background as a biochemist at CalTech, his assignment to Eaton Canyon, and his experiences at Goldstone Lake. He discusses how he came to be at NOTS, the first rocket tests there, and the camp's facilities. Ellis comments on the establishment of NOTS, the location of the lab, its military direction, and its transition to a civil service operation.

Repositories: NWC, DTNSRDC, NHC

Individuals mentioned: Burroughs, ADM Sherman E.
McClaren, CDR

Institutions: Naval Ordnance Test Station
California Institute of Technology

Cities: Inyokern, CA.
Goldstone Lake, CA.
Eaton Canyon, CA.

Dr. Emory L. Ellis (left) and Haskell G. Wilson of the Naval Ordance
Test Station.

Ellis, Dr. Emory L.
Ellis, Marion (Mrs. Emory L.)

Interview of Dr. Emory and Marion Ellis, conducted by
J. D. Gerrard-Gough

Date of Interview: 721100

Documentation: Index, Transcript 31 pp.

Interview number: NWC-75201-S84

Abstract: Dr. and Mrs. Ellis discuss the transfer of
management at NOTS from CalTech to the Navy in late 1944,
the problem of military-civilian relationships, and the
command of CAPT Sykes. They talks about NOTS' principles of
operation and the turnover in personnel. The Ellises
comment on the work of Dr. Louis T. E. Thompson, facilities
at NOTS, and research on submarine guns and rockets. They
also describe living conditions at China Lake and the White
Star Mine.

Repositories: NWC, DTNSRDC, NHC

Individuals mentioned: Beckmann, CAPT Alcorn G.
Armitage, LT John M.
Burroughs, ADM Sherman E.
Hayward, ADM John T.
Hussey, VADM George F.
Lauritsen, Dr. Charles C.
Sykes, RADM James B.
Thompson, Dr. Louis T. E.

Institutions: Naval Ordnance Test Station
California Institute of Technology

Cities: China Lake, CA.

Entwistle, RADM Frederick I.

Interview of RADM Frederick I. Entwistle, conducted by
Albert B. Christman

Date of Inte view: 670300

Documentation: Index, Transcript 48 pp.

Interview number: NOTS-75201-S39

Abstract: This interview was originally conducted as
background for a biography of RADM William S. Parsons. RADM

Entwistle gives his impressions of RADM Parsons as a person and as an officer. He talks about the role of NOTS in the Navy and the role of scientists in the military. Entwistle also reflects on the contributions of Dr. Louis T. E. Thompson.

Repositories: NWC, DTNSRDC, NHC

Individuals mentioned: Sage, Dr. Bruce
Parsons, RADM William S.
Thompson, Dr. Louis T. E.
Tuve, Dr. Merle

Institutions: Naval Ordnance Test Station
Naval Proving Ground
California Institute of Technology
General Tire and Rubber Co.

Cities: Inyokern, CA.
Dahlgren, VA.

Other added entries: Proximity Fuze
Manhattan Project

Eyster, Dr. Eugene H.

Interview of Dr. Eugene H. Eyster, conducted by Albert B. Christman

Date of Interview: 6670100

Documentation: Index, Transcript 21 pp.

Interview number: NOTS-75201-S24

Abstract: Dr. Eyster talks about the weapons produced at Los Alamos, their specifications, and the role of NOTS, Los Alamos, and the Burlington Plant. He discusses the full-scale development and manufacture of atomic weapons. Eyster also comments on the accomplishments of the Salt Wells Pilot Plant and the reasons for its existence.

Repositories: NWC, DTNSRDC, HC

Individuals mentioned: Longwell, Paul
Sage, Dr. Bruce

Institutions: Naval Ordnance Test Station
Salt Wells Pilot Plant

Cities: Los Alamos, NM.

Other added entries: Manhattan Project

Fallgatter, Calvin J.

  Interview of Calvin J. Fallgatter, conducted by Carolyn Ogilvie

Date of Interview: 761006

Documentation: Index, Transcript 33 pp.

Interview number: S-110

Abstract: Mr. Fallgatter comments on housing problems when NOTS opened. He talks about factors in employee turnover and discusses NOTS' first commanders.

Repositories: NWC, DTNSRDC, NHC

Individuals mentioned: Etheridge, CAPT Melvin R.
McLaughlin, Jack
Richmond, CDR John

Institutions: Naval Ordnance Test Station
Naval Weapons Center

Ferguson, Mary

  Interview of Mary Ferguson, conducted by Susan Frutkin

Date of Interview: 740705

Documentation: 1 Tape, Index 4 pp.

Interview number: BA-24

Abstract: This interview is a taped review of a document on Navy financial management put together for Booz-Allen & Hamilton's review of Navy R&D Management 1946-1973. Mrs. Ferguson discusses the effect of the National Security Acts of 1947 and 1949 on the budget process, relationships between the Comptroller of the ONR and the DoD, how funding changes created the program planning process, who controls appropriations, and difficulties for women in the military establishment.

Repositories: NHC, DTNSRDC

Individuals mentioned: Livermore, Cliff

Bennett, RADM Rawson

Institutions: Office of Naval Research
Comptroller of the Office of Naval Research
Comptroller of the Navy

Other added entries: National Security Act
Research and Development Funding
Fiscal Management
Franke Board
Sexual Discrimination

Ferguson, Mary

Interview of Mary Ferguson

Date of Interview: 830219

Other interview date: 830305

Documentation: Tapes, Transcript, 112 pp.

Abstract: This interview is part of the "Women in the Federal Government Project", sponsored by the Arthur and Elizabeth Schlesinger Library on the History of Women in America and funded by the National Endowment for the Humanities. Ms. Ferguson describes her career, beginning as a grade 1 typist in the Department of Agriculture and retiring as a grade 17 Comptroller of the Office of Naval Research. As Comptroller of ONR, she also served as special assistant for financial management to the ASN (R&D) and as a witness in the presentation of the Navy's RDT&E budget proposals submitted to Congress.

Repositories: RAD

Institutions: Office of Naval Research
Comptroller of the Office of Naval Research

Other added entries: Comptroller
Budget
Funding
Research and Development

Fields, Dr. Victor

Interview of Dr. Victor Fields, conducted by Roger Kempler

Date of Interview: 820729

Documentation: Transcript, 33 pp.

Abstract: Dr. Fields relates his initial involvement with Government work, introduction to the Navy personnel research work and the special challenges associated with the military environment, the general Navy attitude toward personnel research in the 1950s and leading researchers in that era, post-war problems for the Research Division and its relationship with Bureau of Naval Personnel. He comments on applied versus basic research, the degree of supervision applied to field activities, problems associated with recruiting and utilizing research people, trends in DoD R&D, the attitude of ONR toward NPRDC, major accomplishments of NPRDC, and the "Center of Excellence" concept.

Repositories: NPRDC, DTNSRDC

Individuals mentioned: Friedman, Sidney
Brundage, Dr. Everett G.
Price, D. George
Carstater, Dr. Eugene D.
Brown, Paul
Sjoholm, Dr. Allan A.
Zimanski, CAPT Frank
Bryan, Dr. Glenn L.

Institutions: Office of Naval Research
Navy Personnel Research and Development Center
Bureau of Naval Personnel

Other added entries: Personnel Research
Center of Excellence

Fitzpatrick, William

   Interview of of William Fitzpatrick

Date of Interview: 780000

Documentation: 1 Tape

Interview number: DNL-T14

Repositories: DTNSRDC

Foladare, Dr. Joseph

   Interview of Dr. Joseph Foladare, conducted by Albert
B. Christman

Date of Interview: 700220

Documentation: Index, Transcript 22 pp.

Interview number: NWC-75201-S70

Abstract: Dr. Foladare discusses the early history of
CalTech in Naval research and the key people involved in it
at the start of World War II. He talks about the tests at
Goldstone Lake and Eaton Canyon, the spirit of the CalTech
people working in weapons research, and the budgeting and
documentation of various programs at NOTS.

Repositories: NWC, DTNSRDC, NHC

Individuals mentioned: Fowler, Dr. William
Gardner, Trevor
Lauritsen, Dr. Charles C.
Millikan, Dr. Robert A.
Potter, Russell
Sage, Dr. Bruce
Watson, Dr. Earnest C.
Winger, Dr. Ralph

Institutions: California Institute of Technology
Naval Ordnance Test Station

Cities: Inyokern, CA.
Goldstone Lake, CA.
Eaton Canyon, CA.

Fowler, Dr. William

Interview of Dr. William Fowler, conducted by Albert B. Christman

Date of Interview: 690100

Documentation: Index, Transcript 45 pp.

Interview number: NWC-75201-S59

Abstract: Dr. Fowler discusses his work before he came to NOTS at the Naval Proving Ground and on the National Defense Research Committee. He talks about the need for rocket rocket research, the CalTech research organization, and the necessity of a West Coast research facility. Fowler describes rocket work at the Goldstone Lake Range and the start of NOTS.

Repositories: NWC, DTNSRDC, NHC

Individuals mentioned: Bowen, Ike
Burroughs, ADM Sherman E.
Ellis, Dr. Emory L.
Hickman, Dr. Roy Scott
Lauritsen, Dr. Charles C.
Lauritsen, Dr. Thomas
Renard, RADM Jack C.
Sage, Dr. Bruce
Skinner, COL

Institutions: Naval Ordnance Test Station
National Defense Research Committee
California Institute of Technology
Naval Proving Ground

Cities: Goldstone Lake, CA.
Inyokern, CA.
Dahlgren, VA.
Indian Head, MD.

Fresh, J. Norman

Interview of J. Norman Fresh, conducted by Dr. David K. Allison

Date of Interview: 840501

Documentation: Three Tapes (5 sides), Index

Abstract: Mr. Fresh reminisces about the history of, and his career with DTNSRDC. He describes the difficulties and political maneuvering involved in getting new wind tunnels at the Carderock laboratory; airflow tests on buildings and bridges, and designs for rigid airships in the old tunnel in the Washington Navy Yard. He talks of coworkers, famed aeronautical engineers, and work on advanced naval vehicles. DTMB's relationship with BUAER, and CAPT Harold Saunders tenure as Commanding Officer. Additional information on the Aerodynamics Laboratory may be found in Mr. Fresh's publication <u>The Aerodynamics Laboratory (The First 50 Years)</u>, DTMB Aero Report 1070, January 1964.

Repositories: DTNSRDC

Individuals mentioned: Saunders, CAPT Harold E.
Truscutt, Starr
Zahm, Dr. Albert F.
Chaplin, Dr. Harvey R.
McCrary, John A.
de los Santos, Dr. Socrates
Saunders, CAPT Harold E.
Keil, Dr. Alfred H.
Diehl, CAPT Walter S.
Richardson, CAPT Holden C.

Institutions: Experimental Model Basin
Bureau of Aeronautics
David Taylor Model Basin
Naval Ship Research and Development Center
National Advisory Committee on Aeronautics
Naval Air Development Center
Bureau of Ships
Bureau of Construction and Repair
David Taylor Naval Ship Research and Development Center

Subjects: Aerodynamics
Hydrodynamics

Cities: Carderock, MD.
Langley, VA.

Other added entries: Wind Tunnels
Air Cushion Vehicles

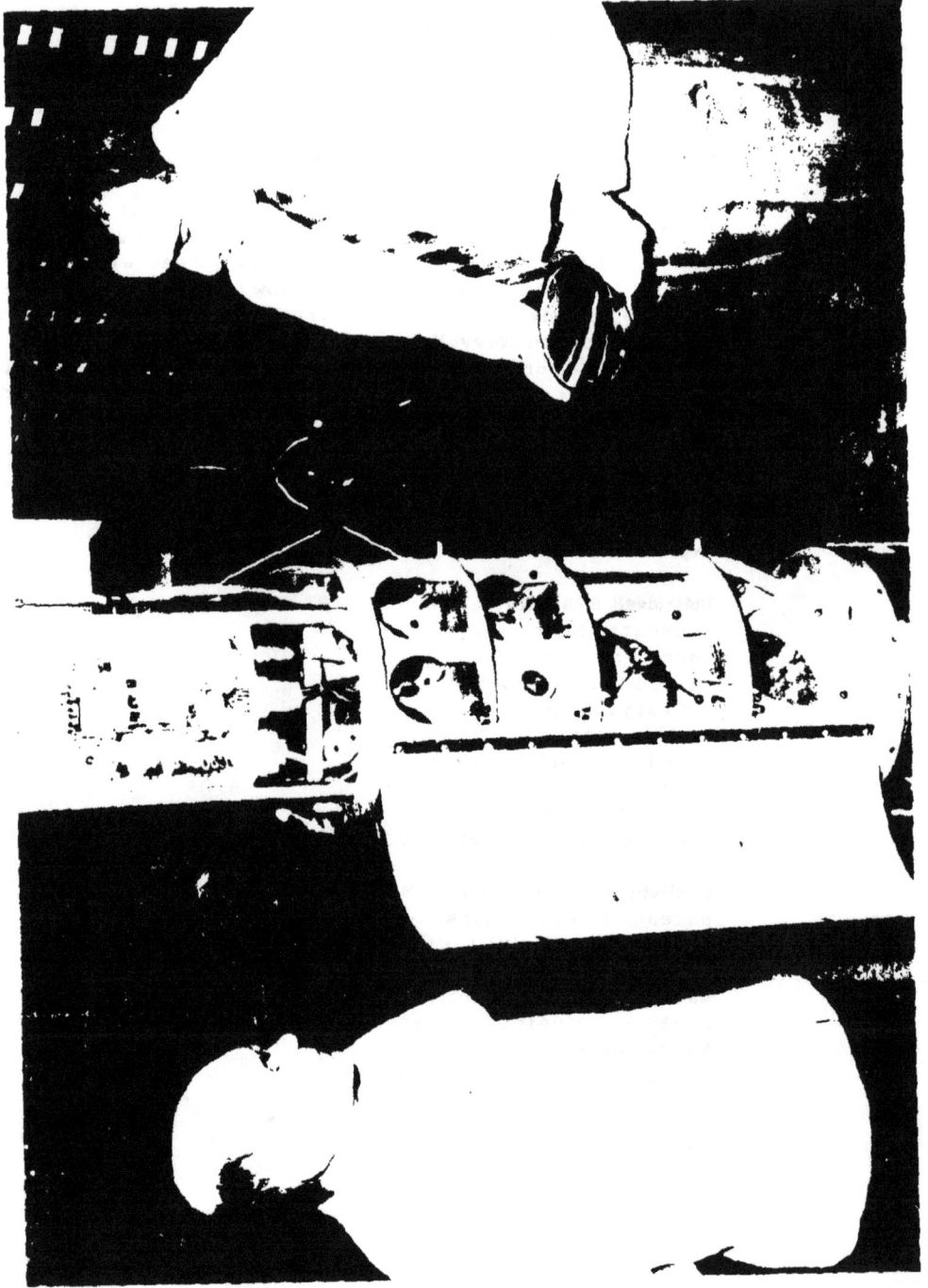

Dr. Herbert Friedman (right) and E.T. Byrum with an Aerobee rocket package.

Repositories: NASM

Individuals mentioned: Wood, R. W.
Franck, Dr. James
Kaiser, Herman F.
Braun, Wernher von
Stuhlinger, E.
Lindsay, John

Institutions: Naval Research Laboratory
Johns Hopkins University

Subjects: Satellites
Optics
Physics
Astrophysics

Other added entries: SOLRAD Program
Solar Spectroscopy
Rockoon
V-2 Rocket
Aerobee Rocket
Project Rainbarrel
Rocket-Sonde

Friedman, Sidney

Interview of Sidney Friedman, conducted by Roger
Kempler

Date of Interview: 8112209

Documentation: Index, Transcript 16 pp.

Abstract: Mr. Friedman discusses his contacts with NPRDC,
Navy personnel research, in general, and the positions he
had held in the Navy.

Repositories: DTNSRDC, NPRDC

Individuals mentioned: Brundage, Dr. Everett G.
Price, D. George
Ramses, Dr. Eugene
Collins, Dr. John J.

Institutions: Navy Personnel Research and Development Center

Other added entries: Personnel Research

Frosch, Dr. Robert A.

Interview of Dr. Robert A. Frosch, conducted by Dr. David H. DeVorkin

Date of Interview: 810710

Documentation: Tapes, 15.5 hours, Transcript, 256 pp.

Abstract: Dr. Frosch discusses his education, work and directorship of Hudson Laboratories, PERT, ocean floor modeling, the search for the THRESHER, his work at ARPA, his position as ASN, the Navy in Space and Naval R&D, SOLRAD and Navy satellites, the effect of the Mansfield Amendment and his decision to leave the Navy. Much of the interview deals with NASA, the Space Shuttle, and the Space Telescope.

Repositories: NASM

Individuals mentioned: Rabi, Isidor I.
Foley, Dr. Henry M.
Press, Frank
Nitze, SECNAV Paul

Institutions: Naval Research Laboratory
Columbia University
Hudson Laboratories
Bell Laboratories
Woods Hole Oceanographic Institute
National Aeronautics and Space Administration
Advanced Research Projects Agency
Assistant Secretary of the Navy

Subjects: Satellites
Space Astronomy
Seismology

Other added entries: Research and Development
Mansfield Amendment
Project Artemis
Project Media
Project Vela
Nuclear Test Detection
Program Evaluation Review Technique
JASON
Ocean Floor Modeling
USS THRESHER

Left to right: ASN (R&D) Dr. Robert A. Frosch; Dr. R.E. Gibson, Director
Johns Hopkins Applied Physics Laboratory; Vice President Hubert H. Humphrey;
Dr. Richard B. Kershner; SECNAV Paul R. Ignatius; RADM Levering Smith,
19 October, 1967.

Frosch, Dr. Robert A.

Interview of Dr. Robert A. Frosch, conducted by Dr. Vincent Ponko

Date of Interview: 810107

Documentation: Index, Transcript 64 pp.

Interview number: NL-T34

Abstract: Dr. Frosch compares Navy and private laboratories in terms of flexibility, mission, size, and the effect of bureaucracy. He describes ARPA's work and comments on the role of the ASN (R&D), including his personnel management philosophy, control over channels of command and R&D Budget, and philosophical observations about the Navy R&D decision-making process. Frosch evaluates the first two DNL/DLP's and talks aobut his influence in selecting TD's and CO's. He describes budget problems, the optimal CO-TD relationship, and McNamara and Laird's influences on Navy R&D.

Repositories: DTNSRDC

Individuals mentioned: Chaffee, John
Connolly, VADM Thomas
Johnson, Dr. Gerald
Laird, SECDEF Melvin
McNamara, SECDEF Robert S.

Institutions: Director of Navy Laboratories
Director of Laboratory Programs
Advanced Research Projects Agency

Other added entries: Technical Director

Fuller, Mrs. Clarissa Parsons

Interview of Mrs. Clarissa Parsons Fuller, conducted by Albert B. Christman

Date of Interview: 670100

Documentation: Index, Transcript 106 pp.

Interview number: NOTS-75201-S32

Abstract: This interview was originally conducted as background for a biography of RADM William S. Parsons. Mrs. Fuller, RADM Parsons' sister, talks about the Parsons' move from Illinois to New Mexico, the Parsons children's early schooling, and RADM Parsons' admission to the Naval Academy at Annapolis. She discusses her brother's role on the Manhattan Project and her contacts with him at the time. Also included are sections on the Proximity Fuze, Parsons' sea duty, and his flight to Hiroshima on the Enola Gay.

Repositories: NWC, DTNSRDC, NHC

Individuals mentioned: Parsons, RADM William S.
Burroughs, Martha Parsons
Oppenheimer, Dr. Robert
Parsons, Clarissa
Parsons, Clare
Parsons, Critchell

Institutions: U. S. Naval Academy

Cities: Annapolis, MD.
Los Alamos, NM.
Ft. Sumner, NM.
Chicago, IL.

Other added entries: Manhattan Project

Furth, RADM Frederick R.
Priori, Dr. E.

Interview of RADM Frederick R. Furth and Dr. E. Priori

Date of Interview: 740723

Documentation: 3 Tapes

Interview number: BA-17

Repositories: DTNSRDC

Gates, SECNAV Thomas S.

Interview of SECNAV Thomas S. Gates

Date of Interview: 720900

Documentation: Transcript 71 pp.

Abstract: Thomas S. Gates was Secretary of the Navy during the development of Polaris. This is one of a series of seven interviews on concept and development of Polaris program conducted by the U. S. Naval Institute Oral History Program.

Repositories: NHC, NWCM, USNA, USNI

Institutions: Secretary of the Navy

Subjects: Submarine Launched Ballistic Missiles
Fleet Ballistic Missiles
Ballistic Missile Submarines
Nuclear Powered Fleet Ballistic Missile Submarines
Nuclear Missiles
Weapons Systems

Other added entries: Polaris Program

Giallorenzi, Dr. Thomas G.

Interview of Dr. Thomas G. Giallorenzi, conducted by Dr. David K. Allison

Date of Interview: 800926

Documentation: 1 Tape, 3 5X7 cards of questions asked

Abstract: NRL pioneered in fiber optics research and has been the Navy's lead laboratory for the tri-service Fiber Optics Sensor System (FOSS) development program.

Repositories: NRL

Institutions: Naval Research Laboratory

Subjects: Fiber Optics

Other added entries: Fiber Optics Sensor System
Acoustics Research
Fiber Optic Hydrophone
Hydrophones

Gebhard, Dr. Louis A.

Interview of Dr. Louis A. Gebhard, conducted by Dr. David K. Allison

Date of Interview: 771003

Documentation: 6 Tapes (11 Tapes), Index, Bound Transcript "An Interview with Dr. Louis Gebhard"

Other interview dates: 770912, 770919

Abstract: Dr. Gebhard discusses radio-electronic research in the Navy and at NRL from 1917-1977. Gebhard joined NRL in 1923 and his research resulted in more than 90 patents and significant advances in radar, radio communications, direction finding, and electronics.

Repositories: NRL

Institutions: Naval Research Laboratory

Subjects: Electronics
Radar
Radio Communications

Gleiter, Werner

Interview of Werner Gleiter, conducted by Tom Misa and Ed Todd

Date of Interview: 820708

Documentation: 1 Tape, Index 2 pp.

Interview number: NADC-8

Abstract: Mr. Gleiter discusses his background, his service in the Navy in World War II, and how and why he came to NADC. He describes NADC sonobuoy research, the SSQ-15 Sonobuoy, cooperation between government and industry, and technical difficulties with sonobuoys. Gleiter talks about the Columbia University Sonobuoy and ASW programs, the rise of Air ASW, and NADC's relations with BUAER. He also mentions NADC's contacts with local universities.

Repositories: NADC, DTNSRDC

Individuals mentioned: Krutter, Dr. Harry
Mason, Russell
Howard, Jim

Wallace, John D.

Institutions: Naval Air Development Center
Underwater Sound Laboratory
Standards and Calibration Laboratory
Bureau of Aeronautics
Columbia University

Subjects: Antisubmarine Warfare
Antisubmarine Aircraft
Sonobuoys

Cities: Orlando, FL.
New London, CT.

Other added entries: SSQ-15 Sonobouy

Goddard, Mrs. Robert

Interview of Mrs. Robert Goddard, conducted by Albert B. Christman

Date of Interview: 710128

Documentation: Index, No transcript, Notes 6 pp.

Interview number: NWC-75201-S75

Abstract: This interview is recorded in note form and not intended for general use. Mrs. Goddard discusses Dr. Robert Goddard's disposition, his relationship with Navy officers, and the influence on him of Prof. Webster of Clark University. She comments on Goddard's rivals at CalTech and his relationship with Dr. Louis T. E. Thompson.

Repositories: NWC, DTNSRDC, NHC

Individuals mentioned: Webster, Dr. A. G.
Karman, Dr. Theodore von
Thompson, Dr. Louis T. E.

Institutions: Naval Proving Ground

Cities: Dahlgren, VA.

Goss, Dr. Wilbur
Porter, Henry

   Interview of Dr. Wilbur Goss and Henry Porter,
conducted by A. B. Christman

Date of Interview: 660504

Documentation: Index, Transcript 40 pp.

Interview number: NOTS-75201-S14

Abstract: This interview was originally conducted as
background for a biography of RADM William S. Parsons. Goss
and Porter discuss Parsons' personal attributes, hi‐
confidence in people, his ability to do a top-flight jou,
and his knack for working with other people. They also
recall the planning, testing, and deployment in Europe and
the Far East of the Proximity fuzes.

Repositories: NWC, DTNSRDC, NHC

Individuals mentioned: Parsons, RADM William S.
Tuve, Dr. Merle

Other added entries: Proximity Fuze

_____

Gould, Gerald

   Interview of Gerald Gould

Date of interview: 780000

Interview number: DNL T-20

Documentation: 1 Tape

Repositories: DTNSRDC

_____

Gouldman, Harold M. Jr.

"Community Relations: Harold M. Gouldman", conducted by
Cynthia Rouse

Date of Interview: 760727

Documentation: Transcript 14 pp.

Note: This interview is Chapter IX of <u>Dahlgren</u>, edited by
Kenneth G. McCollum

Abstract: Mr. Gouldman, a lifelong resident of Dahlgren,
discusses community relations, education for base children,
facilities, and funding.

Repositories: NSWC, DTNSRDC

Institutions: Naval Proving Ground
Naval Surface Weapons Center

Gralla, VADM Arthur R.

Interview of VADM Arthur Gralla, conducted by Vincent
Ponko, Jr.

Date of Interview: 801104

Documentation: 2 Tapes, Index, Transcript 31 pp.

Interview number: DNL-T30

Abstract: VADM Gralla describes his pre-1946 work in R&D,
including torpedo research, time in CNO, a period as CO of
the USS NORTON, and work in BUORD and BUWEPS. He discusses
his tenure as the first head of the Naval Ordnance Systems
Command: his opposition to the formation of DNL/DLP, his
evaluation of Dr. Gerald Johnson as the first DNL/DLP, and
the need for military control of the labs. Gralla questions
the logic of placing the laboratories under the DNL and
states that they should be placed under the Systems
Commands. He adds that he would limit the power of the ASN
(R&D) and the CNM, make the labs compete with private
industry for work, and keep the labs from doing any more
than pure research. Gralla details Naval Ordnance Systems
Command operations, in particular, the funding process and
the problems of the material Navy administratively and
technically. He mentions some key people in Navy R&D -
William Raney, Dr. Joel Lawson, and SECNAV Paul Nitze.

Repositories: DTNSRDC

Individuals mentioned: Frosch, Dr. Robert A.
Johnson, Dr. Gerald
Nitze, SECNAV Paul
Raney, Dr. William

Institutions: Naval Ordnance Systems Command
Chief of Naval Material
Bureau of Ordnance
Bureau of Weapons

Granum, RADM Alfred M.

Interview of RADM Alfred M. Granum, conducted by A. B. Christman

Date of Interview: 670100

Documentation: Index, Transcript 11 pp.

Interview number: NOTS-75201-S29

Abstract: This interview was originally conducted as background for a biography of RADM William S. Parsons. RADM Granum describes Parsons as a young Ensign under his command on the USS IDAHO. He talks about Parsons' practicality, common sense, moral courage, and leadership ability.

Repositories: NWC, DTNSRDC, NHC

Individuals mentioned: Parsons, RADM William S.
Blandy, ADM George

Grodsky, Jim

Interview of Jim Grodsky

Date of Interview: 750122

Documentation: 1 Tape

Interview number: BA-26

Repositories: NHC

Groves, LTGEN Leslie

Interview of LTGEN Leslie Groves, conducted by Albert B. Christman

Date of Interview: 670500

Documentation: Index, Transcript 55 pp.

Interview number: NOTS-75201-S42

Abstract: This interview was originally conducted as background for a biography of RADM William S. Parsons. GEN Groves discusses in detail RADM (then CAPT) Parsons' role in the Manhattan Project from Los Alamos to Alamogordo to Tinian and Hiroshima. He also recalls the dropping of the Nagasaki bomb, in particular, the role of ADM (then CAPT) F. L. Ashworth. Groves talks about military-scientific relations today and during the Manhattan Project.

Repositories: NWC, DTNSRDC, NHC

Individuals mentioned: Ashworth, VADM Frederick L.
Oppenheimer, Dr. Robert
Purnell, RADM William R.
Tibbets, COL Paul

Institutions: Naval Ordnance Test Station

Cities: Inyokern, CA.
Los Alamos, NM.
Alamogordo, NM.
Tinian
Nagasaki, Japan
Hiroshima, Japan

Other added entries: Manhattan Project

Guthrie, Dr. Robert C.

Interview of Dr. Robert C. Guthrie, conducted by Dr. David K. Allison

Date of Interview: 780413

Documentation: 3 Tapes (6 Sides), Index 5 pp.

Abstract: Dr. Guthrie talks about the development of radar at NRL, the first major demonstration of the 25 megacycle equipment in 1936, the installation of an experimental 200 megacycle set on the USS LEARY, the equipment in Britain, and American radar work in the 1930's, and independence from the research of the U. S. Army, the Tizard Mission, NDRC, AEW development in conjunction with the Naval Air Modification Unit, and NRL Research Management.

Repositories: NRL

Institutions: Naval Research Laboratory
Radio Corporation of America
National Defense Research Committee
Naval Air Modification Unit
U. S. Army Signal Corps

Subjects: Radar
Radio Transmitters

Other added entries: Radar Research
Airborne Early Warning Systems
Tizard Mission
USS LEARY

Habicht, Frank

Interview of Mr. Frank Habicht, conducted by Albert B. Christman

Date of Interview: 670500

Documentation: Index, Transcript 54 pp.

Interview number: NOTS-75201-S44

Abstract: Mr. Habicht describes Army rocket tests at Elgin Field in late 1942 and early 1943 and the first American use of rockets in combat. He talks about his arrival at NOTS, his position as Administrative Assistant under CAPT Burroughs, and the leadership at NOTS and in the Bureau of Ordnance. He discusses problems at NOTS, including those of construction and discipline and how NOTS received its funds.

Repositories: NWC, DTNSRDC, NHC

Individuals mentioned: Burroughs, ADM Sherman E.
Hayward, ADM John T.
Parsons, RADM William S.
Richmond, CDR John
Vieweg, RADM Walter V. R.

Institutions: Naval Ordnance Test Station
U. S. Army
Bureau of Ordnance

Cities: Inyokern, CA.

Other added entries: Rocket Research

Haff, CAPT William B.

Interview of CAPT William B. Haff, conducted by Leroy
L. Doig, III

Date of Interview: 810624

Documentation: Transcript 33 pp.

Interview number: S-125

Abstract: CAPT Haff explains the changes in the character of
air-to-air combat, including new weapons and electronic
warfare. He discusses the future of NWC, the place of Navy
labs versus that of the contractor in R&D, and relations
with contractors and people in Washington. Haff comments on
military-civilian relationships at NWC and lab responses to
Fleet needs. He talks about NWC's top management, his
philosophy on RDT&E, and NWC as a command.

Repositories: NWC, DTNSRDC, NHC

Institutions: Naval Weapons Center

Other added entries: Electronic Warfare

Hafstad, Dr. Lawrence R.

Interview of Dr. Lawrence R. Hafstad, conducted by
Albert B. Christman

Date of Interview: 710200

Documentation: Index, Transcript 21 pp.

Interview number: NWC-75201-S76

Abstract: This interview was originally conducted as
background for a biography of RADM William S. Parsons. Dr.
Hafstad discusses his early contacts with Parsons at NRL,
their early atomic work, and the proximity fuze. He talks
about Parsons' leadership and technical ability on the
proximity fuze project, the influence of Dr. Charles C.
Lauritsen on Parsons, and Lewis Strauss' role as Navy
Financial Advisor.

Repositories: NWC, DTNSRDC, NHC

Individuals mentioned: Strauss, Lewis L.
Tuve, Dr. Merle
Lauritsen, Dr. Charles C.

Institutions: Naval Research Laboratory

Subjects: Radar

Other added entries: Proximity Fuze

Hall, Dr. John L.

   Interview of Dr. John L. Hall, conducted by Dr. David
H. DeVorkin

Date of Interview: 790221

Documentation: Tapes, 1 1/2 hrs., Transcript 29 pp.

Abstract: Dr. Hall speaks about his family background and
education, early contacts and interests in photoelectric
photometry, red sensitive cell photometry, work at the
Radiation Laboratory at MIT during World War II, research at
the Naval Observatory, and co-discovery of interstellar
polarization.

Repositories: AIP

Institutions: Naval Observatory
Massachusetts Institute of Technology

Subjects: Astronomy

Other added entries: Photoelectric Photometry

Hardy, CAPT John I.

   Interview of CAPT John I. Hardy, conducted by Albert B.
Christman

Date of Interview: 670213

Documentation: Index, Transcript 39 pp.

Interview number: NOTS-75291-S34

Abstract: CAPT Hardy explains how his Navy background helped him during two tours, one as CO of NOTS. He discusses the role of NOTS as both a quick fix for the Fleet and a long-term R&D Center. Hardy talks about the community surrounding the Center and the support NOTS gets from the Navy Department in Washington.

Repositories: NWC, DTNSRDC, NHC

Institutions: Naval Ordnance Test Station
Naval Weapons Center

Other added entries: Naval Research
Commanding Officer

Hartmann, Dr. Gregory

Interview of Dr. Gregory K. Hartmann, conducted by Mrs. Susan Frutkin and CAPT Robert L. Hansen

Date of Interview: 740000

Documentation: 6 Tapes, Index, Transcript 149 pp.

Interview number: BA-4-74

Abstract: In this extensive and broad ranging interview, Dr. Hartmann recalls a few specific experiments he was involved in, including the Bikini bomb tests. He talks about BUORD's mine and torpedo work, the establishment of NOL, and the Naval Gun Factory and magnetic mines. He talks about R&D in BUORD, particularly the mission of NOL, the Naval Proving Ground at Dahlgren, Va., and Atomic Energy Commission work at NOL. Hartmann comments on laboratory management, the distinction between the CO and TD, the Bureaus' attempts to create a lab management office, laboratory-SYSCOM dialogues, and the Research and Development Board. He discusses Dr. Chalmers Sherwin's opinions of lab project management, DDR&E's drive to improve the labs, and examples of aborted R&D projects.

Repositories: NHC, DTNSRDC

Individuals mentioned: Bennett, Dr. Ralph
Foster, Dr. John S.
Frosch, Dr. Robert A.
Johnson, Dr. Gerald
McLean, Dr. William B.
McNamara, SECDEF Robert S.
Raborn, RADM William F.
Rothman, Dr. Samuel
Sherwin, Dr. Chalmers

Institutions: Director of Defense Research and Engineering
Bureau of Ordnance
Atomic Energy Commission
Naval Ordnance Laboratory
Director of Navy Laboratories
Naval Electronics Laboratory
Systems Commands

Subjects: Limpet Weapons
Antivehicle Weapons
Naval Mine Warfare

Other added entries: Project REFLEX
SUBROC Missile Project
Navy Industrial Fund
Operation Crossroads

Harwit, Dr. Martin
Kondracki, Henry

Interview of Dr. Martin Harwit and Henry Kondracki, conducted by Dr. David H. Devorkin

Date of Interview: 830209

Documentation: Tapes, 1.5 hours, Transcript, 67 pp.

Abstract: This double interview with Kondracki and Harwit centers on their work in the design and construction of an infrared Aerobee rocket payload, and includes discussion of other rocket groups at NRL, use of Atlas missiles, and NASA's doubts about helium-cooled payloads.

Repositories: NASM

Institutions: Naval Research Laboratory
Cornell
National Aeronautics and Space Administration

Subjects: Astronomy

Other added entries: Aerobee Rocket
Atlas Missile

Harwit, Dr. Martin

Interview of Dr. Martin Harwit, conducted by Dr. David
H. DeVorkin

Date of Interview: 830419

Documentation: Tapes, 9 hours, Transcript, 170 pp.

Other dates of interviews: 830620 and 830622

Abstract: Dr. Harwit discusses his background and education,
service in the Army Chemical and Signal Corps, thesis on
interferometry, post-graduate education at Cambridge, work
at Cornell and contact with NRL, building rocket sonde
packages, debate over satellites versus balloons versus
sounding rockets, relationship with NASA, infrared systems
and Hadamard Transform spectroscopy.

Repositories: NASM

Individuals mentioned: Friedman, Dr. Herbert
Gold, Thomas
Bondi, Hermann

Institutions: Naval Research Laboratory
North Atlantic Treaty Organization
U. S. Army Signal Corps
Oberlin College
University of Michigan
Massachusetts Institute of Technology
U. S. Army Chemical Corps
National Aeronautics and Space Administration
Cornell
U. S. Army

Subjects: Infrared Astronomy
Astronomy

Other added entries: Rockoon
Atmospheric Research
Rocket-Sonde
Hadamard Transform Spectroscopy

Hattabaugh, William R.

Interview of William R. Hattabaugh, conducted by Leroy
L. Doig III and Joseph M. Burge

Date of Interview: 810709

Documentation: Index, Transcript 31 pp.

Interview number: S-127

Abstract: Mr. Hattabaugh reflects on his early association
with NWC, NWC's relations with contractors, and changes in
the Center's role in the Navy. He comments on the
interaction of the R&D and T&E sides of the lab and
relations with and support of the Fleet. Hattabaugh also
notes the changes in the type of work at NNWC and talks
about NWC's role in the surrounding community. He discusses
Dr. William B. McLean.

Repositories: NWC, DTNSRDC, NHC

Individuals mentioned: McLean, Dr. William B.
Hillyer, Robert

Institutions: Naval Weapons Center

Havens, Dr. Ralph J.

Interview of Dr. Ralph J. Havens, conducted by Dr.
David H. DeVorkin

Date of Interview: 831006

Documentation: Tapes, 1.25 hours, Transcript, 20 pp.

Abstract: The interview with Havens covers his education,
employment at NRL after World War II, meteorological
research in V-2 and Rockoon experiments, the development of
the Havens cycle gauge for air pressure, his contacts with
NACA, and move to Ford Aeronautics.

Repositories: NASM

Institutions: Naval Research Laboratory
Ford Aeronautics
University of Michigan
National Advisory Committee on Aeronautics

Subjects: Meteorology
Rocketry

Astronomy

Other added entries: V-2 Rocket
Atmospheric Research
Viking Rocket

Hay, Marley Fotheringham

Interview of Marley Fotheringham Hay

Date of Interview: 500000

Documentation: Transcript 19 pp.

Abstract: Concerns submarine construction and submarine warfare in World War I.

Repositories: COL, NHC

Subjects: Naval Architecture

Other added entries: Submarine Design

Hayward, ADM John T.

Interview of ADM John T. Hayward, conducted by Albert B. Christman

Date of Interview: 660500

Documentation: Index, Transcript 38 pp.

Interview number: NOTS-75201-S6

Abstract: This interview was originally conducted as background for a biography of RADM William S. Parsons. Hayward first describes the search for a new ordnance test sight. He talks about Parsons' "technical vision", and their contacts on the Manhattan Project. Hayward talks about ordnance work during and after World War II. Next is the problem of keeping scientists at NOTS after the war. Finally, he discusses Parsons the man - scientist and officer combined.

Repositories: DTNSRDC, NHC

Individuals mentioned: Burroughs, ADM Sherman E.
Lauritsen, Dr. Charles C.
Parsons, RADM William S.

Thompson, Dr. Louis T. E.

Institutions: Naval Ordnance Test Station
Office of Scientific Research and Development
California Institute of Technology

Cities: China Lake, CA.

Other added entries: Manhattan Project
Research Management

Hayward, ADM John T.

Interview of ADM John T. Hayward, conducted by J. D. Gerrard-Gough

Date of Interview: 730726

Documentation: Index, Transcript, Part I 59 pp. Part II 6 pp.

Interview number: NWC-S86

Note: This includes another interview conducted on 731115

Abstract: In part one, VADM Hayward discusses the role of rocket weapons in the Pacific during World War II, the intermixing of ordnance and rocket research, and tests at Armitage Field. Hayward describes his one assignment to NOTS, aircraft armament, and facilities at NOTS. He explains his responsibilities there, his trip to Japan after the war with Dr. Charles Lauritsen, and the choice of a successor for ADM Burroughs at NOTS. He also talks about ADMs Sykes and Switzer. In part two, Hayward makes broad comments about the educational system for dependents for NOTS employees and postwar research programs at NOTS.

Repositories: NWC, DTNSRDC, NHC

Individuals mentioned: Brown, Dr. Ira Sprague
Burroughs, ADM Sherman E.
Fowler, Dr. William
Hussey, VADM George F.
Lauritsen, Dr. Charles C.
Parsons, RADM William S.
Ramsey, RADM DeWitt
Switzer, VADM W. G.
Sykes, RADM James B.
Temple, RADM H. B.
Thompson, Dr. Louis T. E.

Institutions: Naval Ordnance Test Station

Other added entries: Ordnance Research
Rocket Research

Hayward, ADM John T.

Interview of ADM John T. Hayward, conducted by CAPT
Robert L. Hansen, and Dr. Peter Bruton

Date of Interview: 741009

Documentation: Index, Transcript 45 pp.

Interview number: BA-11

Abstract: VADM Hayward discusses the establishment of the
Assistant Chief of Naval Operations (R&D), the ACNO's
relationship with the Bureaus, budget requirement for R&D in
the 1950's, and how the R&D Review Board revised programs.
He comments on the Libby Board study - in particular, the
proposed merger of BUORD and BUAER, how inter-bureau
technical committees operated, and ACNO (R&D)
responsibility. Hayward also describes ACNO's effect on Navy
programs, the impact of DDR&E, DCNO's duties as
appropriations officer, and SECDEF McNamara's feelings on
Navy R&D.

Repositories: NWC, DTNSRDC, NHC

Individuals mentioned: Bennett, RADM Rawson
Burke, ADM Arleigh A.
Franke, William B.
Furth, RADM Frederick R.
Libby, VADM R. E.
McNamara, SECDEF Robert S.

Institutions: Assistant Secretary of Defense (R&D)
Bureau of Ordnance
Bureau of Aeronautics
Deputy Chief of Naval Operations (Development)
Director of Defense Research and Engineering
Office of Naval Research

Other added entries: Libby Board
Technical Development Plan

Hayward, VADM John T.

    Interview of VADM John T. Hayward, conducted by Dr.
Evelyn M. Cherpak

Date of Interview: 770506

Documentation: Transcript 62 pp., 1 vol.

Interview number: O.H. 24

Abstract: VADM Hayward discusses his education at the U. S.
Naval Academy, his flight training, service on the USS
LANGLEY, and work as the Assistant Chief Engineer at the
Naval Aircraft Factory in Philadelphia, PA. He recalls
being Experimental Officer at NOTS, the development of the
atom bomb, and serving as the Commanding Officer of the
Naval Ordnance Laboratory, 1954-1956.

Repositories: NWCM

Institutions: Naval Aircraft Factory
Bureau of Ordnance
Bureau of Aeronautics
Naval Ordnance Laboratory
Naval Ordnance Test Station

Subjects: Naval Aviation
Ordnance

Cities: Inyokern, CA.
Philadelphia, PA.
Pensacola, FL.

Other added entries: Commanding Officer
Manhattan Project

Hayward, ADM John T.

    Interview of ADM John T. Hayward, conducted by Nelson
Wood

Date of Interview: 780815

Documentation: Tapes, Transcript

Abstract: ADM Hayward talks about torpedo research and
development and the Mark 48 Torpedo.

Repositories: ARL

Institutions: Naval Underwater Systems Center

Cities: Newport, RI.

Subjects: Torpedos

Other added entries: Torpedo Mark 48
Torpedos

Henderson, J.

    Interview of J. Henderson, conducted by Nelson Wood

Date of Interview: 770520

Documentation: Tapes, Transcript

Abstract: Mr. Henderson, a former director of the Johns Hopkins Applied Physics Laboratory, describes its operations.

Repositories: APL

Institutions: Johns Hopkins University
Applied Physics Laboratory

Subjects: Physics

Henifin, CAPT Edward E.

    Interview of CAPT Edward E. Henifin, conducted by Dr. David K. Allison

Date of Interview: 800118

Documentation: 1 Tape, 5 pp. summary

Abstract: CAPT Henifin reflects on R&D management in the Navy and at NRL. He also talks about management changes and what led to them.

Repositories: NRL

Institutions: Naval Research Laboratory
Research Management
Laboratory Management

Herget, Dr. Paul

Interview of Dr. Paul Herget, conducted by Dr. David H. DeVorkin

Date of Interview: 770419

Other date of interview: 770420

Documentation: Tapes, 6 1/2 hrs., Transcript 96 pp.

Abstract: Dr. Herget discusses his family, background, schooling, work at the Cincinnati observatory, and the Rechen Institute. He speaks about his work during World War II, his position at the Nautical Almanac Office, and research through the 1950s. [Dr. Herget's papers are in the collection of the U. S. Naval Observatory]

Repositories: AIP

Institutions: Nautical Almanac Office
Naval Observatory

Subjects: Astronomy

Other added entries: Nautical Almanac

Highberg, Dr. Ivar E.

Interview of Dr. Ivar E. Highberg, conducted by Leroy L. Doig, III

Date of Interview: 810401

Documentation: Index, Transcript 26 pp.

Interview number: S-121

Abstract: Dr. Highberg discusses his work at NOTS in the late 1940's, the dedication of the Michelson lab, and changes in the use of NOTS facilities over the years. He describes early rocket missile test work at the lab and NOTS involvement in satellite tracking. Highberg talks about the use of computer simulation, digital fuze control work on missiles and guns, and the political ramifications for NOTS of the 1966 divison of BUWEPS into NAVORDSYSCOM and NAVSHIPSYSCOM. He comments on the leadership of Dr. Louis T. E. Thompson and his personal philosophy of research and development.

Repositories: NHC, DTNSRDC, NWC

Individuals mentioned: McLean, Dr. William B.
Thompson, Dr. Louis T. E.

Institutions: Naval Ordnance Test Station
Naval Weapons Center
Naval Ships Systems Command
Naval Ordnance Systems Command
Michelson Laboratory

Subjects: Computer Simulation

Other added entries: Digital Fuze Control
Satellite Tracking
Systems Commands

Hillyer, Robert

Interview of Mr. Robert M. Hillyer, conducted by Leroy
L. Doig, III

Date of Interview: 820517

Documentation: Index, Transcript 77 pp.

Interview number: S-134

Abstract: Mr. Hillyer talks about the NOTS-Naval Ordnance
Lab-Corona merger, the fuze department at NWC, and gains and
losses of the 1967 lab consolidation. He comments on the
role of the Technical Director at NWC, appropriate and
inappropriate areas of research for the lab, and military-
civilian relationships in the Navy. Hillyer discusses NWC
Commanders, NWC relationships with DON in Washington, and
his reasons for becoming DCNM(L). He describes his
managerial philosophy, the outstanding contributions of NWC
to the Navy, and the problem of declining productivity.
Hillyer also expostulates on NWC's future and offers advise
to NWC's new managers.

Repositories: NWC, DTNSRDC, NHC

Individuals mentioned: Freeman, ADM Rowland G.
Harris, ADM William L.
Lahr, CAPT John Jude
McLean, Dr. William B.

Institutions: Naval Weapons Center
Deputy Chief of Naval Material (Laboratories)
Director of Navy Laboratories

Cities: China Lake, CA.

Retirement party for Dr. Margurite M. "Peggy" Rogers. Left to right:
Robert M. Hillyer, former Technical Director of the Naval Weapons
Center and Director of Navy Laboratories 1982-1984, and Dr. Rogers,
former Laboratory Director (Acting), and Head, Systems Development
Department; March 27, 1980.

Corona, CA.

Other added entries: Technical Director
Commanding Officer
Laboratory Consolidations

Himes, Allen W.

   Interview of Allen W. Himes, conducted by Albert B. Christman

Date of Interview: 780414

Documentation: 1 Tape, Transcript 25 pp.

Interview number: DNL-T13-78

Abstract: Mr. Himes discusses the effect of the Bell Report, Project 97, and the Sherwin Plan. He comments on the establishment of the DNL, the first DNL - Dr. Gerald Johnson, and the SYSCOMs' attitude toward the DNL. Himes talks about the consolidation of the labs, Dr. Joel Lawson as the DNL, and Navy R&D cutbacks and consolidations in the early 1970's. He describes his and Lawson's relations with Dr. Robert A. Frosch, former ASN (R&D), personnel problems in the DNL office, and his term as Deputy Assistant to the DNL.

Repositories: DTNSRDC

Individuals mentioned: Lawson, Dr. Joel
Frosch, Dr. Robert A.
Johnson, Dr. Gerald

Institutions: Chief of Naval Material
Director of Navy Laboratories
Systems Commands

Other added entries: Project 97
Bell Report
Sherwin Report
Laboratory Management
Laboratory Consolidations

Himes, Allen W.

Interview of Allen W. Himes, conducted by Dr. David K. Allison

Date of Interview: 830810

Documentation: 2 Tapes, Transcript 36 pp.

Abstract: Mr. Himes discusses the consolidation of the labs into the eight NAVMAT R&D Centers, headquarters administration of the labs, linkage of the labs to the acquisition process, and the organizational evolution of the DNL from 1965-1983. He comments on the leadership styles of the six DNL's and internal organization of the office.

Repositories: DTNSRDC

Individuals mentioned: Probus, Dr. James H.
Lawson, Dr. Joel
Hillyer, Robert
Parrish, CAPT David
Whittle, ADM Alfred J., Jr.
Law, Howard
Swiggum, George
Huang, Theodore S.
Langille, CAPT John

Institutions: Deputy Chief of Naval Material (Laboratories)
Director of Navy Laboratories
Chief of Naval Material

Subjects: Laboratory Management
Laboratory Consolidations
Laboratory Administration

History of Radio-Radar-Sonar

"History of Radio-Radar-Sonar", papers of RADM Stanford Caldwell Hooper

Documentation: 156 Tapes, Transcripts

Abstract: This series of tape recordings is part of the papers collection of RADM Stanford Caldwell Hooper donated to the Naval Historical Foundation and deposited in the Manuscript Collection of the Library of Congress. Hooper was head of the Radio Division of the Bureau of Engineering (1918-1923). This series contains 156 consecutively numbered tapes recorded by Hooper and his associates concerning the history of naval developments in radio, sonar, and radar. Typed transcripts exist for interviews 1-93, and there are additional notes and background materials. tapes 150 and 151 are interviews with Dr. Leo C. Young of NRL and are duplicated in the NRL oral history collection.

Individuals mentioned: Hooper, RADM Stanford C.
Young, Dr. Leo C.

Institutions: Naval Research Laboratory
Bureau of Engineering

Subjects: Radar
Sonar
Radio Communications
Radio

Hollings, Anthony J.

Interview of Anthony J. Hollings, conducted by Dr. David K. Allison

Date of Interview: 800104

Other interview date: 080108

Documentation: 5 Tapes (9 Sides), typewritten index, 8 pp.

Abstract: Mr. Hollings discusses his career in the Royal Navy, harbor defense and shock and vibration programs at NRL, the difference between American and British methods of research, and the management of the NRL search program for THRESHER. He talks about research at NRL, ONR and NIF funding, and major organizational and management changes there between 1963 and 1980. The interview is supported by a collection of papers.

Repositories: NRL

Individuals mentioned: Klein, Dr. Elias
Bagley, Jim
Berman, Dr. Alan
Cleeton, Dr. Claud E.
Waterman, Dr. Peter
Mutch, Warren
Owen, RADM Thomas B.
Noel, Lee
Henifin, CAPT Edward E.
Sapp, Earl

Institutions: Naval Research Laboratory

Woods Hole Oceanographic Institute
Office of Naval Research
Royal Navy

Subjects: Oceanography

Other added entries: USS THRESHER
Navy Industrial Fund
Shock
Vibration

Hooker, Ruth

Interview of Ruth Hooker, conducted by Dr. David K. Allison

Date of Interview: 791011

Documentation: 2 Tapes (3 Sides)

Abstract: Ms. Hooker discusses the establishment of the NRL technical library. She was originally hired as a physicist.

Repositories: NRL

Institutions: Naval Research Laboratory

Hooper, VADM Edwin B.

Interview of VADM Edwin B. Hooper, conducted by Albert B. Christman

Date of Interview: 710200

Documentation: Index, Transcript 78 pp.

Interview number: S-78

Abstract: This interview was originally conducted as background for a biography of RADM William S. Parsons. Hooper describes his personal background and his contact with Parsons at the Naval Proving Ground at Dahlgren, Va. He discusses Parsons' influence on the post-war structure of Navy R&D. Hooper comments on his post-war contacts with Parsor ¯ on the Atomic Energy Commission, Military Liaison Committee, and socially. He also talks about the Salt Wells Pilot Plant.

Repositories: NWC, DTNSRDC, NHC

Individuals mentioned: Parsons, RADM William S.
Rivero, ADM Horacio
Smith, VADM Levering

Institutions: Naval Ordnance Test Station
Naval Proving Ground
Atomic Energy Commission

Other added entries: Salt Wells Pilot Plant

Hooper, VADM Edwin B.

   Interview of VADM Edwin B. Hooper, conducted by CAPT
Robert L. Hansen, Dr. Peter Bruton, and Mrs. Susan Frutkin

Date of Interview: 740000

Documentation: 4 Tapes, Transcript 135 pp.

Interview number: BA-10

Abstract: This interview contains VADM Hooper's opinions on
management of Navy R&D since the end of World War II. Topics
include Bureau of Ordnance management, inter-bureau
relationships, and the future of Navy R&D.

Repositories: NHC, DTNSRDC

Individuals mentioned: Forrestal, SECNAV James
McNamara, SECDEF Robert S.

Institutions: Naval Weapons Center
Office of Naval Research
Bureau of Ordnance

Other added entries: Foundational Funding

Hooper, ADM Edwin B.

   Interview of ADM Edwin B. Hooper, conducted by Richard
D. Glasow and Nelson Wood

Date of Interview: 780822

Documentation: Tapes, Transcript

Abstract: ADM Hooper discusses his post-graduate ordnance
training at the Naval Post Graduate School, and MIT, and
ordnance research during World War II.

Individuals mentioned: Rivero, ADM Horacio
Ward, ADM A. G.

Institutions: Massachusetts Institute of Technology
U. S. Naval Academy

Subjects: Ordnance

Other added entries: Ordnance Training

Hopper, COMO Grace Brewster (Murray)

Interview of COMO Grace Brewster Hopper, conducted by
Mike Wallace

Date of Interview: 830000

Documentation: Transcript

Abstract: This is a transcript of the "60 Minutes" interview
of COMO Hopper by Mike Wallace. COMO Hopper discusses her
background and training, relatives in the Navy, her work
with the first computers in the Navy, and her contributions
to the development of computer language.

Repositories: RAD

Institutions: Office of Naval Research

Subjects: Computers
Computer Language

Other added entries: COBOL

Hopper, COMO Grace Brewster (Murray)

Interview of COMO Grace Brewster (Murray) Hopper

Date of Interview: 830200

Documentation: 6 Tapes

Abstract: This interview is part of the "Women in the
Federal Government Project", sponsored by the Arthur and
Elizabeth Schlesinger Library on the History of Women in
America and funded by the National Endowment for the
Humanities. COMO Hopper discusses her work with the first

Navy computers and her contributions in developing computer
language.

Repositories: RAD

Institutions: Office of Naval Research

Subjects: Computers
Computer Language

Other added entries: COBOL

Howard, Jim

   Interview of Jim Howard, conducted by Tom Misa and Ed
Todd

Date of Interview: 820609

Documentation: 1 Tape, Index 2 pp.

Interview number: NADC-1

Abstract: Mr. Howard discusses airplane use in antisubmarine
warfare, the systems approach to sonobuoy development from
1952 to the present, and the technical navigator, TACO. He
talks about the design of the P-3C aircraft, including the
incorporation of computers and TACO, LOFAR and DIFAR. Howard
comments on present goals of NADC, including the Advanced
Signal Processor, Very High Speed Integrated Circuitry,
changes in sonobuoy research, and the Julie sonobuoy.

Repositories: NADC, DTNSRDC

Individuals mentioned: Gleiter, Werner

Institutions: Naval Air Development Center

Subjects: Antisubmarine Warfare Research
Antisubmarine Warfare
Sonobouy Research
Sonobuoys
Antisubmarine Aircraft
Low Frequency Radar

Other added entries: Julie Sonobuoy Project

Jim Howard of the Naval Air Development Center.

Hulburt, Dr. Edward O.

Interview with Dr. Edward O. Hulburt, conducted by Dr. David K. Allison

Date of Interview: 770908

Documentation: 5 Tapes (8 Sides), Transcript 49 pp.

Other interview date: 770822

Abstract: Dr. Hulburt talks about his background and education, work with the Signal Corps Radio Laboratory in Paris during World War I, and listening stations at the front, employment at Johns Hopkins and the University of Iowa, early days of working at NRL, short radio waves and skip distances, ionospheric research, naval camouflage, infrared signaling and detection, the Optics Division, laboratory build-up before World War II, rocket studies and the Vanguard Program, work with World War II scientific societies, his involvement with the International Geophysical Year, and comments on on management of research at NRL from 1949-1955.

Repositories: NRL

Individuals mentioned: Taylor, Dr. A. Hoyt
Gunn, Dr. Ross
Tousey, Dr. Richard
Maris, Harry
Dawson, Dr. Leo H.
Bittenger, Charles
Karle, Dr. Jerome
Karle, Dr. Isabella Lugoski

Institutions: Naval Research Laboratory
International Geophysical Year
U. S. Army Signal Corps
Johns Hopkins University

Subjects: Optics
Camouflage

Other added entries: Optics Research
V-2 Rocket
Vanguard Program
Space Research

Dr. Edward O. Hulbert, first Director of Research of the Naval
Research Laboratory.

Hunsaker, Jerome Clarke

Interview with Jerome Clarke Hunsaker

Date of Interview: 600000

Documentation: Transcript 112 pp.

Abstract: This interview mentions the Naval Academy, 1904-1908, naval architecture, MIT, research in Europe, stability analysis and wind tunnels, his Navy duty in World War I, flying boats, the first aircraft carrier 1922, non-rigid air ships, and his position as coordinator of research for the Navy, 1940.

Repositories: COL
Institutions: Coordinator of Research and Development (Navy)

Subjects: Naval Architecture
Aircraft Design
Wind Tunnels

Other added entries: Flying Boats
Airships

Hunt, F. L. "Pete"

Interview of F. L. "Pete" Hunt, conducted by Albert B. Christman

Date of Interview: 801100

Documentation: 2 Tapes, Transcript 45 pp.

Interview number: DNL-T36

Abstract: Mr. Hunt talks about how he came to the New London lab as a scientist from Columbia University, other scientists from Columbia at the time, and the influence of Harvard University there. He describes wartime work done in New London in sonar, submarine research, and the testing of new concepts and discoveries. Other topics include: Dr. Harold Nash, Dr. Horton, the Commanding Officers at New London, postwar R&D, and the merger of the New London and Newport labs into the Naval Underwater Systems Center in 1970.

Repositories: DTNSRDC

Individuals mentioned: Nash, Dr. Harold
Horton, Dr.

Pryor, CAPT William L.
Ide, John

Institutions: Naval Underwater Systems Center
Columbia University
Office of Scientific Research and Development
Harvard University

Subjects: Sonar

Cities: New London, CT.
Newport, RI.

Other added entries: Submarine Research

Hunter, Dr. Hugh

   Interview of Dr. Hugh Hunter, conducted by Elizabeth Babcock

Date of Interview: 750530

Documentation: Index, Transcript 26 pp.

Interview number: S-95

Abstract: Dr. Hunter discusses the formation of the Technical Research Board by Dr. Louis T. E. Thompson at NOTS. He talks about Dr. Frederick W. Brown as Technical Director and the relationship between Levering Smith, the Associate TD, and Dr. Thompson when he was TD. Hunter comments on his own move from the Research Division to the Central Staff at NOTS and how the Ballistics Division at NOTS disappeared. Hunter reflects on his move to the Propulsion Division and the importance of varied career experience at NOTS. There is a second interview with Hunter, numbered S-95A, which was conducted on 14 August 1975.

Repositories: NWC, DTNSRDC, NHC

Individuals mentioned: Brown, Dr. Frederick W.
Smith, VADM Levering
McLean, Dr. William B.
Sage, Dr. Bruce
Shenk, Dr. John H.
Thompson, Dr. Louis T. E.
Wilson, Dr. Haskell G.

Institutions: Naval Ordnance Test Station
Naval Weapons Center

Hunter, Dr. Hugh

Interview of Dr. Hugh Hunter, conducted by Albert B. Christman

Date of Interview: 750814

Documentation: Index, Transcript 21 pp.

Interview number: S-95B

Abstract: Dr. Hunter makes general comments on R&D and NOTS/NWC, including working under Dr. William B. McLean, CAPT Hardy, and Dr. Haskell G. Wilson. He comments on the selection of leadership, organizational changes, and the need to justify research at NOTS/NWC. He comments on the transfer of NOTS research findings to the outside world, travel restrictions for NOTS employees, and the future of R&D in the Navy.

Repositories: NWC, DTNSRDC, NHC

Individuals mentioned: Bennett, Dr. Ira
Hollingsworth, Dr. Guilford L.
LaBerge, Dr. Walter
McLean, Dr. William B.
Wilson, Dr. Haskell G.
Hardy, CAPT John I.

Institutions: Naval Ordnance Test Station
Naval Weapons Center

Hussey, VADM George F.

Interview of VADM George F. Hussey

Date of Interview: 650000

Documentation: Transcript 582 pp.

Abstract: VADM Hussey talks about his education at the Naval Academy, particularily courses in ordnance and ballistics, and the work in the Bureau of Ordnance Armor and Projectile Section. He discusses his service as Proof Officer at the Naval Proving Ground, in Mine research, and as Assistant Chief and Chief of the Bureau of Ordnance, and gives his opinions of contractor-operated ordnance plants and postwar ordnance research.

Repositories: COL, NHC

Institutions: Naval Proving Ground
Bureau of Ordnance

Subjects: Ordnance

Cities: Dahlgren, VA.

Hussey, VADM George F.
Thompson, Dr. Louis T. E.

Interview of VADM George F. Hussey and Dr. Louis T. E.
Thompson, conducted by Albert B. Christman

Date of Interview: 660400

Documentation: Index, Transcript 110 pp.

Interview number: NOTS-75201-S5

Abstract: This extensive interview includes a history of
Navy ordnance bases from around 1910 to after World War II.
It includes a discussion of whether NOTS should be a
research or a test station. Thompson and Hussey also
describe RADM William S. Parsons' relations with scientific
community and his work on the Proximity Fuze Project. They
comment on ADM Hussey's time as head of BUORD and James
Forrestal's tenure as Secretary of the Navy.

Repositories: NWC, DTNSRDC, NHC

Individuals mentioned: Blandy, ADM George
Burroughs, ADM Sherman E.
Forrestal, SECNAV James
Michelson, Dr. Albert A.
Moulton, Prof. Forest Ray
Parsons, RADM William S.
Schoeffel, RADM Malcom F.
Schuyler, CAPT Michael
Tuve, Dr. Merle

Institutions: Naval Ordnance Test Station

Subjects: Ordnance

Other added entries: Proximity Fuze

Hustvedt, VADM Olaf M.

Interview of VADM Olaf M. Hustvedt, conducted by Fred Durant, Paul Garber, Lou Casey, and Erling Hustvedt.

Date of Interview: 720211

Documentation: Transcript 37 pp.

Interview number: S-80

Abstract: VADM Hustvedt comments on his associations with Dr. Robert Goddard and the Navy-Army bombing tests against OSTFRIELAND and FRANKFURT -- old German warships. He discusses the actions of COL (later GEN) Billy Mitchell during those tests and talks about the explosion of the dirigible, SHENANDOAH, in 1925.

Repositories: NWC, DTNSRDC, NHC

Individuals mentioned: Goddard, Dr. Robert
Mitchell, GEN William
Landsdown, Mrs.

Institutions: Bureau of Ordnance
Bureau of Ordnance Experimental Section

Other added entries: Aerial Bombing
Airships
USS SHENANDOAH (ZR)
Rocket Research

Jackson, VADM Andrew McBurney, Jr.

Interview of VADM Andrew McBurney Jackson, Jr.

Date of Interview: 711100

Other interview date: 720400

Documentation: Index, Transcript 385 pp.

Abstract: Naval aviator, project officer in design of Grumman F6F Hellcat at Bureau of Aeronautics, later served with Atomic Energy Commission.

Repositories: NHC, NWCM, USNA, USNI

Institutions: Atomic Energy Commission
Bureau of Aeronautics

Other added entries: Grumman F6F
Aircraft Design

James, Richard

Interview of Richard James, conducted by Tom Misa and
Ed Todd

Date of Interview: 820719

Documentation: 1 Tape, Index 2 pp.

Interview number: NADC-13

Abstract: Mr. James discusses his personal background and
the organization and history of the LAMPS project from 1968
to the present. Included in the LAMPS history are sections
on LAMPS as an air and ship project, the importance of
documentation in the program, and relations between NADC and
NAVAIR on LAMPS. He also talks about IBM's role in LAMPS.

Repositories: NADC, DTNSRDC

Individuals mentioned: Janaco, Tom

Institutions: Naval Air Development Center
Naval Air Systems Command
International Business Machine Company
Sikorsky

Subjects: Antisubmarine Warfare
Antisubmarine Aircraft
Helicopters

Other added entries: Light Airborne Multi-Purpose System

Jennison, James H.

Interview of James H. Jennison, conducted by J. D.
Gerrard-Gough

Date of Interview: 751025

Documentation: Transcript 27 pp.

Interview number: 5313-S-99

Abstract: Mr. Jennison discusses his background, the Mark 13
torpedo, and changes at the NOTS-Pasadena laboratory when

the Navy took it over. He describes his work with Variable Angle Launcher and the benefits of working with the NOTS-China Lake team.

Repositories: NWC, DTNSRDC, NHC

Individuals mentioned: Lindvall, Dr. Frederick C.
Saylor, William
Thompson, Dr. Louis T. E.

Institutions: Naval Weapons Center
Naval Ordnance Test Station
Bureau of Ordnance

Other added entries: Torpedo Mark 13
Variable-Angle Torpedo Launcher

Jennison, James H.

Interview of James H. Jennison, conducted by Albert B. Christman

Date of Interview: 780315

Documentation: 1 Tape, Transcript 17 pp.

Interview number: DNL-T6-78

Abstract: Mr. Jennison discusses the recruitment of qualified scientists for the Navy's West Coast labs - in particular, the role of the Board of Scientists and the Civil Service Commission and competition with private industry. He comments on the increasing amount of bureaucracy involved in running a lab and notes a few examples. In addition, Jennison explains the problems involved in procuring supplies and awarding contracts because of recent government regulations. He talks about his work at the Pasadena Annex of NOTS, the Annex's absorbtion into NUC in San Diego, and his move to San Diego. He describes advantages that small labs like the Annex have over larger labs like NOTS labs still offer good opportunities for scientists and engineers who want to work in R&D and others who want to work in management

Repositories: NHC, DTNSRDC

Institutions: Naval Ordnance Test Station
Naval Undersea Center
Naval Ocean Systems Center
Pasadena Annex
Naval Weapons Center

Cities: Pasadena, CA.
San Diego, CA.

Johnson, Charles Y.

   Interview of Charles Y. Johnson, conducted by Dr. David
K. Allison

Date of Interview: 790525

Documentation: 11 Tapes (22 Sides), Typewritten index 10 pp.

Other dates of interviews: 790108, 790111, 790115

Abstract: Dr. Johnson discusses his background and
education, working conditions and radar development at NRL
during World War II, his transfer to the NRL Communications
Security Group, upper air research, telemetry systems, buzz
bomb defense, V-2 rockets, Aerobee rockets, testing at White
Sands, the Viking rocket on the NORTON SOUND, cryogenic fuel
problems, cosmic ray experimentation, gamma ray detectors,
and the ONR Skyhook Program. He details the effect of
Sputnik on research programs, the exodus from NRL to
Goddard, the loss of NSF and DNA funding, satellite
navigation and communications, use of mass spectrometers,
the SOLRAD Hi satellite, Skylab, and ionospheric research.

Repositories: NRL

Individuals mentioned: Young, Dr. Leo C.
Bourland, Langford
Chubb, Dr. Talbot A.
Reed, Edith
Pressly, Eleanor
Holmes, Julian
Kegley, Larry
Taylor, Dr. A. Hoyt
Gebhard, Dr. Louis A.
Cleeton, Dr. Claud E.
Hagen, Dr. John P.

Institutions: Naval Research Laboratory
Office of Naval Research
National Aeronautics and Space Administration

Subjects: Telemetry
Cosmic Rays
Gamma Rays
Radar
Radio Communications
Radio Transmitters

Satellites

Cities: White Sands, NM.

Other added entries: Atmospheric Research
Viking Rocket
V-2 Rocket
Aerobee Rocket
Kawai Rocket
Saturn Rocket
Skylab
Ionospheric Research
USS NORTON SOUND
Skyhook

Johnson, Charles Y.

Interview of Charles Y. Johnson, conducted by Peg Shea
and Allan Needell

Date of Interview: 820303

Documentation: Tapes, 5.5 hours, Transcript, 61 pp.

Other date of interview: 820421

Abstract: These interviews trace Johnson's work at NRL,
beginning with World War II assignments, his contact with
the atomic bomb, post work in the rocket-sonde division, and
the V-2 program, the organizational structure of NRL, his
involvement with the IGY, Project Vanguard, the formation of
NASA, and NASA's relationship with NRL, the NRL satellite
program, Aerobee and Viking projects, and continuing work in
cosmic ray physics.

Repositories: NASM

Individuals mentioned: Krause, Dr. Ernst H.
Hagen, Dr. John P.
Rosen, Milton
Newell, Dr. Homer E.
Tousey, Dr. Richard
Friedman, Dr. Herbert

Institutions: Naval Research Laboratory
International Geophysical Year
National Aeronautics and Space Administration

Subjects: Ionospheric Physics
Rocketry
Radar

Satellites

Cities: White Sands, NM.

Other added entries: Vanguard Program
Cosmic Ray Physics
Aerobee Rocket
Viking Rocket
Manhattan Project
Rocket-Sonde

Johnson, Dr. Frances Severin

Interview of Dr. Frances Severin Johnson

Date of Interview: 820623

Documentation: Tapes, 3 hours, Transcript, 58 pp.

Abstract: The interview covers Johnson's early life and education in Canada, his training in physics at the University of Alberta, and graduate school at Berkeley and UCLA. He discusses work on the V-2 rocket research program with Tousey, Hulburt, and Krause at NRL.

Repositories: NASM

Individuals mentioned: Hulburt, Dr. Edward O.
Tousey, Dr. Richard
Krause, Dr. Ernst H.

Institutions: Naval Research Laboratory
University of Alberta

Subjects: Solar Physics
Meteorology

Other added entries: V-2 Rocket
Solar Spectrograph

Johnson, ADM Roy L.

   Interview of ADM Roy L. Johnson

Date of Interview: 801200

Documentation: Index, Transcript 350 pp.

Abstract: ADM Johnson, a Naval aviator, discusses the seaplane as weapons system, and the effectiveness of PBY flying boats.

Repositories: NHC, NWCM, USNA, USNI

Subjects: Flying Boats
Seaplanes

Other added entries: PBY Flying Boat

Jones, Dr. Earl

   Interview of Dr. Earl Jones, conducted by Albert B. Christman

Date of Interview: 780315

Documentation: Transcript 27 pp.

Interview number: DNL-T-3-78

Other interview date: 780310

Abstract: Dr. Jones discusses his personal background, personnel research in World War I and World War II, and the rationale behind and need for personnel research. He comments on the effect of policy decisions on the labs, the differences in personnel research in the 1960's and 1970's, manpower problems, and the effect of computers on personnel research. Jones talks about the creation of NPRDC, its equipment needs, and location. He explores the sources for new research, personnel research in wars and crises, and high-tech personnel requirements of the Navy. Jones also reflects on NPRDC's history and the influence of Dr. Edward Dudek.

Repositories: NWC, DTNSRDC, NHC

Individuals mentioned: Dudek, Dr. Edward
Zumwalt, ADM Elmo

Institutions: Navy Personnel Research and Development Center

Other added entries: Personnel Research
Manpower Modeling

Keener, Charles E.

   Interview of Charles E. Keener, conducted by Tom Misa
and Ed Todd

Date of Interview: 820628

Documentation: 1 Tape, Index 2 pp.

Interview number: NADC-3

Abstract: Mr. Keener discusses his arrival at NADC in 1945,
his educational background, and the uses of radar in World
War II. He describes his career at NADC, including work with
AEEL, AWRD, and his position as Director of the Technical
Intelligence Department. Keener comments on NADC from 1945
to the early 1950's, the rise of contract monitoring
functions of NADC, and the re-organization or AWRD into
SAED. He talks about overall re-organizations at the center
and the systems approach.

Repositories: NADC, DTNSRDC

Institutions: Naval Air Development Center
Air Warfare Research Department
Applied Electrical and Electronics Laboratory
Systems Analysis and Electronics Department
Naval Air Modification Unit

Subjects: Systems Approach
Communications
Radar
Aicraft Antennas

Other added entries: Polaris Program
Submarine Communications
Very Low Frequency Communications

Keil, Dr. Alfred H.

Interview of Dr. Alfred H. Keil, conducted by Enid
Kumin

Date of interview: 751010

Documentation: Transcript 79 pp.

Abstract: Dr. Keil describes how he was offered a job by
the United States War Department in 1947 after working for
the German Navy during World War II, how he worked for
BUSHIPS and later the David Taylor Model Basin where he was
in charge of the structures laboratory and later became the
Technical Director, his involvement in long-range planning
for weapons systems, ocean technology, his later work at
MIT, work on various committees, and thoughts on naval
architecture.

Repositories: MIT, DTNSRDC

Institutions: David Taylor Model Basin
Massachusetts Institute of Technology
National Science Foundation
Marine Science Council
Naval Ship Research and Development Center

Other added entries: Ocean Technology
Deep Submersibles
Long Range Planning

Kelly, CAPT James F.

Interview of CAPT James F. Kelly, conducted by Roger
Kempler

Date of Interview: 820922

Documentation: Index, Transcript 32 pp.

Abstract: CAPT Kelly describes his appointment as Commanding
Officer of NPRDC, how NPRDC is perceived in Washington, and
human factors engineering. He talks about orienting the
SYSCOMs, re-organizing NPRDC, and the serious the expansion
of NPRDC, the organizational location of NPRDC, and
competition for funds with R&D labs. He comments on the
possible merger of NOSC and NPRDC, the NAVMAT Inspector
General's report on NPRDC, and major contributions of NPRDC
over the last ten years.

Repositories: DTNSRDC, NPRDC

Dr. Edward O. Hulbert, first Director of Research of the Naval
Research Laboratory.

Dr. James W. Tweedale, Technical Director, and Captain James F. Kelly, Jr., Commanding Officer of the Navy Personnel Research and Development Center.

Individuals mentioned: wnittle, ADM Alfred J., Jr.
Regan, Dr. James J.

Institutions: Navy Personnel Research and Development Center
Naval Ocean Systems Center
Naval Material Command

Cities: San Diego, CA.

Other added entries: Technical Director
Commanding Officer
Inspector General
Personnel Research

Kendig, Dr. Paul M.

   Interview of Dr. Paul M. Kendig, conducted by Richard
D. Glasow

Date of Interview: 800213

Documentation: Tapes, Transcript

Abstract: Dr. Kendig describes his background and education,
and his work at the Harvard Underwater Sound Laboratory and
the Applied Research Laboratory.

Repositories: ARL

Individuals mentioned: Pielemeier, Dr. Walter H.
Walker, Eric A.

Institutions: Pennsylvania State University
Harvard University
Underwater Sound Laboratory
Applied Research Laboratory

Other added entries: Acoustics Research

Kirk, ADM Alan Goodrich

   Interview of ADM Alan Goodrich Kirk

Date of Interview: 610000

Documentation: Transcript 386 pp.

Abstract: ADM Kirk recalls his career in the Navy, including his education at the Naval Academy, and work at the Naval Proving Ground and the Bureau of Ordnance.

Repositories: COL. NHC

Institutions: Naval Proving Ground

Subjects: Ordnance

Cities: Dahlgren, VA.

Koesey, Calvin

   Interview of Calvin Koesey, conducted by Albert B. Christman

Date of Interview: 780000

Documentation: Tape, Transcript 13 pp.

Interview number: DNL-T21-78

Abstract: Mr. Koesey talks about his role at the Naval Underwater Systems Center, including R&D work during the Vietnam War. Research topics covered are mine work, harbor defense, and problems of coastal navies. He also discusses laboratory representatives in Vietnam and the Navy's role in Korea.

Repositories: DTNSRDC

Institutions: Naval Underwater Systems Center

Other added entries: Vietnam Laboratory Assistance Program

Krause, Dr. Ernst H.

   Interview of Dr. Ernst H. Krause, conducted by Dr.
David H. DeVorkin

Date of Interview: 820810

Documentation: Tapes, 6 hours, Transcript, 122 pp.

Other date of interview: 830701

Abstract: Dr. Krause talks about his education, training in
physics, and interests in nuclear physics and spectroscopy.
At NRL during World War II, he worked in the Communications
Security Section, optics, and development of pulse guidance
systems, and was involved in the interrogation of German
missile scientists and Operation Paperclip. He describes the
organization of the Rocket-Sonde section, his role in the
V-2 program, co-workers, contacts with Federal Contract
Research Centers, and his research in cosmic ray physics.

Repositories: NASM

Individuals mentioned: Toftoy, BG Holger N.
Friedman, Dr. Herbert
Malina, Dr. Frank J.
Braun, Wernher von
Tousey, Dr. Richard
Schein, Prof. Marcel
Pickering, Dr. William H.
Schwinger, Dr. Julian S.

Institutions: Naval Research Laboratory
Applied Physics Laboratory
California Institute of Technology
Jet Propulsion Laboratory

Subjects: Physics
Cosmic Rays
Space Astronomy

Cities: White Sands, NM.

Other added entries: Rocket-Sonde
Operation Paperclip
Research Management
Cosmic Ray Research
Dynasoar
V-2 Rocket
Neptune
Viking Rocket
Aerobee Rocket

Kron, Dr. Gerald Edward

Interview of Dr. Gerald Edward Kron, conducted by Dr. David H. DeVorkin

Date of interview: 780520

Documentation: Tapes, 1 1/2 hrs., Transcript 28 pp.

Abstract: Dr. Kron speaks about his education and background, work at Berkeley and Lick Observatory, World War II at MIT and Caltech, post-war employment, and work at the Naval Observatory.

Repositories: AIP

Institutions: Naval Observatory

Subjects: Astronomy

Other added entries: Photoelectric Photometry

Krutter, Dr. Harry

Interview of Dr. Harry Krutter, conducted by Albert B. Christman

Date of Interview: 780400

Documentation: Transcript 23 pp.

Interview number: DNL-T18-78

Abstract: Dr. Krutter talks about his background at the Massachusetts Institute of Technology, his arrival at NADC in 1949, and NADC's early chief scientists. He comments on his time as Technical Director from 1956 to 1972. the direction of Navy R&D work, and the Bureau of Aeronautics and later the Naval Air Systems Command. Dr. Krutter discusses the Navy re-organization of 1965-1966, the cooperation between Navy labs, and his reasons for retiring from NADC. He expostulates in particular on the role of the Director of Navy Laboratories and Chief of Naval Material in running the labs and the major accomplishments of NADC.

Repositories: DTNSRDC, NADC

Institutions: Naval Air Development Center
Director of Navy Laboratories

Naval Air Systems Command
Bureau of Aeronautics
Chief of Naval Material

Other added entries: Technical Director

Krutter, Dr. Harry

Interview of Dr. Harry Krutter, conducted by Tom Misa and Ed Todd

Date of Interview: 820628

Documentation: 2 Tapes, Index 3 pp.

Interview number: NADC-2, 3

Abstract: Dr. Krutter describes his academic background, his time at an NRL field station, and his professorial days at Penn State. He discusses the Bureau of Aeronautics' consolidation of facilities at Johnsville, Pa., the NRL field station's switch to becoming the Radar Division of the Aeronautical Electronics and Electrical Laboratory, and projects of the center in the early 1950's. Krutter comments on the formation of the Anti-Submarine Warfare Laboratory in 1958, BUAER's relationship to NADC, and his appointment as chief scientist of NADC in 1956. He talks about center reorganizations, the systems approach, and Navy lab reorganization, in general, from 1965 to 1968. He mentions the Phoenix Missile System, its predecessor, the Eagle Missile System, and the hybrid digital-analog computer, Typhoon. Krutter reflects on the change in the nature of NADC's work and his career as Technical Director.

Repositories: NADC

Individuals mentioned: Gloeckler, Fred W.
Black, Dr. K. C.
Tremblay, Harold
McNamara, SECDEF Robert S.
Driggs, Ivan

Institutions: Naval Air Development Center
Bureau of Aeronautics
Naval Research Laboratory
Aeronautical Instruments Laboratory
Aircraft Armament Laboratory
Anti-Submarine Warfare Laboratory
Aeronautical Electronics and Electrical Laboratory

Subjects: Antisubmarine Warfare Research

Dr. Harry Krutter of the Naval Air Development Center.

Fire Control Systems
Antisubmarine Warfare
Missile Systems
Airborne Early Warning Radar
Systems Approach
Computers
Radar

Cities: Johnsville, PA.

Other added entries: Technical Director
Airborne Height Finder
Typhoon Project
Eagle Missile Project
Phoenix Missile Project

Kunz, D. A.

   Interview of D. A. ("Bud") Kunz, conducted by J. D.
Gerrard-Gough

Date of Interview: 751023

Documentation: Index, Transcript 9 pp.

Interview number: S-104

Abstract: Mr. Kunz comments on the Navy's problems with
torpedos during World War II and the group put together to
solve them. He talks about the Variable-Angle Launcher and
acoustic torpedo built at Morris Dam. Kunz describes
administration problems at NOTS, his nuclear work and the
role of the General Tire and Rubber Company.

Repositories: NWC, DTNSRDC, NHC

Individuals mentioned: Saylor, William

Institutions: Naval Ordnance Test Station

Subjects: Torpedos
Acoustic Torpedos

Other added entries: Variable-Angle Torpedo Launcher

Land, ADM Emory S.

Interview of ADM Emory S. Land

Date of Interview: 630000

Documentation: Transcript 227 pp.

Abstract: In this interview ADM Land discusses his study at the Naval Academy and MIT, naval architecture, his work in the Bureau of Ships, and Bureau of Aeronautics, Harry Guggenheim and air research, his service as Chief of the Bureau of Ships, and shipbuilding for the National Defense Agency.

Repositories: COL, NHC

Individuals mentioned: Guggenheim, Harry

Institutions: Bureau of Ships
Bureau of Aeronautics
National Defense Agency
Massachusetts Institute of Technology
U. S. Naval Academy

Subjects: Naval Architecture
Naval Construction

Landweber, Dr. Louis

Interview of Dr. Louis Landweber, conducted by Seth Hawkins

Date of Interview: 831028

Documentation: 2 Tapes, 1 Diskette, Transcript 30 pp.

Abstract: Dr. Landweber describes his work at the Experimental Model Basin in the Washington Navy Yard starting in 1932, including coworkers, towing tank conferences, experiments in cable towing and ship rolling, early work by Scott Russell and William Froude, eliminating vibration of submarine periscopes, construction of the model basin at Carderock, and explosives testing.

Repositories: DTNSRDC

Individuals mentioned: Schoenherr, Dr. Karl E.
Tase, Johnny
Russell, Scott
Froude, William

Mumma, RADM Albert G.
Saunders, CAPT Harold E.
Rabinowitz, Leo
Thorne, George
Norley, William
Hewins, Dr. Lyman

Institutions: Experimental Model Basin
David Taylor Naval Ship Research and Development Center
David Taylor Model Basin

Cities: Washington, DC.
Carderock, MD.

Other added entries: Model Testing

Langenbeck, Earl H.

   Interview of Earl H. Langenbeck, conducted by Albert B.
Christman

Date of Interview: 780331

Documentation: 1 Tape, Transcript 16 pp.

Interview number: DNL-T11-78

Abstract: Mr. Langenbeck discusses his time at the Naval Gun
Factory and the Navy Yard during World War II and after and
compares the amount of bureaucracy and the ability to get
things done during the war with the postwar period. He talks
about problems involved in contracting defense research out,
added regulations created for labs by non-R&D oriented
people, and the consolidation of the Navy lab system.
Langenbeck also recommends people for future interviews.

Repositories: DTNSRDC

Individuals mentioned: Probus, Dr. James H.
Bennett, Dr. Ralph
Hartmann, Dr. Gregory

Institutions: Naval Surface Weapons Center
Naval Ordnance Laboratory
Naval Weapons Laboratory
Naval Gun Factory

Cities: White Oak, MD.
Dahlgren, VA.
Washington, DC.

Other added entries: Contracting
Laboratory Consolidations

Laser History

    Laser History, conducted by Dr. David K. Allison

Date of Interview: 810304

Other date of interview: 810312

Documentation: 3 Tapes (6 Sides)

Abstract: This is a series of interviews done to document laser technology at NRL. The interviews consist of descriptions and explanations of individual photographs of equipment. The tapes are keyed to photographs in storage at the Washington National Records Center in Suitland, MD.

Repositories: NRL

Institutions: Naval Research Laboratory

Other added entries: Laser Research
Laser History

Lauritsen, Dr. Charles C.
Hardy, CAPT John I.
Robinson, K. H.

    Dedication of Weapon Exhibit Center

Date of Interview: 641104

Documentation: Index, Transcript 18 pp.

Interview number: NOTS-75201-S3

Abstract: This is a transcript of a speech made at the dedication of Weapon Exhibits Center at NOTS in Inyokern, CA. Among the topics discussed are RADM Parsons' proximity fuze, the submarine as a menace to U. S. ships, and the United Kingdom's use of submarine detectors. In addition, Lauritsen talks about the establishment of NOTS and its top officers.

Repositories: NWC, DTNSRDC, NHC

Individuals mentioned: Burroughs, ADM Sherman E.

Institutions: Naval Ordnance Test Station
National Defense Research Committee

Other added entries: Rocket Research
Submarine Detectors
Proximity Fuze

Lauritsen, Dr. Charles C.

Interview of Dr. Charles C. Lauritsen, conducted by
Albert B. Christman

Date of Interview: 660400

Documentation: Index, Transcript 28 pp.

Interview number: NOTS-75201-S4

Abstract: This interview was originally conducted as
background for a biography of RADM William S. Parsons. Dr.
Lauritsen discusses his overall impression of Parsons, his
early contacts with him, and Parsons' work on the Proximity
Fuze Project. In addition, Lauritsen reflects on Parsons'
Manhattan Project involvement and his early connection with
NOTS. He talks about CAPT Burroughs' role at NOTS and
British-American scientific cooperation during World War II.

Repositories: NWC, DTNSRDC, NHC

Individuals mentioned: Parsons, RADM William S.
Burroughs, ADM Sherman E.
Thompson, Dr. Louis T. E.

Institutions: Naval Ordnance Test Station
Office of Scientific Research and Development
California Institute of Technology

Other added entries: Proximity Fuze
Manhattan Project

Lauritsen, Dr. Thomas

Interview of Dr. Thomas Lauritsen, conducted by Albert
B. Christman

Date of Interview: 690626

Documentation: Index, Transcript 20 pp.

Interview number: NWC-75201-S68

Abstract: Dr. Thomas Lauritsen comments on his father, Dr.
Charles Lauritsen - his allegiance to the U. S., his ability
to make decisions, his personal characteristics, and his
international outlook. Thomas Lauritsen discusses Nils Bohr,
British rocket research, and NDRC and OSRD. He talks about
project work at CalTech, propellant problems for rockets,
and a disappointing rocket test at Goldstone Lake. He also
describes RADM William S. Parsons' influence on Navy R&D and
military-civilian relationships, in general.

Repositories: NWC, DTNSRDC, NHC

Individuals mentioned: Bohr, Dr. Nils
Fowler, Dr. William
Lauritsen, Dr. Charles C.
Parsons, RADM William S.

California Institute of Technology
Naval Ordnance Test Station

Cities: Goldstone Lake, CA.

Other added entries: Rocket Research
Rocket Propellents

Law, Howard

Interview of Howard Law, conducted by Dr. David K.
Allison

Date of Interview: 830812

Documentation: 2 Tapes, Diskette, Transcript 41 pp.

Abstract: Mr. Law describes his education, military
experience in the Bureau of Ordnance, work at NWC and the
Naval Ordnance Plant in Georgia, and employment in 1965 with
BUWEPS in Washington, DC. He comments on the difference
between BUWEPS laboratory management and the early days of
the DNL organization, his work in 6.5 funding, management

styles and changes, "shore establishment realignments" - the consolidations of NSRDC, NOSC, NSWC, and NUSC, the role of the Facilities Division, the FCRCs, program reviews, Corporate Planning, the VLAP and NSAP programs, SHORESTAMPS, and the need for the laboratories to work harder at developing leaders.

Repositories: DTNSRDC

Individuals mentioned: Lawson, Dr. Joel
Hillyer, Robert
Kidd, ADM Issac C., Jr.
Kleback, Thomas
Johnson, Dr. Gerald
Smith, Howard
Towle, CAPT Bernard
Probus, Dr. James H.

Institutions: Director of Navy Laboratories
Federal Contract Research Centers
Systems Commands
Bureau of Ordnance
Bureau of Weapons
Naval Ship Research and Development Center
Naval Ocean Systems Center
Naval Surface Weapons Center
Naval Underwater Systems Center

Other added entries: Shore Establishment Realignments
Vietnam Laboratory Assistance Program
Navy Science Assistance Program
Corporate Plan
Navy Industrial Fund
Laboratory Consolidations

Lawson, Dr. Joel

Interview of Dr. Joel Lawson, conducted by Dr. Samuel Rothman and Mrs. Susan Frutkin

Date of Interview: 750000

Documentation: 2 Tapes, Transcript 64 pp.

Interview number: BA-2-75

Abstract: Dr. Lawson comments on his position as Special Assistant for Electronics, and on Robert A. Frosch as ASN (R&D). He talks about becoming Director of Navy Laboratories, his views on the DNL/DLP charter, block funding, and his management objectives. Lawson discusses his role as DNL, competition between the labs, and bringing CO's and TD's together. He describes the impact of the consolidation of the labs, the DNL as intercessor between the labs and their resources, and the labs problems in general. He explains lab budgeting, talks about work that is contracted out, and the relationship between the DNL and the Chief of Naval Operations. He comments on the effects of the SYSCOMs losing control of the labs. Also included are sections on Project REFLEX, the effect of numerous studies of the labs, and trends in lab management.

Repositories: DTNSRDC, NHC

Individuals mentioned: Foster, Dr. John S.
Frosch, Dr. Robert A.
Morse, Dr. Robert W.
Zumwalt, ADM Elmo
Kidd, ADM Issac C., Jr.

Institutions: Director of Navy Laboratories
Chief of Naval Material
Assistant Secretary of the Navy (R&D)
Chief of Naval Development
Director of Defense Research and Development
Systems Commands

Other added entries: Project REFLEX
Laboratory Consolidations

Lewis, Russell

Interview of Russell Lewis, conducted by Albert B. Christman

Date of Interview: 780000

Documentation: 1 Tape, Transcript 21 pp.

Interview number: DNL-T16-78

Abstract: Mr. Lewis comments on his work with sonar during World War II at New London, CT., his time on the USS ISLAND, and the influence of Columbia University and Harvard University scientists on the New London lab. He talks about the consolidation of the New London and Newport labs into NUSC, Navy sonar work at New London in the postwar era and its use in the Fleet, and the labs' role in the Vietnam War.

Repositories: DTNSRDC

Individuals mentioned: Clearwater, Walter

Horton, Dr.

Institutions: Naval Underwater Systems Center

Subjects: Sonar

Other added entries: Vietnam War
Laboratory Consolidations

Lockhart, Dr. Luther

   Interview of Dr. Luther Lockhart, conducted by Dr.
David K. Allison

Date of Interview: 790703

Documentation: 4 Tapes, Index 6 pp.

Other interview date: 790710

Abstract: Dr. Lockhart talks about his background and
education, conditions at NRL during World War II, airplane
anti-static wicks, lense coatings for binoculars,
restructuring of Chemistry Division after the war, research
in atmospheric radioactivity, laser research, work on
chemical coatings.

Repositories: NRL

Individuals mentioned: Zisman, Dr. William A.

Institutions: Naval Research Laboratory

Other added entries: Spectroscopy
Polymers
Spectrometry
Laser Technology
Chemical Coatings

Lockwood, VADM Charles A.

Interview of VADM Charles A. Lockwood

Date of Interview: 650000

Documentation: Transcript 720 pp.

Abstract: VADM Lockwood recalls his career and developments in submarine technology, including captured German submarines, SQUALUS rescue operations, periscope photography, the inventions of sonar, radar, and nuclear propulsion, and the development of the atomic submarine.

Repositories: COL, NHC

Subjects: Nuclear Propulsion
Sonar
Radar

Other added entries: USS SQUALUS
Atomic Submarines
Captured German Equipment

McDowell, Rensler

Interview of Rensler McDowell, conducted by Richard D. Glasow

Date of Interview: 800820

Documentation: Tapes, Transcript

Abstract: Mr. McDowell describes his role in acoustics research at the Newport Naval Torpedo Station.

Repositories: ARL

Institutions: Naval Torpedo Station

Cities: Newport, RI.
Goat Island, RI.

Subjects: Torpedos

Other added entries: Acoustics Research
Ordnance Research

Lyddane, Dr. Russell H.

"Times of Crisis: Dr. Russell H. Lyddane", conducted by Cynthia Rouse

Date of Interview: 770124

Documentation: Transcript 14 pp.

Abstract: This interview is Chapter VII in <u>Dahlgren</u>, edited by Kenneth G. McCollum

Abstract: Dr. Lyddane discusses the work environment at Dahlgren, the work of the Naval Gun Factory, ballistics tables, projectile testing, torpedo fuzes, the Computation Laboratory, the Armor and Projectile Laboratory, problems in position classification, the Fleet Ballistic Missile Program, the change in name in 1959 and relationship with NOL, White Oak.

Repositories: NSWC, DTNSRDC

Institutions: Naval Proving Ground
Naval Ordnance Laboratory
Naval Gun Factory

Subjects: Ordnance
Ballistics

Other added entries: Fleet Ballistic Missile Program
Technical Director

McKibbin, Mrs. Joseph (Dorothy)

Interview of Mrs. Joseph McKibbin, conducted by Albert B. Christman

Date of Interview: 670100

Documentation: Index, Transcript 29 pp.

Interview number: NOTS-75201-S28

Abstract: This interview was originally conducted as background for a biography of RADM William S. Parsons. Mrs. McKibbin discusses Parsons' attitude toward the office, his family life, his appearance, and what others thought of him.

Repositories: NWC, DTNSRDC, NHC

Individuals mentioned: Carmondy, Hazel

Parsons, RADM William S.
Oppenheimer, Dr. Robert
Parsons, Martha

Cities: Los Alamos, NM.

Other added entries: Manhattan Project

McLean, Edith LaVerne (Mrs. William B.)

  Interview of Mrs. LaVerne McLean, conducted by William F. Wright

Date of Interview: 800318

Documentation: Index, Transcript 48 pp.

Interview number: S-113

Abstract: Mrs. McLean discusses Dr. William B. McLean's personal habits, social abilities, and relationships with Navy personnel. She describes his work habits, his role in the Sidewinder Missile Project, and his appointment as Technical Director of NWC. Mrs. McLean conveys McLean's feelings on war, in general, and on the use of Sidewinder in Korea and Vietnam. She also talks about McLean's delegation of authority when necessary, particularly to Dr. Haskell G. Wilson.

Repositories: NWC, DTNSRDC, NHC

Individuals mentioned: McLean, Dr. William B.
McLean, Edith LaVerne (Mrs. William B.)
Wilson, Dr. Haskell G.

Institutions: Naval Ordnance Test Station
Naval Weapons Center

Other added entries: Sidewinder Missile Project
Korean War
Vietnam War

McLean, Edith LaVerne (Mrs. William B.)

Interview of Mrs. Edith LaVerne ("LaV") McLean, conducted by Starla E. Hall

Date of Interview: 800617

Documentation: Transcript 38 pp.

Interview number: DNL-T23-80

Abstract: Mrs. McLean discusses the personal life of her husband, Dr. William B. McLean, who was the Technical Director of NOT/NWC and NUC. Included are sections on McLean's relationships with his sons, his hobbies at home, McLean as a husband. Mrs. McLean comments on life at NOTS, her husband as TD there, and the other scientists that made up the NOTS/NWC team. She talks about their family's move to San Diego, the establishment of NUC, and her husband's health; also his interests outside of science and the Sidewinder Missile Project.

Repositories: DTNSRDC

Individuals mentioned: McLean, Dr. William B.
McLean, Mark
McLean, Edith LaVerne (Mrs. William B.)
McLean, Jack

Institutions: Naval Ordnance Test Station
Naval Weapons Center
Naval Undersea Center

Other added entries: Sidewinder Missile Project

McLean, Dr. William B.

Interview with Dr. William B. McLean, conducted by Albert B. Christman

Date of Interview: 731116

Documentation: Index, Transcript 30 pp.

Interview number: S-88

Abstract: Dr. McLean discusses the development of various Naval missile projects at NOTS, including the Sidewinder and Walleye Missiles. He describes their tracking and launching methods and the politics involved in developing a missile.

Military-civilian conference at Armitage Field, Naval Ordnance Test
Station. Fourth from left, Dr. Louis T.E. Thompson (NOTS Technical
Director); fifth from left, Dr. William B. McLean (Head, Aviation
Ordnance Department); far right, Captain Walter V.R. Vieweg (NOTS
Commander); April 1950.

Naval Ordnance Test Station Code 40 (Weapons Development Department)
principals. Left to right: Frank Knemeyer, Leroy L. Doig II,
Leroy Riggs, circa 1964.

Repositories: NWC, DTNSRDC, NHC

Individuals mentioned: Crawford, Jack A.
Ward, Dr. Newton E.

Institutions: Naval Ordnance Test Station
Naval Weapons Center

Subjects: Guided Missiles
Air to Air Missiles

Other added entries: Sidewinder Missile Project
Walleye Missile Project

McLean, Dr. William B.

Interview of Dr. William B. McLean, conducted by Albert
B. Christman

Date of Interview: 750700

Documentation: Index, Transcript 44 pp.

Interview number: 5313-S-97

Abstract: Dr. McLean recalls his first association with
NOTS, his work in the Fire Control Laboratory, and the need
for the Sidewinder Missile. He details his role in the
Sidewinder design, his tenure as Head of Aviation Ordnance,
and comments on technical layering at NOTS. McLean remembers
his time as Technical Director of NOTS, reflects on the role
of a TD, and his management style. McLean states that the
laboratory re-organization of 1967 failed and talks about
the Navy's future; in particular, the need for more
submarines.

Repositories: NWC, DTNSRDC, NHC

Individuals mentioned: Hussey, VADM George F.
Lauritsen, Dr. Charles C.
Thompson, Dr. Louis T. E.

Institutions: Naval Ordnance Test Station
Naval Weapons Center
Naval Undersea Center
Fire Control Laboratory

Other added entries: Sidewinder Missile Project
Submarine Research
Technical Director

McLean, Dr. William B.

Interview of Dr. William B. McLean, conducted by Dr. Samuel Rothman and Mrs. Susan Frutkin

Date of Interview: 741212

Documentation: 2 Tapes, Transcript 33 pp.

Interview number: BA-1-75

Abstract: Dr. McLean gives a broad overview of naval laboratories since World War II. First, he comments on the state of NOTS and NOL at the end of World War II. McLean discusses the transfer of the labs to the chief of Naval Material in 1966, the Sherwin Plan, and changes in the Office of the Director of Navy Laboratories. He talks about the effect Congress has on the labs, NIF Funding, and Special Project Offices and Project Managers. He also explains the effect of frequent leadership changes on R&D, significant lab problems from 1958 to 1973, and how to evaluate the results of R&D in peacetime. In addition McLean details the effect of civil service regulations on the labs and how to attract qualified civilians to work on military programs.

Repositories: DTNSRDC, NHC

Individuals mentioned: Thompson, Dr. Louis T. E.
Sherwin, Dr. Chalmers
Lawson, Dr. Joel
Rexroth, John
Hayward. ADM John T.
Kidd, ADM Issac C., Jr.

Institutions: Director of Navy Laboratories
Chief of Naval Material
Systems Commands
Naval Ordnance Test Station
Naval Ordnance Laboratory
Department of Defense Research and Engineering

Other added entries: Navy Industrial Fund
Sherwin Plan

McMillan, Dr. Edwin M.

 Interview of Dr. Edwin M. McMillan, conducted by Albert B. Christman

Date of Interview: 670300

Documentation: Index, Transcript 22 pp.

Interview number: NOTS-75201-S36

Abstract: This interview was originally conducted as background for a biography of RADM William S. Parsons. Dr. McMillan describes his and Dr. Robert Oppenheimer's early connections with the Manhattan Project. He reflects on ADM (then CAPT) Parsons' arrival at Los Alamos, NM. and the time he spent working with him. McMillan discusses Parsons' personal character and Parsons' relationship with Oppenheimer.

Repositories: NWC, DTNSRDC, NHC

Individuals mentioned: Parsons, RADM William S.
Groves, GEN Leslie
Oppenheimer, Dr. Robert

Cities: Los Alamos, NM.

Other added entries: Manhattan Project

Martell, VADM Charles B.

 Interview of VADM Charles B. Martell

Date of Interview: 740000

Documentation: 3 Tapes

Interview number: BA-16

Repositories: DTNSRDC

Marten, William H.

Interview of William H. Marten, conducted by Roger Kempler

Date of interview: 820730

Documentation: Transcript, 42 pp.

Abstract: Mr. Marten describes his initial exposure to Navy personnel research, the early efforts at billet analysis in the Fleet, beginning and problems in organizing the Navy Personnel Research Activity in San Diego, typical work assignments. describing movie industry jobs for applications in Armed Forces Radio and Television, program development in the 1950s, establishment of NPRDC, NRAC's involvement, coordination with Washington, chosing a Technical Director, and major accomplishments.

Repositories: DTNSRDC

Individuals mentioned: Van Swearingen, CAPT Earl K.
Turney, Robert F.
Rimland, Dr. Bernard
Jones, Dr. Earl
Price, D. George
Sprague, ADM Thomas L.
Zumwalt, ADM Elmo

Institutions: Navy Personnel Research and Development Center
Naval Research Advisory Committee

Other added entries: Personnel Research
Billet Analysis

Masterson, VADM Kleber S.

Interview of VADM Kleber S. Masterson

Date of Interview: 721100

Other date of interview: 730400

Documentation: Index, Appendices, Transcript 493 pp.

Abstract: VADM Masterson served as executive member of the Navy Ballistic Missiles Committee, which played a major role in developing Polaris, Chief of the Bureau of Weapons, and as Director of the Weapons Systems Evaluation Group, OSD.

Repositories: NHC, NWCM, USNA, USNI

William H. Marten of the Navy Personnel Research and Development Center.

Institutions: Navy Ballistic Missiles Committee
Bureau of Weapons
Secretary of Defense
Weapons Systems Evaluation Group

Subjects: Submarine Launched Ballistic Missiles
Ballistic Missile Submarines
Nuclear Powered Fleet Ballistic Missile Submarines
Nuclear Missiles
Weapons Systems

Other added entries: Polaris Program

Meyers, Wesley W.

"The Manhattan and Elsie Projects: Wesley W. Meyers,
conducted by Cynthia Rouse

Date of Interview: 761201

Documentation: Transcript 13 pp.

Note: This interview is Chapter VIII of Dahlgren, edited by
Kenneth G. McCollum

Abstract: Mr. Meyers discusses the Manhattan Project and the
part Dahlgren and Dahlgren personnel played, the "Sewer
Pipe" bomb, testing of atomic projectiles (the Elsie
Project), security of atomic devices, and dropping the test
bombs.

Repositories: NSWC, DTNSRDC

Institutions: Naval Proving Ground

Other added entries: Manhattan Project
Elsie Project
Atomic Weapons

Miller, Laymon N.

Interview of Laymon N. Miller, conducted by Richard D. Glasow

Date of Interview: 800821

Documentation: 2 Tapes, Transcript

Abstract: Mr. Miller talks about his work in acoustics and torpedo quieting at the Ordnance Research Laboratory.

Repositories: ARL

Institutions: Ordnance Research Laboratory
Pennsylvania State University

Subjects: Torpedos

Other added entries: Acoustics Research

Moran, VADM William J.

Interview of VADM William J. Moran, conducted by CAPT Robert L. Hansen,

Date of Interview: 750000

Documentation: 1 Tape, Index, Transcript 31 pp.

Interview number: BA-5-75

Abstract: VADM Moran comments on his relationships with various ASN (R&D)'s, changes in the relationship between the ASN (R&D) and OPNAV, and ADM Zumwalt's use of the CNO Executive Board. He recalls his time at NOTS and talks about the shift of lab control to the CNM, the roles of CO's and TD's, and the Navy's success in working with civilians. Moran discusses his tenure as Director of the Office of RDT&E - Particularly the need to increase interaction with the DCNM's Office, the Ordnance Systems Command's ability to response to new requirements, and the layering of management in Navy R&D.

Repositories: DTNSRDC, NHC

Individuals mentioned: Foster, Dr. John S.
Zumwalt, ADM Elmo

Institutions: Assistant Secretary of the Navy (R&D)
Chief of Naval Material

Chief of Naval Operations
Defense Systems Acquisition Review Council
Naval Ordnance Systems Command
Chief of Naval Operations

Other added entries: Technical Director

Morton, RADM Thomas

Interview of RADM Thomas Morton

Date of Interview: 751090

Other interview date: 760290

Documentation: Index, Transcript 484 pp.

Abstract: RADM Morton served as a gunnery officer on the USS NORTH CAROLINA during World War II, and was the Commanding Officer of the Naval Weapons Laboratory at Dahlgren, Va. from 1960-1961.

Repositories: NHC, NWCM, USNA, USNI

Individuals mentioned: McNamara, SECDEF Robert S.

Institutions: Naval Weapons Laboratory
Naval Surface Weapons Center

Subjects: Ballistic Research Laboratories
Ordnance Laboratories
Ordnance

Cities: Dahlgren, VA.

Other added entries: Commanding Officer

Naval Research Laboratory Meeting

Naval Research Laboratory Meeting

Date of Interview: 810700

Documentation: Tapes, Transcript, 112 pp.

Repositories: NASM

Subjects: Astronomy

Newell, Dr. Homer E.

   Interview of Dr. Homer E. Newell, conducted by Dr.
Richard F. Hirsh

Date of interview: 8007018

Documentation: Tapes, 3 hrs., Transcript

Abstract: Dr. Newell discusses war work and the rocket-
sonde program at NRL, the atomic bomb, upper atmospheric
research, establishment of the V-2 Panel, Edward Hulburt and
Herbert Friedman, the Vanguard Satellite Program, IGY,
reaction to the launch of Sputnik, creation of NASA in 1958,
his career with NASA, the effects of Vietnam on the space
program, and the Space Telescope and Space Shuttle.

Repositories: AIP

Individuals mentioned: Hulburt, Dr. Edward O.
Friedman, Dr. Herbert

Institutions: Naval Research Laboratory
International Geophysical Year
National Aeronautics and Space Administration

Subjects: *Astronomy*
Space Astronomy
Space Telescope

Other added entries: Rocket-Sonde
Atmospheric Research
Sputnik
V-2 Rocket
Vietnam War
Vanguard Program
Space Shuttle

Niedermair, John Charles

Interview of John Charles Niedermair

Date of Interview: 750600

Other interview date: 760400

Documentation: Index, Appendices, Transcript 349 pp.

Abstract: Mr. Niedermair discusses his role in the salvage of the S-4 and S-51 submarines during the 1920's, his many years in the Bureau of Ships, and his design of the tank landing ship (LST). He mentions RADM David W. Taylor's work at the Experimental Model Basin, Taylor's book "The Speed and Power of Ships", and CAPT Harold Saunders' contributions to naval architecture and the science of hydrodynamics.

Repositories: NHC, NWCM, USNA, USNI
Individuals mentioned: Taylor, RADM David W.
Saunders, CAPT Harold E.

Institutions: Bureau of Ships
Experimental Model Basin
David Taylor Model Basin

Subjects: Submarines
Salvage
Naval Architecture
Hydrodynamics
Ship Design
Tank Landing Ships

Other added entries: S-4 Submarine
S-51 Submarine

Niemann, Ralph A.

"Development of Computer Technology: Ralph A. Niemann", conducted by Cynthia Rouse

Date of Interview: 781026

Documentation: Transcript 15 pp.

Note: This interview is Chapter X of _Dahlgren_, edited by Kenneth G. McCollum

Abstract: Mr. Niemann discusses the first IBM card-feed computers at Dahlgren, the Aiken Relay Computer, computer-generated ballistics tables, the 60 desk calculators used by

WAVES in World War II, the NORC, and advances in speed of computers, use of the NORC in NRL's Vanguard Program, the IBM STRETCH computer, the effect of the Fleet Ballistic Missile Program on computer work at Dahlgren, constructing a facility to house the computers, and management problems.
Repositories: NSWC, DTNSRDC

Individuals mentioned: Cohen, Dr. Charles J.
Bramble, Dr. Charles C.
Ryland, Robert
Walker, John
Gleissner, Gene H.
Burke, William

Institutions: Naval Research Laboratory
Naval Proving Ground
Naval Weapons Laboratory
International Business Machine Company

Subjects: Computers
Fire Control Computers

Cities: Dahlgren, VA.

Other added entries: Naval Ordnance Research Calculator
Fleet Ballistic Missile Program
Vanguard Program
Polaris Program

Nutt, Mr. Harold V.

Interview of Harold V. Nutt, conducted by Dr. David K. Allison

Date of Interview: 821022

Documentation: 7 Tapes, 2 Diskettes, Transcript 125 pp.

Abstract: Mr. Nutt tells about his background and education, his work in private industry developing greases and lubricating oils, and his interest in aeronautical engineering. He accepted a job at the Engineering Experiment Station in 1938, and speaks of the change during the war years from testing material manufactured by industry to research, testing captured equipment, the post-war reduction in force, and becoming superintendent of the Internal Combustion Laboratory. He also discusses the relationship between EES and BUSHIPS, the Metallurgical Laboratory, experimental submarine engines, early work with titanium, and how the loss of the THRESHER stimulated the development of SDRVs. He speaks of his involvement in VLAP, the

reorganization during the 1960s, and the change in name to
Marine Engineering Laboratory, and the consolidation of MEL
and NSRDC.

Repositories: DTNSRDC

Individuals mentioned: Joakim, W. F.
Argora, Larry
Zumwalt, ADM Elmo
Vincent, CAPT Manuel da Costa
Smith, Clane
Smith, Watt
King, FADM Ernest
Taylor, RADM David W.

Institutions: Marine Engineering Laboratory
Office of Naval Research
Engineering Experiment Station
David Taylor Naval Ship Research and Development Center
Bureau of Ships

Subjects: Fuel
Metallurgy
Bearings
Submarine Propulsion Systems
Lubrication
Titanium

Other added entries: Submarine Snorkels
Vietnam Laboratory Assistance Program
USS THRESHER
Submarine Deep Rescue Vehicles
Ship Storage
Hydrogen Peroxide Engines
Technical Director

O'Neill, William

Interview of William O'Neill, conducted by Dr. David K.
Allison

Date of Interview: 811214

Documentation: 1 Tape, Index

Abstract: This interview centers on the history of hydrofoil
development in the Navy. Mr. O'Neill mentions the original
mission studies and testing by NELC of the ships PLAINVIEW
and HIGH POINT, and the propulsion system and design of the
hydrofoil gunboats TUCUMCARI and FLAGSTAFF. He discusses
early work by ONR and MIT, the program at DTNSRDC, how it

was funded, and key players at the Center.

Repositories: DTNSRDC

Individuals mentioned: Johnson, Robert
Ellsworth, William
Buckley, William H.
Schab, Henry
Kelly, Jim

Institutions: Naval Electronics Laboratory Center
David Taylor Model Basin
Naval Ship Research and Development Center
David Taylor Naval Ship Research and Development Center
Boeing Airplane Company
Office of Naval Research

Subjects: Hydrofoils
Hydroelasticity
Cavitation
Hydrodynamics

Other added entries: Hydrodynamic Research
USS HIGH POINT
USS FLAGSTAFF
USS TUCUMCARI
USS PLAINVIEW

Owen, RADM Thomas B.

Interview of RADM Thomas B. Owen

Date of Interview: 740000

Documentation: 3 Tapes

Interview number: BA-20

Repositories: DTNSRDC

Page, Dr. Robert Morris

Interview with Dr. Robert Morris Page, conducted by Dr. David K. Allison

Date of Interview: 781027

Documentation: 9 Tapes (16 Sides), Transcript 217 pp.

Other interview date: 781026

Abstract: Dr. Page discusses his background and education, taking the Civil Service Examination and being offered a job at NRL, work on frequency measurement and the invention of the frequency meter, work on radar from 1930-1934, assignment to radio detection in 1934, pulse radar, the Signal Corps radar project, microwave radar, invention of the radar duplexer, test of equipment on the LEARY, NEW YORK, and TEXAS, the Tizard Mission, airborne radar, British radar development, and opposition to the NDRC Radiation Laboratory. He also talks about the publication of the Ridenour Report, fire control radar, monopulse radar, the effect of ONR on research money, over-the-horizon radar, administrative problems at NRL, patents to NRL employees, his feelings about being Director of Research, reflections on the relationships between civilian scientists and naval officers, Vanguard Project, the Long Range Modernization Program, and his role in bringing ocean sciences to NRL.

Repositories: NRL

Individuals mentioned: Crosley, Al
Friedman, Dr. Herbert
Hulburt, Dr. Edward O.
Bowen, ADM Harold G.
Guthrie, Dr. Robert C.
Gebhard, Dr. Louis A.
Philpott, LaVerne
Davis, Tommy
Adams, SECNAV Charles F.
Taylor, Dr. A. Hoyt
Young, Dr. Leo C.

Institutions: Naval Research Laboratory
Radio Corporation of America
Bureau of Engineering
National Defense Research Committee
U. S. Army Signal Corps
Bureau of Ships

Subjects: Radar
Radio Detection
Fire Control Radar

Dr. Robert Morris Page with an early radar antenna.

Airborne Radar
Microwave Radar

Other added entries: Radar Research
USS NEW YORK
USS TEXAS
USS LEARY
Tizard Mission
Ridenour Report

Parsons, Harry R.

   Interview of Harry R. Parsons, conducted by Albert B.
Christman

Date of Interview: 670100

Documentation: Index, Transcript 29 pp.

Interview number: NOTS-75201-S31

Abstract: This interview was originally conducted as
background for a biography of RADM William S. Parsons. Harry
Parsons describes his relationship with his brother, his
father's influence on the family, and the family's move West
from Chicago to Ft. Sumner, NM. He recalls his father's
career, the social life of Ft. Sumner, and RADM Parsons
around the time of his death.

Repositories: NWC, DTNSRDC, NHC

Individuals mentioned: Parsons, RADM William S.
Parsons, Clarissa
Parsons, Critchell

Cities: Ft. Sumner, NM.

Pehrson, Gordon

   Interview of Gordon Pehrson

Date of Interview: 720200

Documentation: Transcript 66 pp.

Abstract: Mr. Pehrson headed the Plans and Program Division
of the Special Projects Office for Polaris. He developed
program management concepts, and the Program Evaluation
Review Technique (PERT). This is one of a series of seven
interviews on concept and development of Polaris *program*
conducted by the U. S. Naval Institute Oral History Program.

Repositories: NHC, NWCM, USNA, USNI

Subjects: Submarine Launched Ballistic Missiles
Fleet Ballistic Missiles
Ballistic Missile Submarines
Nuclear Powered Fleet Ballistic Missile Submarines
Nuclear Missiles
Weapons Systems

Other added entries: Polaris Program
Program Evaluation Review Technique

Peterkin, Ernest W.

   Interview of Ernest W. Peterkin, conducted by Dr. David
K. Allison

Date of Interview: 810720

Documentation: 1 Tape (2 Sides)

Abstract: Mr. Peterkin discusses the SOLRAD (solar
radiation) satellite program. The interview is supplemented
by a collection of papers on research management.

Repositories: NRL

Institutions: Naval Research Laboratory

Other added entries: SOLRAD Program

Petersen, ADM Forrest Silas

Interview of ADM Forrest Silas Petersen, conducted by
Dr. William J. Armstrong

Date of Interview: 800407

Documentation: 1 Tape

Note: ADM Petersen was COMNAVAIR from 1976-1980

Repositories: NAVAIR

Institutions: Naval Air Systems Command

Plain, Dr. Gilbert

Interview of Dr. Gilbert Plain, conducted by Elizabeth
Babcock

Date of Interview: 7512909

Documentation: Index, Transcript 30 pp.

Interview number: S-108

Abstract: Dr. Plain comments on his move from MIT to NOTS
and on Dr. Brode, Dr. Sage, and Dr. Warner. He talks about
Aircraft Sights work, the start of the Sidewinder Missile
Project, and his position as Head of Properties of Matter.
Plain describes the NOTS/NWC commanders since 1949 and the
various aspects of base operation, including the effect of
the Freedom of Information Act, morale problems at NOTS, and
Equal Employment Opportunity.

Repositories: NWC, DTNSRDC, NHC

Individuals mentioned: Hunter, Dr. Hugh
LaBerge, Dr. Walter
McLean, Dr. William B.
Brode, Dr. Wallace C.
Sage, Dr. Bruce
Wilson, Dr. Haskell G.
Warner, Dr. Arthur H.

Institutions: Naval Ordnance Test Station
Naval Weapons Center

Cities: China Lake, CA.

Polin, Jerry

Interview of Jerry Polin, conducted by Tom Misa and Ed
Todd

Date of Interview: 820713

Documentation: 1 Tape, Index 2 pp.

Interview number: NADC-9

Abstract: Mr. Polin talks about human factors engineering,
his personal background, and his work for Martin Marietta.
He comments on his work for the state of Pennsylvania doing
statistical highway modeling, his time at Philco-Ford, and
his arrival at the Philadelphia Navy Yard as a GS-7
management analyst. Polin discusses the Defense Logistics
Agency, the Centrifuge Department at AMRD, and NADC's
outside appearance. He describes what it meant to win an
NADC fellowship for graduate work at Temple University and
his project assignments in human engineering at NADC.

Repositories: NADC, DTNSRDC

Individuals mentioned: Polis, Dr. David
Lazo, John

Institutions: Naval Air Development Center
Martin Marietta
Philadelphia Navy Yard
Defense Logistics Agency
Philco-Ford Corporation
Temple University

Subjects: Sonobuoys
Antisubmarine Warfare
Antisubmarine Aircraft

Other added entries: Human Factors Engineering
Human Centrifuge
F-14 Project
Light Airborne ASW Vehicle
Light Airborne Multi-Purpose System
A-NEW Program

Polin, Jerry

Interview of Jerry Polin, conducted by Tom Misa and Ed Todd

Date of Interview: 920718

Documentation: 1 Tape, Index, 1 p.

Interview number: NADC-12

Abstract: Mr. Polin discusses the Navy Scientist Training Exchange Program, (NSTEP) which was set up as a NAVMAT function under the DNL in 1978, and relations between NADC and NAVMAT. He describes his assignment at NAVMAT in the laboratories management area and his work with the SHORESTAMPS manpower needs assessment program.

Repositories: NADC, DTNSRDC

Individuals mentioned: Law, Howard

Institutions: Naval Air Development Center
Naval Material Command

Other added entries: Navy Scientist Training Exchange Program
Laboratory Management

Pollak, George

Interview of Mr. George Pollak, conducted by J. D. Gerrard-Gough

Date of Interview: 751024

Documentation: Index, Transcript 8 pp.

Interview number: 5313-S-100

Abstract: Pollak describes his first, short tenure at NOTS, his two years in the Army, and his return to NOTS-Pasadena Annex as a management analyst. He recalls becoming Deputy of Administration at NOTS and the Navy re-organization of 1967. Pollak comments on relations between NOTS-China Lake and Pasadena, the duties of the officer-in-charge, and Douglas Wilcox's role as Deputy for Administration.

Repositories: NWC, DTNSRDC, NHC

Individuals mentioned: Wilcox, Douglas

Institutions: Naval Weapons Center
Naval Ordnance Test Station
Pasadena Annex

Cities: Pasadena, CA.
China Lake, CA.

Pollock, CAPT Thomas

Interview of CAPT Thomas Pollock, conducted by Albert B. Christman

Date of Interview: 670500

Documentation: Index, Transcript 41 pp.

Interview number: NOTS-75201-S45

Abstract: CAPT Pollock explains his background in rocket research and the initial work by the Navy and CalTech on forward firing rockets. He discusses rocket testing procedures, the uses of rockets in combat in the Atlantic and the Pacific during World War II, and the results of test conducted at Inyokern and Goldstone Lake. He comments on his crew, the naming of NOTS, and the risks involved in rocket research.

Repositories: NWC, DTNSRDC, NHC

Individuals mentioned: Anderson, Dr. Carl
Burroughs, ADM Sherman E.
Lauritsen, Dr. Charles C.
Renard, RADM Jack C.

Institutions: Naval Ordnance Test Station
California Institute of Technology
Bureau of Ordnance

Cities: Inyokern, CA.
Goldstone Lake, CA.

Subjects: Rocket Research

Pollock, CAPT Thomas

   Pollock Review Comments, Vol 2, conducted by Albert B.
Christman

Date of Interview: 730730

Documentation: 3 Tapes, Transcript 53 pp.

Interview number: NOTS-75201-S45-A

Abstract: This is a taped review of the first six chapters
of <u>The Grand Experiment at Inyokern</u>, Naval History Division,
Government Printing Office, Washington, DC., 1978, by Albert
B. Christman, and J. D. Gerrard-Gough.

Repositories: NWC, DTNSRDC, NHC

Powers, Kenneth

   Interview of Kenneth Powers, conducted by Elizabeth
Babcock

Date of Interview: 810518

Documentation: Index, Transcript 34 pp.

Interview number: S-123

Abstract: Mr. Powers comments on his first assignments at
NOTS, problems with contractors for the Sidewinder Missile,
and relations with the Bureau of Weapons and the Bureau of
Ships. He talks about the development of Sidewinder,
differences between NOTS and NWC, and his time in Europe
working on NATO Sidewinder. Powers describes NOTS/NWC's
relationship with Navy people in Washington, the motivations
of military decision makers and industry, and the reasons
for the success of the Sidewinder Program. He also makes
suggestions on improving management of Sidewinder.

Repositories: NWC, DTNSRDC, NHC

Individuals mentioned: Cartwright, Dr. Frank W.
Knemeyer, Franklin H.
LaBerge, Dr. Walter
Smith, Chuck
Wilcox, Dr. Howard A.

Institutions: Naval Ordnance Test Station
Naval Weapons Center

Price, D. George

   Interview of D. George Price, conducted by Roger Kempler

Date of Interview: 820728

Documentation: Index, Transcript 53 pp.

Abstract: Mr. Price discusses his early background in the Navy Personnel Research Program, World War II and Personnel Research, and postwar establishment of the Personnel Research Division. He describes major figures in NPRDC, his personal philosophy, and the need for NPRDC. Price discusses funding, personnel research activities in San Diego and Washington, and relations between NPRDC and ONR. He also comments on the move toward "centers of excellence" and ADM Elmo Zumwalt.

Repositories: DTNSRDC, NPRDC

Individuals mentioned: McDowell, Perceval E. (Pete)
Herron, RADM Edwin W.
Van Swearingen, CAPT Earl K.
Daley, Dr. John
Zumwalt, ADM Elmo

Institutions: Chief of Naval Material
Office of Naval Research
Navy Personnel Research and Development Center

Cities: San Diego, CA.
Washington, DC.

Other added entries: Personnel Research
Center of Excellence

Probus, Dr. James H.

Interview of Dr. James H. Probus, conducted by Dr. David K. Allison

Date of Interview: 830727

Documentation: 3 Tapes, 3 diskettes, Transcript 47 pp.

Abstract: Dr. Probus discusses how he became DNL and his impressions of the laboratories on assuming the position, LUS and resulting RIFs, the evolution of the center concept, problems with program oriented funding, implementing the systems approach, the role of COs and TDs in program management, career development for laboratory personnel, the influence of Dr. William McLean, Dr. Chalmers Sherwin, and Robert Morse on the office of the DNL, selection of COs and TDs, the role of the laboratories in the DSARC-DNSARC process, ATOWG, NSAP and the Corporate Plan, the value of the DNL's military deputy, laboratory inspections, and laboratories and the assessment of fleet readiness.

Repositories: DTNSRDC

Individuals mentioned: Berman, Dr. Alan
Galantin, ADM Ignatius J.
Hillyer, Robert
Johnson, Dr. Gerald
Keach, CAPT Donald
Lawson, Dr. Joel
Michaelis, ADM Frederick
Parrish, CAPT David
Whittle, ADM Alfred J., Jr.
Morse, Dr. Robert W.

Institutions: Director of Navy Laboratories
Defense Systems Acquisition Review Council
Systems Commands
Department of the Navy Systems Acquisition Review Council

Other added entries: Navy Industrial Fund
Corporate Plan
Laboratory Utilization Study
Program Management
Reduction in Force
Advanced Technical Objectives Working Groups
Navy Science Assistance Program

Director of Navy Laboratories and staff, circa 1976. Left to right: Captain Williamson, Bud Shull, Theodore S. Huang, Dr. James Probus, Director of Navy Laboratories, Captain Don Walsh, Allen Himes, and Howard Law.

Pryor, CAPT William L.

   Interview of CAPT William L. Pryor, conducted by Albert
B. Christman

Date of Interview: 780400

Documentation: Tape, Transcript 22 pp.

Interview number: DNL-T14-78

Abstract: CAPT Pryor discusses the establishment of the New
London, CT., Laboratory, pre-World War II sonar testing, and
conflicts between ADM Bowen and Dr. Vannevar Bush. He talks
about the establishment of the San Diego research center,
NOSC, the impact on R&D of Dr. Vern Knudson, and
specifications for NOSC. Pryor describes how he came to New
London, the shift of OSRD work to NRL, and his duty with the
Pacific Fleet. He talks about problems at New London upon
his return as CO, the need for accountability in R&D, and
the failures of the previous CO. Pryor talks about the Navy
officer in R&D, including dealing with civilians, officers
with technical backgrounds, and the differences between
officers of different bureaus. He discusses RADM William S.
Parsons and the differences between laboratories.

Repositories: DTNSRDC

Individuals mentioned: Bowen, Dr. Ira S.
Bush, Dr. Vannevar
Parsons, RADM William S.
Knudson, Dr. Vern

Institutions: Naval Research Laboratory
Naval Ocean Systems Center
Office of Scientific Research and Development

Pryor, CAPT William L.

   Interview of CAPT William L. Pryor, conducted by Albert
B. Christman

Date of Interview: 810626

Documentation: 2 Tapes, Transcript 56 pp.

Interview number: DNL-T37

Abstract: CAPT Pryor discusses his work in sonar, radio, and
submarine research. He talks about his fleet duty, both in
submarines and aboard the USS WEST VIRGINIA. Pryor describes

his tenure at NRL and as Head of NUSL/New London.

Repositories: DTNSRDC

Individuals mentioned: Rickover, ADM Hyman

Institutions: Naval Underwater Sound Laboratory
Naval Research Laboratory

Subjects: Sonar
Radio
Submarines

Purcell, D.

Interview of D. Purcell, conducted by David H. Devorkin

Date of interview: 820329

Documentation: Tapes, Transcript, 85 pp.

Repositories: NASM

Subject: Astronomy

Quarles, Gilford G.

Interview of Gilford G. Quarles, conducted by Nelson Wood

Date of Interview: 780424

Documentation: Tapes, Transcript

Abstract: Mr. Quarles, a former director of the Ordnance Research Laboratory, speaks of his work there.

Repositories: ARL

Institutions: Ordnance Research Laboratory
Pennsylvania State University

Subjects: Torpedos

Other added entries: Acoustics Research

Raborn, VADM William F., Jr.

Interview of VADM William F. Raborn, Jr.

Date of Interview: 720900

Documentation: Transcript 71 pp.

Abstract: VADM Rayborn served as the Director of the Special Projects Division to develop Polaris. This is one of a series of seven interviews on concept and development of the Polaris program conducted by the U. S. Naval Institute Oral History Program.

Repositories: NHC, NWCM, USNA, USNI

Subjects: Submarine Launched Ballistic Missiles
Fleet Ballistic Missiles
Ballistic Missile Submarines
Nuclear Powered Fleet Ballistic Missile Submarines
Nuclear Missiles
Weapons Systems

Other added entries: Polaris Program

Ramras, Eugene M.

Interview of Eugene M. Ramras, conducted by Albert B. Christman

Date of Interview: 780309

Documentation: 1 Tape, Transcript 16 pp.

Interview number: DNL-T4-78

Abstract: Mr. Ramras discusses the evolution of NPRDC from several field activities. He describes how a particular project works, military interfaces with NPRDC, and the impact of computers on people. Ramras explains that the Navy's main problems of the 1970's are in personnel management and comments on laboratory consolidation, significant breakthroughs, and the future of the laboratory system.

Repositories: NHC, DTNSRDC

Individuals mentioned: Frosch, Dr. Robert A.
Probus, Dr. James H.

Institutions: Navy Personnel Research and Development Center
Navy Personnel and Training Research Center

Ramsey, Dr. Norman

Interview of Dr. Norman F. Ramsey

Date of Interview: 600000

Documentation: Index, Transcript 358 pp.

Abstract: Dr. Ramsey talks about his education, research
with Isidor Rabi, and Enrico Fermi, the NDRC Radiation
Laboratory, MIT, the development of radar, and the Manhattan
Project. He speaks of work at Los Alamos, and discussions on
use of the atomic bomb and possible targets, the Trinity
test, and estimates of the damage at Hiroshima.

Repositories: COL

Individuals mentioned: Oppenheimer, Dr. Robert
Fermi, Enrico
Rabi, Isidor I.

Institutions: National Defense Research Committee
Radiation Laboratory

Subjects: Radar

Cities: Los Alamos, NM.
Tinian
Hiroshima, Japan

Other added entries: Manhattan Project
Trinity Test

Raney, Dr. William

Interview of Dr. William P. Raney, conducted by Dr.
Vincent Ponko

Date of Interview: 801125

Documentation: 3 Tapes, Index, Transcript 47 pp.

Interview number: DNL-T31

Abstract: Dr. Raney discusses the role of the National
Research Council of the National Academy of Science in

military R&D and his early years as Special Assistant to the Assistant Secretary of the Navy (R&D). This includes contacts with Dr. Chalmers Sherwin, lack of support for the Sherwin Plan, and the role of the DNL in dealing with the Sherwin Plan. Raney describes the beginnings of the DNL/DLP and its first heads, Dr. Gerald Johnson and Dr. Joel Lawson. He comments on exploratory development in Navy R&D, the systems approach to lab operations, and the role of management studies under SECDEF McNamara. Raney assesses Dr. Robert A. Frosch as ASN (R&D), his work in ONR, and talks about Thomas Amlie as Technical Director of NWC.

Repositories: DTNSRDC

Individuals mentioned: Foster, Dr. John S.
Frosch, Dr. Robert A.
McNamara, SECDEF Robert S.
Johnson, Dr. Gerald
Sherwin, Dr. Chalmers
Lawson, Dr. Joel
Amlie, Dr. Thomas S.

Institutions: Chief of Naval Operations
Director of Navy Laboratories
Office of Naval Research
National Academy of Science
Director of Laboratory Programs
Naval Weapons Center
National Science Foundation

Other added entries: Sherwin Plan

Rees, Mina

    Interview of Mina Rees

Date of Interview: 840100

Documentation: 8 Tapes

Abstract: This interview is part of the "Women in the Federal Government Project", sponsored by the Arthur and Elizabeth Schlesinger Library on the History of Women in America and funded by the National Endowment for the Humanities. Ms. Rees describes her career with the Navy.

Repositories: RAD

Institutions: Office of Naval Research

Regan, Dr. James J.

Interview of Dr. James J. Regan, conducted by Roger Kempler

Date of interview: 820716

Other interview date: 821117

Documentation: Transcript, 49 pp.

Abstract: Dr. Regan describes becoming NPRDC's first Technical Director, the special problems of the first year of operation, difficulties associated with full consolidation of the Navy's personnel R&D efforts and responsibility for coordinating all personnel research, the origin of the Center concept, NRAC's impact on Center development, the Sub-Panel on Personnel, and location of NRAC records, funding of NPRDC, his Center management philosophy, the appropriateness of a civilian Technical Director managing a military laboratory, becoming a NAVMAT laboratory, the differences in operational philosophy between NPRDC and the material laboratories, his concerns relative to changing modes in R&D funding, reports by the Inspector General and GAO, and an overview of the last ten years.

Repositories: NPRDC, DTNSRDC

Individuals mentioned: Rigney, Dr. Joseph
Kinnear, RADM George E. R.
Bagley, VADM David H.
Collins, Dr. John J.
Probus, Dr. James H.
Ramras, Eugene M.
Bryan, Dr. Glenn L.
Frosch, Dr. Robert A.
Smith, Dr. Robert

Institutions: Naval Research Advisory Committee
General Accounting Office
Navy Personnel Research and Development Center

Other added entries: Technical Director
Personnel Research

Dr. James J. Regan, Technical Director of the Navy Personnel
Research and Development Center, 1974-1981.

Reich, VADM Eli T.

Date of Interview: 750210

Documentation: 1 Tape

Interview number: BA-23

Repositories: NHC, DTNSRDC

Reich, VADM Eli T.

   Interview of VADM Eli T. Reich, Volume I

Date of Interview: 780400

Other date of interview: 790100

Documentation: Index, Transcript 520 pp.

Abstract: VADM Reich discusses his submarine experience in World War II, command of the missile cruiser USS CANBERRA, and his role in the investigative study of the Tartar, Terrier and Talos missile programs.

Repositories: NHC, USNA, USNI, NWCM

Subjects: Surface to Air Missiles
Antiaircraft Missiles
Weapons Systems

Other added entries: Terrier Missile
Tartar Missile
Talos Missile
Surface Missile Systems Project

Reich, VADM Eli T.

   Interview of VADM Eli T. Reich, Volume II

Date of Interview: 790200

Other date of interview: 800100

Documentation: Index, Appendices, Transcript 681 pp.

Abstract: Continues career in 1963, when VADM   ich was Director of the Surface Missile Systems Project. Prior to his retirement, he served as Deputy Assistant Secretary of

Defense (Production, Engineering, and Acquisition).

Repositories: NHC, USNA, USNI, NWCM

Subjects: Surface to Air Missiles
Antiaircraft Missiles
Weapons Systems

Other added entries: Terrier Missile
Tartar Missile
Talos Missile
Surface Missile Systems Project

Renard, RADM Jack C.

   Interview of RADM Jack C. Renard, conducted by Albert
B. Christman

Date of Interview: 690521

Documentation: Index, Transcript 52 pp.

Interview number: NOTS-75201-S64

Abstract: RADM Renard comments on his position as Magnetic
Airborne Director at NOTS, test facilities at Goldstone
Lake, and the search for a new rocket test sight. He talks
about acquiring land for a new test facility, the turn of
events that led to it, and CalTech's participation in the
war effort under Dr. Charles Lauritsen. Renard describes
RADM Mitscher's influence, the first rocket tests, and the
opening of NOTS.

Repositories: NWC, DTNSRDC, NHC

Individuals mentioned: Burroughs, ADM Sherman E.
Fowler, Dr. William
Hayward, ADM John T.
King, FADM Ernest
Lauritsen, Dr. Charles C.
Mitscher, ADM Marc
Pollock, CAPT Thomas
Russell, ADM James S.

Institutions: Naval Ordnance Test Station
California Institute of Technology
Ryan Aircraft

Subjects: Naval Research
Rocket Research

Cities: Goldstone Lake, CA.
Inyokern, CA.

Renne, Clarence J.

Interview of Clarence J. Renne, conducted by Michelle
Kilikauskas and Susan Priest

Date of Interview: 801219

Documentation: Index, Transcript 30 pp.

Interview number: S-114

Abstract: Renne discusses his early career, relationships
between blue and white collar employees at NOTS, and the
employee services board there. He comments on the difficulty
in firing poor employees, difficulty getting work done, and
his management philosophy. Renne talks about who really got
work done at NOTS/NWC, Dr. Haskell G. Wilson, and
contracting work to outside companies. He also speaks on the
importance of trusting government workers.

Repositories: NWC, NHC, DTNSRDC

Individuals mentioned: Hays, Burrell
Printy, Rich
Wilson, Dr. Haskell G.

Institutions: Naval Ordnance Test Station
Naval Weapons Center

Rexroth, John

Interview of Mr. John Rexroth, conducted by Dr. Vincent
Ponko

Date of Interview: 801205

Documentation: 3 Tapes, Index, Transcript 46 pp.

Interview number: DNL-T33

Abstract: Mr. Rexroth discusses his work as a project
officer in the Bureau of Ordnance, including fire control,
liaison officer with contractors, target designation work,
and the Research and Development Board. He talks about
support for applied research, in particular, the work of Dr.
Frank Tanczoz, the adverse influence of Polaris and other

projects, and the establishment of ASN (R&D). Rexroth comments on the Bureau of Weapons, his tenure as TD there, his contact with the Applied Physics Labs, and relations with in-house labs. He also discusses the negative impact of releasing the labs from the Bureaus/SYSCOMs, the lack of benefit derived from CNM control of the labs, and project management in the Systems Commands. Rexroth states that labs should only handle technical management responsibility, private industry should remain part of the R&D picture, and evaluates Dr. Robert A. Frosch and Dr. William Raney as R&D leaders. He explains the impact SECDEF Robert S. McNamara had on R&D procedures, the role of the CNO in Naval R&D, and the problems the Navy faced in the mid-1970's.

Repositories: DTNSRDC

Individuals mentioned: Parham, CAPT John S.
Tanczoz, Dr. Frank I.
Wilson, Dr. Haskell G.
Raney, Dr. William
Frosch, Dr. Robert A.
McNamara, SECDEF Robert S.

Institutions: Bureau of Ordnance
Bureau of Weapons
Chief of Naval Material
Chief of Naval Operations
Director of Navy Laboratories
Applied Physics Laboratory
Systems Commands

Other added entries: Technical Director
Polaris Program

_____ _____

Rich, Harry L.

   Interview of Harry L. Rich, conducted by Dr. David K. Allison

Date of Interview: 840514

Documentation: 3 Tapes, Index

Abstract: Mr. Rich reminisces about his thirty-three years at DTNSRDC, he mentions his initial interview with Dr. Lyman Hewins and CAPT Alvey Wright, and his job as scientific assistant at the Experimental Model Basin. Rich was more interested in Structures and was able to transfer to that Department in 1941. He discusses the development of strain gauges, different types of hull strength testing, his memories of Operation Crossroads and how DTMB simulated the

tests. He describes conditions at DTMB during World War II -
the Marine guard force living in the Structural Mechanics
Laboratory, and unusual tests with cadavers. He mentions the
role of the Center in the full scale shock test of the
THRESHER, involvement in testing the "3 T" missile systems,
improvements in submarines and surface ships due to research
in shock and vibration studies, his position as the Navy's
Shock Coordinator, and his work as an NSAP advisor to the
Korean Navy.

Repositories: DTNSRDC

Individuals mentioned: Johnson, Everatt Emmil
Hewins, Dr. Lyman
Hartmann, Dr. Gregory
Keil, Dr. Alfred H.
Kell, ADM Claude O.
Saunders, CAPT Harold E.
Windenburg, Dr. Dwight F.
Crook, Mary Charlotte
Heller, CDR S. K.
Allen, Dr. Robert
Lawson, Dr. Joel

Institutions: Navy Science Assistance Program
David Taylor Naval Ship Research and Development Center
Naval Ship Research and Development Center
David Taylor Model Basin
Structures Department
Applied Mechanics Laboratory
Bureau of Ordnance
Bureau of Ships
Structural Mechanics Department
Shock and Vibration Centralization Activity

Subjects: Shock
Vibration

Other added entries: Korean War
Strain Gauges
Shock Testing
Shock Hardening
Navy Industrial Fund
Polaris
USS TROUT
Terrier Missile
Operation Paperclip
Talos Missile
Tartar Missile
USS THRESHER
USS DRAGONET
USS BOSTON
USS OMAHA

Manhattan Project
Operation Crossroads

Richmond, CDR John

   Interview of CDR John Richmond, conducted by Albert B.
Christman

Date of Interview: 670100

Documentation: Index, Transcript 125 pp.

Interview number: NOTS-75201-S33

Abstract: CDR Richmond reminisces about the construction and
expansion of NOTS during the two years he was in charge. He
discusses the birth of the community at China Lake, CA. and
the construction of permanent housing, schools, and
recreational facilities. Richmond sketches the personalities
of NOTS there during his time and describes the military
function of the base.

Repositories: NWC, DTNSRDC, NHC

Individuals mentioned: Appleton, Robert
Blandy, ADM George
Byrnes, CAPT James
Duncan, CAPT James
Hayward, ADM John T.
Hussey, VADM George F.
Lauritsen, Dr. Charles C.
Sage, Dr. Bruce
Sandquist, CAPT Oscar
Switzer, VADM W. G.
Sykes, RADM James B.
Thompson, Dr. Louis T. E.
Zimmerman, LT

Institutions: Naval Ordnance Test Station

Cities: China Lake, CA.

Other added entries: Manhattan Project
Commanding Officer

Ricketts, COMO Myron V.

Interview of COMO Myron V. Ricketts, conducted by Dr.
David K. Allison

Date of Interview: 820210

Documentation: 1 Tape, Transcript 22 pp.

Abstract: COMO Ricketts comments on the role of a military
commanding officer in the Navy laboratories, his work at
NRL, the establishment of the Fleet Support Office at
DTNSRDC, NSAP, financial management at DTNSRDC, the
relationship between the laboratories and Systems Commands,
contacting out of commercial activities, and incentives to
keep competent technical people in the laboratories.

Repositories: DTNSRDC

Institutions: Fleet Support Office
Naval Research Laboratory
David Taylor Naval Ship Research and Development Center
Navy Science Assistance Program

Other added entries: Commercial Activities
Navy Industrial Fund
Contracting

Roach, James

Date of Interview: 750203

Documentation: 1 Tape

Interview number: BA-27

Repositories: NHC, DTNSRDC

Robinson, ADM Samuel M.

Interview of ADM Samuel M. Robinson

Date of Interview: 630000

Documentation: Transcript 56 pp.

Abstract: ADM Robinson recalls his career in Naval engineering, discussing electric ship propulsion, the development of the high speed diesel engine, his service at the Puget Sound Navy Yard, and as Chief of the Bureaus of Engineering and Ships.

Repositories: COL, NHC

Institutions: Bureau of Ships
Bureau of Engineering

Subjects: Diesel Engines
Electric Ship Propulsion
Naval Engineering

Roman, Nancy Grace

Interview of Nancy Grace Roman, conducted by Dr. Richard F. Hirsh

Date of Interview: 7606300

Documentation: Tape, 1 hr.

Repositories: AIP

Subjects: Astronomy

Roman, Nancy Grace

Interview of Nancy Grace Roman, conducted by Dr. David DeVorkin

Date of Interview: 8008019

Documentation: Tapes, 4 hrs., Transcript 70 pp.

Abstract: Ms. Roman speaks mainly about her career with NASA and the astronomy and space astronomy programs there, she also discusses her early life, education, and positions at the Yerkes Observatory and the Naval Research Laboratory.

Institutions: Naval Research Laboratory
National Aeronautics and Space Administration
Yerkes Observatory

Subjects: Astronomy
Space Astronomy

Rosen, Milton

   Interview of Milton Rosen, conducted by Dr. David H.
DeVorkin

Date of Interview: 830325

Documentation: Tapes, 3.5 hours, Transcript, 90 pp.

Abstract: This interview covers Mr. Rosen's education,
employment at Westinghouse and the Federal Power Commission,
and move to NRL in 1940. At NRL Rosen was involved in
general atmospheric research, including the Rocket-Sonde
Division, the V-2 rocket program, and his year at JPL. He
describes the V-2 rocket and later programs, and discusses
basic versus applied research at NRL.

Repositories: NASM

Individuals mentioned: Braun, Wernher von
Tombaugh, Clyde
McLaughlin, R. B.
Krause, Dr. Ernst H.

Institutions: Naval Research Laboratory
Jet Propulsion Laboratory
University of Pennsylvania
Westinghouse Corporation
Federal Power Commission

Subjects: Radar
Rocketry

Cities: White Sands, NM.

Other added entries: V-2 Rocket
Viking Rocket
Aerobee Rocket
Rocket-Sonde
Missile Research
Redstone Rocket
Convair Rocket

Atmospheric Research

Roy, Dr. Max

   Interview of Dr. Max Roy, conducted by Albert B.
Christman

Date of Interview: 670100

Documentation: Index, Transcript 10 pp.

Interview number: NOTS-75201-S25

Abstract: Dr. Roy speaks about the establishment of the Salt
Wells Pilot Plant and the types of bombs made there. He
discusses the establishd of the atom bomb plant at
Inyokern, CA., and the different components made at Inyokern
and Albuquerque, NM. Roy also tells why SWPP was closed.

Repositories: NWC, DTNSRDC, NHC

Individuals mentioned: Parsons, RADM William S.

Institutions: Naval Ordnance Test Station
Salt Wells Pilot Plant

Cities: Inyokern, CA.
Albuquerque, NM.
Los Alamos, NM.

Ruckner, RADM Edward A.

   Interview of RADM Edward A. Ruckner

Date of Interview: 731000

Other interview date: 750500

Documentation: Index, Transcript 571 pp.

Abstract: RADM Ruckner discusses his education at the Naval
Postgraduate School and MIT, his work on radar with ADM
Rivero, and his tenure as Deputy CNO for Development. He
also describes his tours of duty on the Ships
Characteristics Board, and as Ordnance Officer at the Naval
Proving Ground.

Repositories: NHC, USNA, USNI, NWCM

Individuals mentioned: Rivero, ADM Horacio

Institutions: Massachusetts Institute of Technology
Deputy Chief of Naval Operations (Development)
Bureau of Ordnance
Naval Proving Ground
Ship Characteristics Board
Naval Postgraduate *School*

Subjects: Ordnance
Radar

Cities: Annapolis, MD.
Dahlgren, VA.

Ruckner, RADM Edward A.

   Interview of RADM Edward A. Ruckner, conducted by Peter Bruton and an unknown interviewer

Date of Interview: 740900

Documentation: 3 Tapes, Index, Transcript 87 pp.

Interview number: BA-6

Abstract: RADM Ruckner discusses Bureau of Ordnance R&D objectives, differences between BUORD's operation and those of other bureaus, and technical direction in BUORD labs. He explains the BuOrd lab evaluation process, how contractors were selected, and how ordnance was inspected. Ruckner describes trends and issues in BUORD from 1940 to 1948 and his tenure as Asst. Chief for R&D-BUORD. He talks about how R&D money was obtained, BuOrd's relations with ONR, and the establishment of the ASN (R&D). Ruckner also mentions BUORD's relations with OPNAV, DCNO, and ASN (R&D) and relates how DCNO (Development) was created and what its functions are. Lastly, he also discusses major trends and issues in R&D from 1958 to 1973, including important program successes, expansion of the DDR&E staff, and the centralization of Navy labs into the Centers.

Repositories: NHC, DTNSRDC

Individuals mentioned: Bennett, RADM Rawson
Foster, Dr. John S.
Frosch, Dr. Robert A.
McNamara, SECDEF Robert S.
Wakelin, *Dr. James H.*

Institutions: Assistant Secretary of the Navy (R&D)

Chief of Naval Material
Deputy Chief of Naval Operations (Development)
Office of Naval Research
Bureau of Ordnance
Director of Defense Research and Engineering

Russell, ADM James S.

   Interview of ADM James S. Russell, conducted by Albert
B. Christman

Date of Interview: 700500

Documentation: Index, Transcript 17 pp.

Interview number: NWC-75201-71

Abstract: ADM Russell first details his own background at
CalTech and the Bureau of Aeronautics. He discusses Dr.
Theodore von Karman and how - with the help of Andrew Haley
- he began to manufacture things for the Army. Russell also
comments on the relationship between BUAER and BUORD. That
includes the influence of ADM McCain in Navy R&D and the
battle over cognizance at NOTS/NWC.

Repositories: NWC, DTNSRDC, NHC

Individuals mentioned: Burroughs, ADM Sherman E.
Haley, Andrew
McCain, ADM John S.
Karman, Dr. Theodore von

Institutions: California Institute of Technology
Bureau of Aeronautics
Bureau of Ordnance
North Atlantic Treaty Organization

Other added entries: Rocket Engines

Sagdahl, John

    Interview of John Sagdahl, conducted by Nelson Wood

Date of Interview: 7705211

Documentation: Tapes, Transcript

Abstract: Mr. Sagdahl speaks of his work as general foreman for the Mark 43 Torpedo.

Repositories: ARL

Subjects: Torpedos

Other added entries: Torpedo Mark 43
Aircraft Launched Torpedos

Sage, Dr. Bruce

    Interview of Dr. Bruce Sage, conducted by Albert B. Christman

Date of Interview: 661100

Documentation: Index, Transcript 30 pp.

Interview number: NOTS-75201-S22

Abstract: Dr. Sage discusses the selection of NOTS sites for pilot plant operations, the construction of the Salt Wells and China Lake Pilot Plants. He talks about the Michelson Laboratory at China Lake, the land selection for the plants, and Dr. Charles C. Lauritsen's motivations.

Repositories: DTNSRDC, NWC, NHC

Individuals mentioned: Byrnes, CAPT James
Lauritsen, Dr. Charles C.
Parsons, RADM William S.
Sabin, Palmer

Institutions: Salt Wells Pilot Plant
China Lake Pilot Plant
Michelson Laboratory

Cities: Inyokern, CA.
Pasadena, CA.

Sanderson, Dr. John A.

Interview of Dr. John A. Sanderson, conducted by Dr. David K. Allison

Date of Interview: 770831

Documentation: 3 Tapes (5 Sides), Index 4 pp.

Abstract: This interview is a supplement to the oral history interview with Dr. Edward O. Hulburt and talks about Hulbert's associates.

Repositories: NRL

Individuals mentioned: Hulburt, Dr. Edward O.

Institutions: Naval Research Laboratory

Subjects: Optics

Sandquist, CAPT Oscar

Interview of CAPT Oscar Sandquisc, conducted by Albert B. Christman

Date of Interview: 660706

Documentation: Index, Transcript 26 pp.

Interview number: NOTS-75201-S13

Abstract: CAPT Sandquist tells about the birth of NOTS in Inyokern, CA., the recruitment of labor, and contractors at NOTS. He describes the logistics of construction, and at the same time cooperating with the CalTech scientists on the missile ranges nearby. Next, he discusses the master plan of the site, water problems, labor problems, budgets, postwar plans and construction. Sandquist also reflects on the first weapons systems to come out of NOTS, including the Sidewinder missile.

Repositories: NWC, DTNSRDC, NHC

Individuals mentioned: Burroughs, ADM Sherman E.
Michelson, Dr. Albert A.
Byrnes, CAPT James

Institutions: Naval Ordnance Test Station
California Institute of Technology

Other added entries: Sidewinder Missile Project

Sawyer, Dr. Ralph A.

   Interview of Dr. Ralph A. Sawyer, conducted by Albert
B. Christman

Date of Interview: 670500

Documentation: Index, Transcript 55 pp.

Interview number: NOTS-75201-S46

Abstract: This interview was originally conducted as
background for a biography of RADM William S. Parsons and
also partly to record the history of NOTS at Inyokern, CA.
Dr. Sawyer discusses his work at the Armor and Projectile
Laboratory at the Naval Proving Ground at Dahlgren, VA., his
relations with CAPT Hedrick, the CO there, and his
impressions of Parsons. He describes subsequent promotion to
Head of Research at NOTS, his work on Crossroads, and other
research at NOTS. He evaluates Parsons as a man and as an
officer and comments on Dr. Louis T. E. Thompson.

Repositories: NWC, DTNSRDC, NHC

Individuals mentioned: Blandy, ADM George
Bradbury, Dr. Norris E.
Hedrick, CAPT David
Loeb, Dr. Leonard
Parsons, RADM William S.
Thompson, Dr. Louis T. E.

Institutions: Naval Ordnance Test Station
Armor and Projectile Laboratory
Naval Proving Ground

Cities: Inyokern, CA.
Dahlgren, VA.

Other added entries: Operation Crossroads

Sawyer, Dr. Ralph A.

   "Development of the Armor and Projectile Laboratory:
Dr. Ralph A. Sawyer", conducted by Jack Brooks, Jr.

Date of Interview: 740522

Documentation: Transcript 7 pp.

Note: This interview is the Chapter V of D_a_h_l_g_r_e_n, edited by
Kenneth G. McCollum

Abstract: Dr. Sawyer tells how he came to Dahlgren as a
Naval Officer to do spectrographic analysis at the newly
constructed Armor and Projectile Laboratory, mentions his
co-workers, Dr. L. T. E. Thompson and CAPT Leonard Loeb, the
size of his staff, the most significant achievements of the
A&P Laboratory, his latter work on the Manhattan Project.

Repositories: NSWC, DTNSRDC

Individuals mentioned: Thompson, Dr. Louis T. E.
Loeb, Dr. Leonard

Institutions: Naval Proving Ground
Armor and Projectile Laboratory

Subjects: Ordnance

Schneider, RADM R. J.

   Interiew of RADM R. J. Schneider

Date of Interview: 750107

Documentation: 2 Tapes

Interview number: BA-18

Repositories: DTNSRDC

Schoeffel, RADM Malcom F.

Interview of RADM Malcom Schoeffel, conducted by Albert
B. Christman

Date of Interview: 660421

Documentation: Index, Transcript 11 pp.

Interview number: NOTS-75201-S8

Abstract: This interview was originally conducted as
background for a biography of RADM William S. Parsons. RADM
Schoeffel reflects on NOTS and the Michelson laboratory. He
comments on RADM Parsons as Deputy Chief of Bureau of
Ordnance.

Repositories: MWC, DTNSRDC, NHC

Individuals mentioned: Hussey, VADM George F.
Parsons, RADM William S.
Thompson, Dr. Louis T. E.

Institutions: Naval Ordnance Test Station
Michelson Laboratory

Cities: Inyokern, CA.

Schoenherr, Dr. Karl E.

Interview of Dr. Karl E. Schoenherr, conducted by Dr.
David K. Allison

Date of Interview: 820415

Documentation: 8 Tapes, 5 Diskettes, Transcript 153 pp.

Abstract: Dr. Schoenherr talks about his background and
education, serving as an apprentice seaman, entering MIT to
study naval architecture, and his first experience with the
Experimental Model Basin - testing yacht models for a school
project. He discusses the EMB in 1922, his coworkers, the
carriage, the size and type of staff, RADM David Taylor, the
relationship between EMB and the Bureau of Construction and
Repair, testing procedures, and the inadequacy of the EMB.
He mentions the importance of the development of the bulbous
bow and Taylor's Standard Series, cavitation studies in the
1930s, the search for a new basin site, acoustic decoys for
World War II German torpedos, torpedo and submarine research
and development during World War II, the wind tunnel, and
the influence of airship design on on torpedos. He gives his

Dr. Karl E. Schoenherr (left) and Mr. Krebs at the controls of the
model towing carriage of the Experimental Model Basin, late 1920s.

impressions of CAPT Saunders and CMDR Wright, NSRDCs
relations with BUSHIPS, post-war changes in organization,
speaks of leaving the Center to become Dean of Engineering
at Notre Dame, returning to the Model Basin in 1958, work on
underwater acoustics, and the balance between testing and
research.

Repositories: DTNSRDC

Individuals mentioned: Hewins, Dr. Lyman
Rickover, ADM Hyman
Keil, Dr. Alfred H.
St. Denis, Manley
Karman, Dr. Theodore von
Gertler, Morton
Wright, RADM Edward Alvey
Landweber, Dr. Louis
Saunders, CAPT Harold E.
Eggert, CAPT Ernest F.
McEntee, CAPT William
Taylor, RADM David W.
Sam, Dr. Albert

Institutions: Massachusetts Institute of Technology
Notre Dame
Bureau of Construction and Repair
Bureau of Ships
Johns Hopkins University
Experimental Model Basin

Subjects: Airships
Propellers
Torpedos

Other added entries: Naval Architecture
Mine Mark 24
Bulbous Bow
Model Testing

Schoman, Dr. Charles M.

Interview of Dr. Charles M. Schoman, conducted by Dr.
David K. Allison

Date of Interview: 820726

Documentation: 1 Tape, Index

Abstract: Dr. Schoman describes the organizational structure
of DTNSRDC, his position as Director of Plans & Programs,
the Five Year Planning process, and the work of Center

committees.

Repositories: DTNSRDC

Individuals mentioned: Powell, Dr. Alan
Allen, Dr. Robert C.

Institutions: David Taylor Naval Ship Research and Development Center
Director, Plans & Programs
Director of Technology
Technical Director

Other added entries: Five Year Plan
Laboratory Management

Sette, Dr. William J.

   Interview of Dr. William J. Sette, conducted by Dr.
David K. Allison

Date of Interview: 821015

Documentation: 1 Tape, Index

Abstract: Dr. Sette talks about his background, initial
impression of the Experimental Model Basin, early work on
shock testing and propeller cavitation, involvement of the
Basin in World War II operations, airblast and gunblast
effects, Operation Crossroads, and his view of the Carderock
- Annapolis Laboratory merger.

Repositories: DTNSRDC

Individuals mentioned: Mumma, RADM Albert G.
Windenburg, Dr. Dwight F.
Strasberg, Dr. Murray
Keil, Dr. Alfred H.

Institutions: Experimental Model Basin
David Taylor Model Basin
Marine Engineering Laboratory
David Taylor Naval Ship Research and Development Center
Underwater Explosives Research Division
Applied Mechanics Laboratory
Hydrodynamics Division

Subjects: Shock
Cavitation

Cities: Los Alamos, NM.
Woods Hole, MA.

Other added entries: Operation Crossroads
Airblast
Independent Research/Independent Exploratory Development
Gunblast

Sewell, Robert G. S.

   Interview of Robert G. S. Sewell, conducted by Mickey
Strang

Date of Interview: 751200

Documentation: Index, Transcript 27 pp.

Interview number: S-105

Abstract: Mr. Sewell comments on the Vietnam Laboratory
Assistance Program - how men were selected to go, how they
travelled to Vietnam with lab equipment, and technical
support from NOTS. He discusses being a civilian in uniform,
life in the Navy at sea and in Saigon, and cutting military
red tape. Sewell also talks about the Sidewinder and Walleye
Missile Projects.

Repositories: NWC, DTNSRDC, NHC

Individuals mentioned: Gould, Al
Johnson, Dr. Gerald

Institutions: Naval Ordnance Test Station

Other added entries: Vietnam Laboratory Assistance Program
Sidewinder Missile Project
Walleye Missile Project
Vietnam War

Sewell, Robert G. S.

   Interview of Robert G. S. Sewell, conducted by Mickey
Strang

Date of IntVview: 750826

Documentation: Index, Not Transcribed, but in note form.

Interview number: S-106

Abstract: Mr. Sewell explains why he came to NOTS-China
Lake, why testing there is more expensive than other labs.

He comments on the role of William B. McLean at NOTS and an engineer's pursuit of excellence - he cannot stand to be wrong. Sewell talks about changes in NOTS organization and Junior Professional Training, as well as the initial team recruited for NOTS. He noted that by 1950, NOTS original projects had been completed and the lab had to find new things to do.

Repositories: NWC, DTNSRDC, NHC

Individuals mentioned: McLean, Dr. William B.
Thompson, Dr. Louis T. E.

Institutions: Naval Ordnance Test Station
Naval Weapons Center

Cities: China Lake, CA.

Seymour, VADM Ernest R.

Interview of VADM Ernest R. Seymour, conducted by Leroy L. Doig III and Dr. David K. Allison

Date of Interview: 830612

Documentation: Tapes, Transcript, 36 pp.

Interview number: S-149

Abstract: VADM Seymour was COMNAVAIR from 1980-1983. Discussion includes concept and place of the laboratories, contractors versus laboratories, organization, NAVMAT versus NAVAIR activities, military-civilian relationships, projects - including Maverick and Skipper; uses NWC as example of good and bad in laboratories.

Repositories: NWC

Institutions: Naval Weapons Center
Naval Material Command
Naval Air Systems Command

Other added entries: Laboratory Management
Maverick Missile

Seymour, VADM Ernest R.

    Interview of VADM Ernest R. Seymour, conducted by Dr. William J. Armstrong

Date of Interview: 830713

Documentation: 1 Tape

Note: VADM Seymour was COMNAVAIR from 1980-1983.

Repositories: NAVAIR

Institutions: Naval Air Systems Command

Seymour, Dr. Harry R.

    Interview of Dr. Harry R. Seymour, conducted by Roger Kempler

Date of Interview: 820629

Other interview date: 820818

Documentation: Transcript, 27 pp

Abstract: Dr. Seymour describes his perception of NRAC, the establishment of NPRDC, the relative merits of BUPERS and NAVMAT sponsorship, the changing role of NPRDC's Washington representative, its major accomplishments, the influence of his military service on his decision to enter personnel research, the Special Projects Units, personnel research programs of the 1950s, the general attitude of the Navy toward personnel research, major figures in research during the post-war era, and his thoughts on improving management of Naval R&D. He talks of his major goals as NPRDC's Washington liaison officer, basic versus applied research, problems associated with justifying personnel R&D in relation to hardware R&D, the relative impact of personnel R&D in the fleet today, the NRAC sub-panel's concern over the amount of applied research performed by NPRDC, his views on the GAO review, and NPRDC's size as a key to its effectiveness

Repositories: NPRDC, DTNSRDC

Individuals mentioned: Price, D. George
Watkins, ADM James
Clarkin, CAPT James J.
Wiskoff, Dr. Martin
Carstater, Dr. Eugene D.

Sjoholm, Dr. Allan A.
Regan, Dr. James J.
Parker, CAPT Donald F.
Collins, Dr. John J.
Marcy, ASN (R&D) H. Tyler
Rostker, Dr. Bernard
Elster, Dr. Richard
Bryan, Dr. Glenn L.

Institutions: Naval Research Advisory Committee
Navy Personnel Research and Development Center

Subjects: Personnel Research

Sheehy, Myles

Interview of Myles Sheehy, conducted by Albert B.
Christman

Date of Interview: 780300

Documentation: 1 Tape, Transcript 12 pp.

Interview number: DNL-T7-78

Abstract: Mr. Sheehy describes his years at NEL in San
Diego, in particular, his role during World War II. Note:
The transcription of this interview is poor. Key terms are
repeatedly omitted either purposefully of because poor tape
quality. There is no page 11.

Repositories: DTNSRDC

Institutions: Naval Electronics Laboratory

Sherwin, Dr. Chalmers

Interview of Dr. Chalmers Sherwin, conducted by Dr.
Samuel Rothman

Date of Interview: 740000

Documentation: Index, Transcript 30 pp.

Interview number: BA-3-74

Abstract: Dr. Sherwin talks about the original purpose of
DDR&E, funding for labs, and the dissatisfaction that led to
lab re-organization. He comments on the image on Navy labs,

the reason for the McNamara memo concerning lab re-organization, and and new innovations in technology. He also discusses the management of the labs, basic research done by labs, DDR&E, and centralization in DoD. Sherwin sees the need for a Historical Evaluation Group to continually evaluate technical and management decisions.

Repositories: NWC, DTNSRDC, NHC

Individuals mentioned: Glass, Dr. Edward
McLean, Dr. William B.
McNamara, SECDEF Robert S.

Institutions: Director of Defense Research and Engineering

Other added entries: Laboratory Consolidations
Laboratory Management

Shugg, Carleton

    Interview of Carleton Shugg

Date of Interview: 731100

Documentation: Transcript 25 pp.

Abstract: Mr. Shugg was President of Electric Boat Company, a sub-systems contractor and builder of FBM submarines for Polaris. This is one of a series of seven interviews on concept and development of Polaris program conducted by the U.S. Naval Institute Oral History Program.

Repositories: NHC, NWCM, USNA, USNI

Subjects: Submarine Launched Ballistic Missiles
Fleet Ballistic Missiles
Ballistic Missile Submarines
Nuclear Powered Fleet Ballistic Missile Submarines
Nuclear Missiles
Weapons Systems

Other added entries: Polaris Program

Smith, Bernard

Interview of Barney Smith, conducted by Mrs. Susan
Frutkin and Dr. Peter Bruton

Date of Interview: 740000

Documentation: 4 Tapes, Index, Transcript 120 pp.

Interview number: BA-7-74

Abstract: Mr. Smith explains how management of R&D
facilities in DoD worked: The Pentagon formulated programs,
the TD at a laboratory went to a desk man at a Bureau for
money, and the desk man allocated it according to a set
budget. He discusses the establishment of the ASN (R&D),
quotes Sidewinder as an example of a program not managed
well, and describes how foundational research money was
misused. Smith comments on bureau-lab dialogues and how an
individual can make a big difference in laboratory
management. He explains the Bureau's feelings at the labs
being place under the CNM, the role of the DNL, and the
SYSCOMs' dialogues with industry. He notes that the DNL was
not an innovative force and was a poor contact between the
labs and their customers. Smith states that RDT&E
appropriations were not a serious problem, evaluates the
success of Project 97, and says that the CNO is not competent
enough to set exploratory development goals. He finds that
block funding was an improvement over specific grants to the
labs, Sidewinder was a success that broke all the rules, and
Navy labs can afford mistakes more than private industry.
Smith believes that rotation of personnel improves R&D
management, that labs should be on the same level as the
SYSCOMs, and that education of lab personnel should be
continuous.

Repositories: NHC, DTNSRDC

Individuals mentioned: Davies, RADM Thomas
Kidd, ADM Issac C., Jr.

Institutions: Bureau of Ordnance
Assistant Secretary of the Navy (R&D)
Chief of Naval Material
Chief of Naval Development
Naval Weapons Laboratory
Systems Commands

Other added entries: Sidewinder Missile Project
Technical Development Plan
Navy Industrial Fund

Smith, Bernard

"Rapid Development: Bernard Smith", conducted by
Cynthia Rouse

Date of Interview: 760608

Documentation: Transcript 17 pp.

Note: This interview is Chapter XII of <u>Dahlgren</u>, edited by
Kenneth G. McCollum

Abstract: Mr. Smith discusses his early interest in rockets,
his appointment as Technical Director of the Naval Weapons
Laboratory in 1964, his opinion of work at Dahlgren in the
1950s, reorganizations and mission changes, dealings with
the Systems Commands, military-civilian relationships, the
effect of civil rights legislation at Dahlgren, professional
development, management training, the significance of the
merger with NOL, White Oak, other proposed mergers, co-
workers.

Repositories: NSWC, DTNSRDC

Individuals mentioned: Colvard, Dr. James E.
Lydanne, Dr. Russell H.
Chase, ADM John Dawson
Bernard, Charles W.
Thompson, Dr. Louis T. E.

Institutions: Naval Ordnance Laboratory
Naval Surface Weapons Center
Naval Weapons Laboratory
Systems Commands

Cities: White Oak, MD.
Dahlgren, VA.

Other added entries: Technical Director

Smith, Howard

    Interview of Howard Smith, conducted by Dr. Vincent
Ponko

Date of Interview: 800916

Documentation: Index, Transcript 34 pp.

Interview number: DNL-T26

Abstract: Mr. Smith talks about military civilian
relationships, the formation of the DNL/DLP, and the work of
the first two DNL/DLP's. He comments on financial controls
of in-house laboratories, labs under the DNL and the
bureaus, and key people in Navy R&D, including Dr. Chalmers
Sherwin, Dr. Robert A. Frosch, and SECDEF Robert S.
McNamara. Smith discusses organizational changes in Navy
R&D; in particular, the politicizing of R&D under President
Kennedy, and the role of the DNL/DLP. He describes the
technical ability of Navy R&D headquarters personnel,
decentralization of DoD under SECDEF Laird, and lack of
incentive for technical people in the labs.

Repositories: DTNSRDC

Individuals mentioned: Johnson, Dr. Gerald
Lawson, Dr. Joel
Laird, SECDEF Melvin
Kennedy, PRES John F.
Sherwin, Dr. Chalmers
Frosch, Dr. Robert A.
Towle, CAPT Bernard

Institutions: Director of Navy Laboratories
Director of Laboratory Programs

Smith, VADM Levering

    Interview of VADM Levering Smith, conducted by Albert
B. Christman

Date of Interview: 670500

Documentation: Index, Transcript 18 pp.

Interview number: NOTS-75201-S48

Abstract: This interview was originally conducted as
background for a biography of RADM William S. Parsons. Smith
discusses Parsons as an officer on the USS TEXAS and as a

proponent of the Proximity Fuze. He talks about Parsons'
knack for spotting people's talents and his tenure as Deputy
Chief of the Bureau of Ordnance. Smith also compares Parsons
to Engineering Duty officers and notes Parsons' role in Navy
nuclear research.

Repositorie: NWC, DTNSRDC, NHC

Individuals mentioned: Parsons, RADM William S.
Sides, ADM
Thompson, Dr. Louis T. E.

Institutions: Naval Ordnance Test Station
Bureau of Ordnance

Other added entries: Proximity Fuze
Engineering Duty Officers

Smitley, Charles Raymond

Interview of Charles Raymond Smitley, conducted by
Nelson Wood

Date of Interview: 790126

Documentation: Tapes, Transcript

Abstract: Mr. Smitley describes his background and
education, and his work with the Harvard Underwater Sound
Laboratory.

Repositories: ARL

Institutions: U. S. Army Signal Corps
Harvard University
Underwater Sound Laboratory

Other added entries: Acoustics Research
Electronics Research
Ordnance Research

Snyder, RADM J. Edward

   Interview of RADM J. Edward Snyder

Date of Interview: 741223

Documentation: 1 Tape

Interview number: BA-19

Repositories: DTNSRDC

Spangenburg, George

   Interview of George Spangenburg

Date of Interview: 751210

Documentation: 1 Tape

Interview number: BA-25

Repositories: NHC, DTNSRDC

Stone, Dr. Harris B.

   Interview of Dr. Harris B. Stone, conducted by Booz-Allen & Hamilton

Date of Interview: 741128

Documentation: 1 Tape (1 Side), Index

Interview number: BA-15

Abstract: This interview is part of Booz-Allen & Hamilton's review of Navy R&D Management 1943-1973. Dr. Stone discusses leaving the Army laboratory system to work for the Navy, feeling that the Navy had better military/civilian relations and more opportunities in in-house research. He describes his work coordinating electronics warfare and intelligence research in ONR, and the reorganization that placed his group under the CNO. He emphasizes the need to analyze Navy R&D programs in totality.

Repositories: NHC, DTNSRDC

Individuals mentioned: Zumwalt, ADM Elmo
Burns, Dr. Robert O.

Institutions: Office of Naval Research
U. S. Army
Ft. Monmouth
Ft. Huachuca
Chief of Naval Operations
Director of Research, Development, Test & Evaluation

Other added entries: Long Range Planning
Naval Research

Stoner, Donald W.

   "Range Operations: Donald W. Stoner", conducted by
Cynthia Rouse

Date of Interview: 760914

Documentation: Transcript 19 pp.

Note: This interview is the Chapter IV of <u>Dahlgren</u>, edited
by Kenneth G. McCollum

Abstract: Mr. Stoner describes the work he did on
bombsights and fuzes at Dahlgren between 1935 and 1941,
experiments with armor-piercing bombs, general ordnance work
during World War II, funding problems, change in emphasis to
guided missiles, re-working World War II ammunition during
the Vietnam War, problems with the local community,
accidental deaths during ordnance tests, and co-workers.

Repositories: NSWC, DTNSRDC

Individuals mentioned: Dement, Roger
Kemper, Dr. William
Tubman, Benjamin
Reynolds, Dr. Melvin F.

Institutions: Naval Proving Ground
Bureau of Ordnance
Naval Weapons Laboratory

Subjects: Ordnance
Ballistics
Armor
Fuzes
Bombs
Bombsights
Projectiles

Strand, Dr. Kai Aa.

   Interview of Dr. Kai Aa. Strand, conducted by Dr. David
H. DeVorkin

Date of Interview: 821208

Documentation: Tapes, 7.5 hours, Transcript, 140 pp.

Other interview date: 830103

Abstract: Mr. Strand's early life and training in Copenhagen
are discussed, his work for the U. S. Army during World War
II, and his time at the Sproul, Yerkes, and U. S. Naval
Observatories.

Repositories: NASM

Institutions: Naval Observatory
Yerkes Observatory
Northwestern University
Sproul Observatory
U. S. Army

Subjects: Astronomy

Strauss, RADM Louis L.

   Interview of RADM Louis L. Strauss, conducted by Albert
B. Christman

Date of Interview: 670500

Documentation: Index, Transcript 13 pp.

Interview number: NOTS-75201-S47

Abstract: This interview was originally conducted as
background for a biography RADM William S. Parsons. RADM
Strauss recalls his first acquaintance with Parsons, in the
Manhattan Project, and Parsons' feelings on the United
States' atomic strategy. He details Parsons' relationship
with SECNAV James Forrestal, his and Parsons' roles on the
Atomic Energy Commission, and Dr. Robert Oppenheimer's loss
of clearance.

Repositories: NWC, DTNSRDC, NHC

Individuals mentioned: Oppenheimer, Dr. Robert
Forrestal, SECNAV James
Parsons, RADM William S.

Institutions: Atomic Energy Commission
Naval Proving Ground

Cities: Dahlgren, VA.

Other added entries: Manhattan Project

Stump, ADM Felix Budwell

    Interview of ADM Felix Budwell Stump

Date of Interview: 650000

Documentation: Transcript 364 pp.

Abstract: This interview concerns the Naval Academy, naval aviation training at Pensacola in 1919, aeronautical engineering 1922-1924, and the Naval Air Maintenance Procurement Division, Bureau of Aeronautics.

Repositories: COL, NHC

Institutions: Bureau of Aeronautics

Subjects: Naval Aviation

Cities: Pensacola, FL.

Other added entries: Aeronautical Engineering

Sullivan, ADM William

    Interview of ADM William Sullivan

Date of Interview: 650000

Documentation: Transcript 1,784 pp.

Abstract: ADM Sullivan recalls his career in the Navy, with special mention of Naval construction, Navy yards in United States, the Trans-Siberian Railroad, his work at the Model Basin and Washington Naval Gun Factory, diving technology and mine-sweeping.

Repositories: COL, NHC

Institutions: Experimental Model Basin
Naval Gun Factory

Cities: Washington, DC.

Subjects: Naval Construction

Sykes, RADM James B.

   Interview of RADM James Sykes, conducted by Albert B. Christman

Date of Interview: 670427

Documentation: Index, not taped 23 pp.

Interview number: NOTS-75201-S41

Abstract: RADM Sykes discusses his tenure as Commanding Officer at NOTS - his operating philosophy for the station, his relationship with scientists there, and the building of a neighborhood community. He recalls how he got his appointment to the Naval Academy and compares his other tours of duty with his time at NOTS.

Repositories: NWC, DTNSRDC, NHC

Individuals mentioned: Burroughs, ADM Sherman E.
Sykes, Mrs. James

Institutions: Naval Ordnance Test Station
Salt Wells Pilot Plant

Cities: Inyokern, CA.

Thompson, Arthur

   Interview of Arthur Thompson, conducted by Richard D. Glasow

Date of Interview: 800822

Documentation: Tapes, Transcript

Abstract: Mr. Thompson speaks of his his work with the Ordnance Research Laboratory.

Repositories: ARL

Institutions: Ordnance Research Laboratory
Pennsylvania State University

Thompson, Dr. Louis T. E.

   Interview of Dr. L. T. E. Thompson, conducted by Albert B. Christman

Date of Interview: 651107

Documentation: Index, Transcript 54 pp.

Interview number: NOTS-75201-S1

Other interview date: 651106

Abstract: This interview was originally conducted as background for a biography of RADM William S. Parsons. Dr. Thompson discusses Parsons' background, his early days at the Naval Proving Ground at Dahlgren, VA., and Parsons at NRL and NOTS. Thompson also includes an account of Parsons' work on the Manhattan Project, his thoughts on in-house labs, and his role in the Naval hierarchy.

Repositories: NWC, DTNSRDC, NHC

Individuals mentioned: Burroughs, ADM Sherman E.
Duncan, CAPT James
Hussey, VADM George F.
Lauritsen, Dr. Charles C.
Moulton, Prof. Forest Ray
Parsons, RADM William S.

Institutions: Naval Surface Weapons Center
Naval Proving Ground
Naval Research Laboratory
Naval Ordnance Test Station
Bureau of Ordnance

Cities: Dahlgren, VA.

Other added entries: Manhattan Project

Thompson, Dr. Louis T. E.

    Interview of Dr. L. T. E. Thompson., conducted by Albert B. Christman

Date of Interview: 681110

Documentation: Transcript 40 pp.

Interview number: NWC-75201-S55

Abstract: Dr. Thompson comments informally on pre-World War II research at the Naval Proving Ground, weapons design, and the Naval bureaucracy.

Repositories: NWC, DTNSRDC, NHC

Individuals mentioned: Goddard, Dr. Robert
Hedrick, CAPT David
Schuyler, CAPT Michael

Institutions: Naval Proving Ground

Thompson, Dr. Louis T. E.

    "Dahlgren's First Leading Scientist: Dr. L. T. E. Thompson", conducted by Cynthia Rouse

Date of Interview: 761208

Documentation: Transcript 8 pp.

Note: This interview is Chapter II of <u>Dahlgren</u>, edited by Kenneth McCollum

Abstract: Dr. Thompson explains his decision to come to Dahlgren in 1923, comments on his personal goals, the environment at the Proving Ground, support from BUORD, his friendship with RADM Parsons, his theories on the value of experimental and developmental work.

Repositories: NSWC, DT. 3RDC

Individuals mentioned: Parsons, RADM William S.
Stark, ADM Harold R.

Institutions: Bureau of Ordnance
Naval Proving Ground

Tibbitts, CAPT Barrick F.

Interview of CAPT Barrick F. Tibbitts, conducted by Dr. David K. Allison

Date of Interview: 800716

Documentation: Three Tapes (5 Sides), Index

Abstract: At the end of his tour at DTNSRDC, CAPT Tibbitts reviews his three years at the Center and his major accomplishments. He describes the Center's role in relation to other NAVMAT laboratories and its customers, the Systems Commands.

Repositories: DTNSRDC

Individuals mentioned: Powell, Dr. Alan
Ricketts, COMO Myron V.

Institutions: David Taylor Naval Ship Research and Development Center
Naval Sea Systems Command

Other added entries: Navy Industrial Fund
Ship Design
Engineering Duty Officers
Long Range Planning
Laboratory Management
Military Construction

Tousey, Dr. Richard

Interview of Dr. Richard Tousey, conducted by Dr. David H. DeVorkin

Date of Interview: 811100

Other interview dates: 820108 and 820406

Documentation: Tapes, 9.5 hours, Transcript, 160 pp.

Abstract: Dr. Tousey talks about his education, interest in the UV solar spectrum, contact with E. O. Hulburt, and research in optics at the Naval Research Laboratory during World War II. After the war, Hulburt brought Tousey into the V-2 rocket program, and he designed a new UV spectrograph. He describes his involvement with and objectives of the V-2 program, and designs of Aerobee and Viking spectroscopic equipment.

Repositories: NASM

Individuals mentioned: Friedman, Dr. Herbert
Van Allen, Dr. James
Menzel, Dr.Donald
Roberts, Dr. Walter Orr
Krause, Dr. Ernst H.
Hulburt, Dr. Edward O.
Goldberg, Dr. Leo

Institutions: Naval Research Laboratory
Harvard University
Bureau of Aeronautics
Applied Physics Laboratory
Upper Air Rocket Research Panel

Subjects: Satellites
X-Ray Astronomy
Experimental Physics
Solar Physics
Optics
Solar X-Ray Radiation

Other added entries: Coronagraphic Studies
Aerobee Rocket
Photographic Emulsions
Lyman-Alpha
V-2 Rocket
Nike Missile
Ultra Violet Solar Spectroscopy
Photoelectric Sensors
Infrared Sensors

Towle, CAPT Bernard

Interview of CAPT Bernard Towle, conducted by Dr. Samuel Rothman, Dr. Peter Bruton, and Mrs. Susan Frutkin

Date of Interview: 741217

Documentation: 3 Tapes, Index, Transcript 54 pp.

Interview number: BA-14

Abstract: CAPT Towle discusses lab management under SECDEF Robert S. McNamara, the philosophies of different Navy bureaus, and the combination of the Bureau of Ordnance and Bureau of Aeronautics. He talks about the establishment of the DNL, particularly why the labs should report to CNM. Towle explains the influence of outside sources on R&D, including the Sherwin Plan, the Mansfield Amendment, the National Science Foundation, and congressional input. He also comments on problems in the use of labs, in decision making, and trends in top-level laboratory management.

Repositories: NHC, DTNSRDC

Individuals mentioned: Johnson, Dr. Gerald
Sherwin, Dr. Chalmers
McNamara, SECDEF Robert S.

Institutions: Bureau of Aeronautics
Bureau of Ordnance
Chief of Naval Material
Director of Navy Laboratories
National Science Foundation

Other added entries: Mansfield Amendment
Sherwin Plan

Towle, CAPT Bernard

Interview of CAPT Bernard Towle, conducted by Albert B.
Christman

Date of Interview: 780314

Documentation: 1 Tape, Transcript 32 pp.

Interview number: DNL-T1-78

Abstract: CAPT Towle comments on his positions in the Navy
in the 1960's, the pre-DNL lab management, and the
introduction of the Sherwin Plan. He explains the Navy's
compromise plan for re-organization of the labs - changes
dictated by technology, SYSCOM resistance, and ADM Rivero's
decision that military command of the labs is not essential.
Towle talks about the DNL charter, concepts of the DNL
position, and the first DNL. He describes the problems in
selecting lab managers, SECDEF McNamara and the DNL, and
DDR&E's influence. Towle discusses the Navy's loss of
flexibility in controlling money and effect of SYSCOM
opposition to the establishment of the DNL. He comments on
the second DNL, ADM Kidd's view of the labs, and the future
of the lab system.

Repositories: NWC, DTNSRDC, NHC

Individuals mentioned: Rivero, ADM Horacio
Rothman, Dr. Samuel
McNamara, SECDEF Robert S.
Kidd, ADM Issac C., Jr.
Andrews, CAPT Albert
Smith, Howard

Institutions: Assistant Secretary of the Navy (R&D)
Chief of Naval Material
Director of Navy Laboratories
Director of Defense Research and Engineering
Systems Commands

Other added entries: Sherwin Plan

Tremblay, Harold

Interview of Mr. Harold Tremblay, conducted by Tom Misa and Ed Todd

Date of Interview: 820706

Documentation: 1 Tape, Index 2 pp.

Interview number: NADC-7

Abstract: Mr. Tremblay describes his personal background and his early NAMU work, including the V-2 Missile Studies, glider research, and early television projects, leading to airborne video cameras. He discusses Project Typhoon, his relations with RCA, and BUAER's role at NADC. Tremblay talks about Typhoon's construction as a vacuum tube computer, its applications, and its size.

Repositories: NADC, DTNSRDC

Institutions: Naval Air Development Center
Radio Corporation of America
Princeton University
Bureau of Aeronautics
Naval Air Modification Unit

Subjects: Computer Simulation
Guided Missile Computers
Missile Systems

Other added entries: Typhoon Project
Whirlwind Project
Hurricane Project
Computer Research
REAC Computers
V-2 Rocket

Tremblay, Harold

Interview of Harold Tremblay, conducted by Tom Misa and
Ed Todd

Date of Interview: 820720

Documentation: 1 Tape, Index 2 pp.

Interview number: NADC-14

Abstract: Mr. Tremblay discusses the relationship between
NADC and the University of Pennsylvania, the creation of the
Numerical Analysis Branch at NADC in 1953, and the re-
organization of computer work there in 1955 and 1956. He
talks about the ambiguity in the term "systems concept",
establishment of the Aeronautical Computer Lab at NADC, and
connections between computers and centrifuges. Tremblay
describes computer work in the 1960's and the development of
advanced software in the 1970's.

Repositories: NADC, DTNSRDC

Individuals mentioned: Hardy, Dr. James D.

Institutions: Naval Air Development Center
University of Pennsylvania
Naval Proving Ground
Aeronautical Computer Laboratory
U. S. Army

Subjects: Computer Softwear
Space Simulation
Aerospace Medicine
Computer Simulation
Fire Control Computers
Ballistic Trajectories

Cities: Dahlgren, VA.

Other added entries: ENIAC Computer
X-15 Project
Mercury Project
Gemini Project
Human Centrifuge

Harold Tremblay of the Naval Air Development Center.

Trexler, James Hugh

Interview of James Hugh Trexler, conducted by Dr. David
K. Allison

Date of Interview: 801020

Documentation: 5 Tapes (10 Sides), Background and list of
questions asked

Abstract: Mr. Trexler talks about radio telescope projects
done at Stump Neck, MD, and Sugar Grove, WV, and research in
electronic counter-measures at NRL. The interview is
supplemented by a collection of papers on research
management.

Repositories: NRL

Institutions: Naval Research Laboratory

Cities: Stump Neck, MD.
Sugar Grove, WV.

Other added entries: Radio Telescope Research
Electronic Counter-measures

Truax, CAPT Robert

Interview of CAPT Robert Truax, conducted by Albert B.
Christman

Date of Interview: 720316

Documentation: Index, Transcript 27 pp.

Interview number: NWC-751-S82

Abstract: CAPT Truax talks about his own research at the
Naval Academy and his early contacts in Maryland. He
describes his work in California during World War II, the
competition between himself and Dr. Robert Goddard, and the
s-milarities and differences in their work. Truax comments
on Goddard's general disposition, his penchant for secrecy,
his poor health, and his research methods.

Repositories: NWC, DTNSRDC, NHC

Individuals mentioned: Cox, ADM
Fischer, LTC Frank
Goddard, Dr. Robert

Institutions: U. S. Naval Academy

Other added entries: Rocket Research

Upgren, A.

   Interview of A. Upgren, conducted by David H. DeVorkin

Date of Interview: 770000

Documentation: Tapes

Repository: AIP

Subjects: Astronomy

Van Allen, Dr. James

   Interview of Dr. James Van Allen, conducted by Dr.
David H. DeVorkin and Allan Needell

Date of Interview: 810218

Documentation: Tapes, 18.5 hours, Transcript, 362 pp.

Other interview dates: 810712, 810618, 810622, 810715, 810116,
810728, 810806

Abstract: Dr. Van Allen talks about his family and life
during World War I in Iowa, his educational background,
thesis subjects, and post-graduation job at the Department
of Terrestrial Magnetism in Washington and interest in
cosmic ray studies. He describes his work in World War II
in the Pacific, Merle Tuve and the development of the
Proximity Fuze, post-war years at the APL, work with NRL on
the V-2 rockets, and achievements of the V-2 experiments,
the development of the Rockoon, the Rocket Panels'
involvement during the International Geophysical Year, the
effect of Sputnik and the rush to launch Vanguard, the
establishment of NASA, satellites, the "Van Allen" radiation
belts, and the outlook for space science.

Repositories: NASM

Tousey, Dr. Richard
Tuve, Dr. Merle
Krause, Dr. Ernst H.
Toftoy, BG Holger N.
Zwicky, Prof. Fritz

Braun, Wernher von
Johnson, PRES Lyndon B.
Millikan, Dr. Robert A.

Institutions: Naval Research Laboratory
Bureau of Ordnance
Applied Physics Laboratory
International Geophysical Year

Subjects: Satellites
Cosmic Rays
Physics
Magnetospherics

Other added entries: Proximity Fuze
Van Allen Radiation Belt
USS *NORTON SOUND*
V-2 Rocket
Sputnik
Aerobee Rocket
Vanguard Program
Explorer Program
Project Sherwood
Rockoon

Vossler, RADM Curtis F.

   Interview of RADM Curtis F. Vossler, conducted by J. D. Gerrard-Gough

Date of Interview: 730400

Documentation: Index, Transcript 34 pp.

Interview number: NOTS-75201-S85

Abstract: RADM Vossler explains how he came to be in the Navy and talks about his early career. He describes testing rockets and new planes at NOTS and comments on the command structure at NOTS-in particular, the tenures of CAPTs John T. Hayward and James Sykes as Commanding Officer.

Repositories: NWC, DTNSRDC, NHC

Individuals mentioned: Armitage, LT John M.
Burroughs, ADM Sherman E.
Hayward, ADM John T.
Pollock, CAPT Thomas
Sykes, RADM James B.

Institutions: Naval Ordnance Test Station

Other added entries: Rocket Testing
Aircraft Testing
Commanding Officer

Wakelin, Dr. James H.

Interview of Dr. James H. Wakelin, conducted by Dr. Peter Bruton, Mrs. Susan Frutkin, and CAPT Robert L. Hansen

Date of Interview: 740900

Documentation: 2 Tapes, Index, Transcript 110 pp.

Interview number: BA-9

Abstract: Dr. Wakelin discusses R&D programs in the 1950's, establishment of the ASN (R&D), the Polaris Program, and DDR&E as a pressure mechanism for ASN (R&D). He discusses the ONR-Blue Suit Navy relationship, management responsibilities for DDR&E appropriations, and the need for a coherent R&D program. Wakelin describes the Navy R&D planning system and program structure. He also mentions ideas for improving lab operations, the creation of the DNL, and the ASN (R&D) as a liaison between the Navy and DoD, and the difficulty of attracting qualified technical people.

Repositories: NHC, DTNSRDC

Individuals mentioned: Franke, William B.
Hayward, ADM John T.
McNamara, SECDEF Robert S.

Institutions: Director of Defense Research and Engineering
Assistant Secretary of the Navy (R&D)
Bureau of Ordnance
Department of Defense

Other added entries: Polaris Missile
Tentative Specific Organizational Requirement

Ward, Dr. Newton E.

   Interview of Dr. Newton E. Ward, conducted by J. D.
Gerrard-Gough and Max R. Smith

Date of Interview: 740524

Documentation: Index, Transcript 36 pp.

Interview number: S-91

Abstract: Dr. Ward describes the early NOTS organizational
structure and talks about problems with air-to-ground
missiles like Sidewinder and Dove. He comments on the first
proposals for Walleye, its funding, and its building
problems. Ward recalls its early launchings and production
problems and conflicts with Martin Company.

Repositories: NWC, DTNSRDC, NHC

Individuals mentioned: Crawford, Jack A.
McLean, Dr. William B.

Institutions: Naval Ordnance Test Station
Martin Company

Subjects: Missiles

Other added entries: Sidewinder Missile Project
Walleye Missile Project
Dove Missile Project

Walker, Eric A.

   Interview of Eric A. Walker

Date of Interview: 791128

Documentation: Tapes, Transcript

Abstract: Mr. Walker desᵣ   es his background and education,
and his work at the Harvard Underwater Sound Laboratory.

Repositories: ARL

Institutions: Harvard University
Underwater Sound Laboratory

Other added entries: Acoustics Research

Ward, Dr. Newton E.

Interview of Dr. Newton E. Ward, conducted by Albert B. Christman

Date of Interview: 741023

Documentation: Index, Transcript 46 pp.

Interview number: S-94

Abstract: Dr. Ward discusses the management of NOTS when he first arrived, and Dr. Louis T. E. Thompson as NOTS' first technical director. He comments on the leadership abilities and roles of other technical directors, including Dr. Brown, Dr. William B. McLean, and Dr. Thomas Amlie, and Dr. Haskell G. Wilson. Ward reflects on the commanding officers who have been at NOTS, military-civilian relationships there, and the trend towards more bureaucracy in R&D.

Repositories: NWC, DTNSRDC, NHC

Individuals mentioned: Amlie, Dr. Thomas S.
Brown, Dr. Frederick W.
Frosch, Dr. Robert A.
LaBerge, Dr. Walter
McLean, Dr. William B.
Thompson, Dr. Louis T. E.
Wilson, Dr. Haskell G.

Institutions: Naval Ordnance Test Station
Naval Weapons Center

Warner, Dr. Arthur H.

Interview of Dr. Arthur H. Warner, conducted by J. D. Gerrard-Gough

Date of Interview: 751211

Documentation: Index, Transcript 10 pp.

Interview number: 5313 S-102

Abstract: Dr. Warner discusses NOTS history, including a housing shortage problem, SECNAV Forrestal's visit to NOTS in 1947, and the role of ADMs Switzer and Vieweg in shaping NOTS. He comments on Dr. Bruce Sage, Dr. Wallace C. Brode, the need for a better computing center at NOTS, and Dr. Willaim McLean's work on the Sidewinder Missile.

Repositories: NWC, DTNSRDC, NHC

Individuals mentioned: Brode, Dr. Wallace C.
Hayward ADM John T.
McLean, Dr. William B.
Switzer, VADM W. G.
Sykes, RADM James B.
Forrestal, SECNAV James
Vieweg, RADM Walter V. R.

Institutions: Naval Ordnance Test Station

Other added entries: Sidewinder Missile Project

Waterman, Dr. Peter

    Interview of Dr. Peter Waterman

Date of Interview: 740000

Documentation: 1 Tape, Transcript 32 pp.

Interview number: BA-12

Abstract: Dr. Waterman speaks about the maintenance of Navy
R&D facilities and programs, cost effectiveness of programs,
and Navy R&D, in general, from World War II to the present.

Repositories: NWC, DTNSRDC, NHC

Individuals mentioned: Clements, William

Other added entries: Laboratory Management

Watson, Dr. Earnest C.

    Interview of Dr. Earnest C. Watson, conducted by Albert
B. Christman

Date of Interview: 700220

Documentation: Index, Transcript 68 pp.

Interview number: NWC-75201-S69

Note: Other date: 700219

Abstract: Dr. Watson talks about scientists in World War I,
Dr. Robert Millikan, and Dr. Richard C. Tolman. He describes

CalTech's role in research during World War II, Dr. Charles
C. Lauritsen, and Dr. Vannevar Bush. Watson comments on the
development of rocket propellents and the proximity fuze and
Dr. Max G. Mason, He details the development of NOTS and
CalTech's role there after World War II.

Repositories: NWC, DTNSRDC, NHC

Individuals mentioned: Bush, Dr. Vannevar
Fowler, Dr. William
Hale, George Ellery
Lauritsen, Dr. Charles C.
Mason, Dr. Max G.
Michelson, Dr. Albert A.
Millikan, Dr. Robert A.
Noyer, Arthur
Sage, Dr. Bruce
Tolman, Dr. Richard C.

Institutions: Naval Ordnance Test Station
California Institute of Technology

Cities: Inyokern, CA.

Other added entries: Proximity Fuze
Rocket Propellents

Watson, Clement

    Interview of Clement Watson

Date of Interview: 721100

Documentation: Transcript 65 pp.

Abstract: Mr. Watson was Presentation/Public relations
contractor for Polaris. This is one of a series of seven
interviews on concept and development of Polaris program
conducted by the U. S. Naval Institute Oral History Program.

Repositories: NHC, NWCM, USNA, USNI

Subjects: Submarine Launched Ballistic Missiles
Fleet Ballistic Missiles
Ballistic Missile Submarines
Nuclear Powered Fleet Ballistic Missile Submarines
Nuclear Missiles
Weapons Systems

Other added entries: Polaris Program

Watson-Watt, Sir Robert Alexander

    Interview of Sir Robert Alexander Watson-Watt

Date of Interview: 610000

Documentation: Transcript 568 pp.

Abstract: Watson-Watt reminisces about his involvement in meteorological work, World War I, radio and static studies, director finders, the Department of Scientific and Industrial Research, airborne radar, planned position indicators, secondary radar devices, interallied intelligence missions, and V-1 and V-2 raids.

Repositories: COL

Individuals mentioned: Tizard, Henry

Subjects: Radar
Airborne Radar

Waynick, Arthur H.

    Interview of Arthur H. Waynick, conducted by Richard D. Glasow

Date of Interview: 800321

Documentation: Tapes, Transcript

Abstract: Mr. Waynick describes his background and education, his work at the Harvard Underwater Sound Laboratory and the Applied Research Laboratory.

Repositories: ARL

Institutions: Pennsylvania State University
Harvard University
Underwater Sound Laboratory
Applied Research Laboratory

Other added entries: Acoustics Research

Weaver, Dr. Warren

Interview of Dr. Warren Weaver

Date of Interview: 610000

Documentation: Transcript 783 pp.

Abstract: Mr. Weaver discusses World War II, the NDRC, range finders, fuzes, bomb sights, gun directors, electrical predictors, computers, and the Applied Mathematics Panel.

Repositories: COL

Institutions: Applied Mathematics Panel
National Defense Research Committee

Individuals mentioned: Tizard, Henry
Millikan, Dr. Robert A.

Subjects: Range Finders
Fuzes
Bomb Sights
Ordnance

Welford, Randolph

Interview of Randolph Welford, conducted by Albert B. Christman and Dr. Marjorie Ciarlante

Date of Interview: 820700

Documentation: 1 Tape (15 Minutes Total)

Interview number: ABC-1

Note: Mr. Welford is the nephew of Dr. Louis T. E. Thompson

Repositories: DTNSRDC

Individuals mentioned: Thompson, Dr. Louis T. E.

White, Dr. Howard J., Jr.

Interview of Dr. Howard A. J. White, Jr., conducted by
Dr. Vincent Ponko

Date of Interview: 801200

Documentation: 4 Tapes, Index, Transcript 27 pp.

Interview number: DNL-T32

Abstract: Dr. White discusses the background to his
appointment as Special Assistant for Research to the ASN
(R&D). He describes his duties, including budgeting 6.1 and
6.2 funds, working as a liaison between the labs and ASN
(R&D), and studying the problem of laboratory management in
a military-civilian matrix. White comments on the impact of
the Task Force 97 Project Report, the Dillon Review of 1962,
and the Furnes and Austin Reports. He talks about the
Sherwin Plan and the Navy R&D community's reaction to it,
and key R&D people like Dr. William B. McLean, Dr. Haskell
G. Wilson, and SECNAV Paul Nitze. White discusses the needs
the Navy's in-house labs must meet, the justification for
in-house labs, and Navy labs in the early 1960's. He also
comments on SECDEF McNamara.

Repositories: NWC, DTNSRDC, NHC

Individuals . entioned: McLean, Dr. William B.
Wilson, Dr. Haskell G.
Nitze, SECNAV Paul
McNamara, SECDEF Robert S.
Sherwin, Dr. Chalmers
Wakelin, Dr. James H.

Institutions: Secretary of Defense
Secretary of the Navy

Other added entries: Sherwin Plan
Task Force 97
Dillon Report
Furnes Report
Austin Report

Whitmarsh, David

   Interview of David Whitmarsh, conducted by Nelson Wood

Date of Interview: 790126

Documentation: Tapes, Transcript

Abstract: Mr. Whitmarsh talks about his work at the Ordnance Research Laboratory.

Repositories: ARL

Institutions: Naval Torpedo Station
Ordnance Research Laboratory
Pennsylvania State University
Bureau of Ordnance

Cities: Newport, RI.

Subjects: Torpedos

Other added entries: Acoustics Research
Ordnance Research

Wiegand, Dr. James

   Interview of Dr. James Wiegand, conducted by Michelle Ballenger

Date of Interview: 720800

Documentation: Index, Transcript 28 pp.

Interview number: S-111

Abstract: Dr. Wiegand talks about his association with the Solid Propellent Branch at NOTS. He describes the China Lake Pilot Plant, social interaction between military and civilian personnel, and Dr. Louis T. E. Thompson. Wiegand comments on program direction from Washington, relations with Aerojet and major problems encountered by the rocket department. He also explains his reasons for leaving NOTS.

Repositories: NWC, DTNSRDC, NHC

Individuals mentioned: Ellis, Dr. Emory L.
Gould, Al
McLean, Dr. William B.
Patton, Harold

Sage, Dr. Bruce
Smith, VADM Levering
Thompson, Dr. Louis T. E.

Institutions: Naval Ordnance Test Station
Naval Weapons Center
China Lake Pilot Plant
Aerojet General Corporation

Cities: China Lake, CA.

Other added entries: Rocket Research

Wilcox, Douglas

Interview of Douglas Wilcox, conducted by J. D. Gerrard-Gough

Date of Interview: 751223

Documentation: Index, Transcript 11 pp.

Interview number: 5313 S-103

Abstract: Mr. Wilcox recalls his entry at NOTS-Pasadena as an "NP" (New Professional) and his later appointment as Head of the Underwater Ordnance Department. He describes the communication problems between China Lake and Pasadena and how they were solved. Wilcox comments on problems in the military-civilian relationships at NOTS, the emphasis there on the Junior Professional Program, and his switch to the Naval Undersea Center at San Diego, CA. He also states that he did not favor the break-up of the China Lake-Pasadena arrangement.

Repositories: NWC, DTNSRDC, NHC

Individuals mentioned: McLean, Dr. William B.
Wilson, Dr. Haskell G.

Institutions: Naval Ordnance Test Station
Naval Undersea Center

Cities: China Lake, CA.
Pasadena, CA.
San Diego, CA.

Wilcox, Douglas

    Interview of Douglas Wilcox, conducted by Albert B. Christman

Date of Interview: 780313

Documentation: 1 tape, Transcript 22 pp.

Interview number: DNL-T5-78

Abstract: Wilson comments on his early work at NOTS, his move from NOTS to NUC, and his stint as Technical Director there. He talks about the influence of Dr. William B. McLean; in particular, his ability at NOTS/NWC to cut through red tape and achieve real progress in weapons systems. Wilson also describes the problem of layering in the federal bureaucracy, the need for greater trust and flexibility in the laboratory system, and for a better recorded history of what happened at Navy laboratories.

Repositories: NHC, DTNSRDC

Individuals mentioned: McLean, Dr. William B.
Wilson, Dr. Haskell G.

Institutions: Naval Ordnance Test Station
Naval Ocean Systems Center

Other added entries: Technical Director

Wilcox, Dr. Howard A.

    Interview of Dr. Howard A. Wilcox, conducted by Mickey Strang

Date of Interview: 760525

Documentation: Index, Transcript 13 pp.

Interview number: S-107

Abstract: Dr. Wilcox comments on the projects he was involved in NOTS, including NOTSNIK, a response to Sputnik, and ASROC. He also talks about satellites as collectors of solar energy and their extremely high cost.

Repositories: NWC, DTNSRDC, NHC

Institutions: Naval Ordnance Test Station
Naval Weapons Center

Subjects: Satellites

Other added entries: Sputnik
NOTSNIK
Antisubmarine Rocket

Wilcox, Dr. Howard A.

   Interview of Dr. Howard A. Wilcox, conducted by Albert
B. Christman with Bert Larson

Date of Interview: 780315

Documentation: 1 Tape, Transcript 23 pp.

Interview number: DNL-T9-78

Abstract: Dr. Wilcox describes various problems with Navy
labs before World War II, including increasing bureaucracy,
the insertion of new managers without wartime lab
experience, and budget constraints. He commments on lack of
innovative weapons ideas and narrowly defined lab missions.
He discusses Dr. William B. McLean's leadership qualities,
his ability to cut red tape, and his technical and
administrative skills. Wilcox comments on Dr. Walter LaBerge
as an R&D leader, good aspects of the Navy lab system, and
the roles of headquarters, labs, and industry in Navy R&D.
He states that there is a need for more vigorous prosecution
of Navy R&D, talks about the effect of Sputnik and the
Navy's role in Vietnam.

Repositories: DTNSRDC

Individuals mentioned: McLean, Dr. William B.
LaBerge, Dr. Walter
Thompson, Dr. Louis T. E.

Institutions: Naval Ordnance Test Station
Naval Weapons Center

Other added entries: Sputnik
Vietnam War

Wilcox, Dr. Howard A.

Interview of Dr. Howard A. Wilcox, conducted by Starla
Hall

Date of Interview: 800900

Documentation: Transcript 36 pp.

Interview number: DNL-T25

Abstract: Dr. Wilcox gives his impressions of his longtime
colleague Dr. William B. McLean. He talks about McLean's
involvement on the Sidewinder Missile Project; in
particular, his leadership style, technical problems
involved, and problems of Air Force acceptance of the
missile. Wilcox comments on McLean as NOTS Technical
Director and as a lobbyist in Washington. He discusses
McLean's frustration with increasing government bureaucracy,
his move to NUC as TD, and problems in combining NOTS and
NEL functions at NUC. He comments on officers' attitudes
toward McLean, McLean's retirement, and the role of Edith
LaVerne McLean.

Repositories: NWC, DTNSRDC, NHC

Individuals mentioned: McLean, Dr. William B.
McLean, Edith LaVerne (Mrs. William B.)

Institutions: Naval Ordnance Test Station
Naval Undersea Center
Naval Electronics Laboratory
Naval Weapons Center
U. S. Air Force

Other added entries: Sidewinder Missile Project

Willey, Thomas

Interview of Tom Willey, conducted by Tom Misa and Ed
Todd

Date of Interview: 820715

Documentation: 2 Tapes, Index 3 pp.

Interview number: NADC-10,11

Abstract: Mr. Willey discusses his personal background and
his work in Systems Engineering at NADC, including the A-NEW
Program, Airborne Computer Development Systems in the

Thomas Willey of the Naval Air Development Center.

1960's, and the Proteus System of Signal Processing. He
talks about the impact of Systems Engineering, the Polaris
Submarine and its effect on ASW, and re-organization of NADC
in the early 1970's. Willey comments on audits of programs
over 6-12 year periods.

Repositories: NADC, DTNSRDC

Individuals mentioned: Aslo, Izzy
Cody, Harold

Institutions: Naval Air Development Center
Naval Air Systems Command
Anti-Submarine Warfare Laboratory

Subjects: Systems Engineering
Antisubmarine Warfare
Antisubmarine Aircraft

Other added entries: Polaris Submarines
Proteus System
A-NEW Program

Williams, ADM Henry

    Interview of ADM Henry Williams

Date of Interview: 630000

Documentation: Transcript 251 pp.

Abstract: ADM Williams recalls his career in the Navy,
remembering the Spanish-American War, taking a graduate
course in naval architecture in Paris, 1899-1901, his work
as a naval construction specialist dealing with launching
problems, the developments of plastic ship bottom paint, and
submarine rescue chambers.

Repositories: COL, NHC

Individuals mentioned: Sims, ADM William
Taylor, ADM Henry
Robinson, ADM Samuel M.
Land, ADM Emory S.

Institutions: Bureau of Ships

Subjects: Naval Construction
Naval Architecture
Polymers

Other added entries: Submarine Rescue Chambers

Williams, ADM John G. Jr.

 Interview of ADM John G. Williams Jr., conducted by Leroy L. Doig III, and Dr. David K. Allison

Date of Interview: 830712

Documentation: Diskette, Transcript 9 pp.

Interview number: DNL-T38

Abstract: ADM Williams discusses the purpose of R&D Centers, and changes that occurred during his tenure as CNM, the Corporate Plan for NAVMAT, selection of Technical Directors, selection of good personnel, the laboratories' role as "smart buyers" for the Navy, and the laboratories as part of NAVMAT.

Repositories: NWC, DTNSRDC

Individuals mentioned: Colvard, Dr. James E.
Hillyer, Robert
Paisley, Dr. Melvyn R.
Whittle, ADM Alfred J., Jr.

Institutions: Director of Navy Laboratories
Deputy Chief of Naval Material
Chief of Naval Material
Chief of Naval Operations
Naval Material Command

Other added entries: Navy Industrial Fund
Corporate Plan

Wills, James R.

 Interview of James R. Wills, conducted by Leroy L. Doig III

Date of Interview: 810107

Documentation: Index, Transcript 29 pp.

Interview number: S-116

Abstract: Mr. Wills comments on the closure of the NOTS branch at Corona and its move to China Lake in 1970. He talks about fuzing projects, in general, and the Air Force, Navy, and NWC's contact with NATO. Wills extols NWC's safety record and reflects on the work of Mr. Robert Hillyer, the lack of continuity at the Technical Director level at NWC, and NWC as a national asset.

Repositories: NWC, DTNSRDC, NHC

Individuals mentioned: Hillyer, Robert
Nastromeno, John

Institutions: Naval Ordnance Test Station
Naval Weapons Center
North Atlantic Treaty Organization
U. S. Air Force

Cities: China Lake, CA.
Corona, CA.

Other added entries: Fuze Research

Wilson, Dr. Haskell G.

Interview of Dr. Haskell G. Wilson, conducted by Albert B. Christman

Date of Interview: 700911

Documentation: Transcript 13 pp.

Interview number: S-93

Abstract: Dr. Wilson discusses in a general way public attitudes towards the Navy and the armed services as a whole. He comments on the future of R&D installations and the changing military role of the Navy and the Marines.

Repositories: NWC, DTNSRDC, NHC

Individuals mentioned: Zumwalt, ADM Elmo

Wilson, CAPT Eugene Edward

    Interview of CAPT Eugene Edward Wilson

Date of Interview: 620000

Documentation: Transcript 974 pp.

Abstract: Naval Academy; Engineering School, Columbia; Aviation Mechanics School, Great Lakes; Bureau of Aeronautics; private industry.

Repositories: COL, NHC

Individuals mentioned: Sikorsky, Igor
Boeing, William
Moffett, ADM William A.
King, *FADM* Ernest
Forrestal, SECNAV James

Wingo, Carl H., Jr.

    "Naval Guns: Carl H. Wingo, Jr.", conducted by Cynthia Rouse

Date of Interview: 760930

Documentation: Transcript 13 pp.

Note: This interview is Chapter XI of Dahlgren, edited by Kenneth G. McCollum

Abstract: Mr. Wingo describes the changes in ammunition testing since he came to Dahlgren in 1951, the effect of the Korean War, refitting the guns of the NEW JERSEY, the development of shipboard missiles and guided projectiles, lightweight guns, the *Naval Gunnery Improvement Program*, HIFRAG rounds, and EOSS.

Repositories: NSWC, DTNSRDC

Individuals mentioned: Kitterman, Warren
Kirschke, Jim

Institutions: Naval Ordna ce Laboratory

Subjects: Ordnance
Projectiles
Guided Projectiles

Other added entries: Naval Gunnery

Electro-Optical Sensor System
USS *NEW JERSEY*

Winnick, Robert L.

Interview of Robert L. Winnick, conducted by Albert B. Christman

Date of Interview: 780000

Documentation: 1 Tape, Transcript 26 pp.

Interview number: DNL-T17-78

Abstract: Mr. Winnick discusses sonar and torpedo R&D work conducted at NUSC, including torpedo research during World War II. He talks about the effect of the Bureaus and Systems Commands on torpedo development and his position as Director of Fleet Readiness. Winnick also comments on Naval re-organization in the late 1960's and 1970's.

Repositories: DTNSRDC

Institutions: Naval Underwater Systems Center
Naval Sea Systems Command
Systems Commands

Other added entries: Torpedos
Sonar

Wislicenus, Dr. George F.

Interview of Dr. George F. Wislicenus, conducted by Nelson Wood

Date of Interview: 800821

Documentation: Tapes, Transcript

Abstract: Dr. Wislicenus speaks of his background and education, his work with the OSRD and his research in acoustics.

Repositories: ARL

Institutions: Office of Scientific Research and Development
National Defense Research Committee
California Institute of Technology

Withington, RADM Frederick S.

   "Dahlgren in Perspective: RADM Frederick S. Withington", conducted by Cynthia Rouse

Date of Interview: 761103

Documentation: 12 pp.

Note: This interview is Chapter XIII of <u>Dahlgren</u>, edited by Kenneth G. McCollum

Abstract: RADM Withington describes his education, tours of different ordnance facilities in the 1920s, the primitive facilities at Dahlgren when he began work there, his work at the Naval Gun Factory on torpedo directors and gunfire control directors from 1934-1936, his work with the Bureau of Ordnance, his position as OIC at the Naval Ordnance Laboratory, White Oak MD, and later positions with AEC and Chief of BUORD, and individuals who had particular influence on Naval R&D.

Repositories: NSWC, DTNSRDC

Individuals mentioned: Johnson, Dr. Ellis
Lauritsen, Dr. Charles C.
Bradbury, Dr. Norris E.
Tuve, Dr. Merle
Leary, VADM Herbert F.

Institutions: Naval Proving Ground
Naval Gun Factory
Bureau of Ordnance
Naval Weapons Laboratory
Atomic Energy Commission

Subjects: Ordnance
Torpedo Directors
Gun Directors

Cities: White Oak, MD.
Washington, DC.
Dahlgren, VA.

Other added entries: Laboratory Consolidations
Defense Spending
Funding

Wolff, Dr. Irving

Interview of Dr. Irving Wolff, conducted by Dr. David
K. Allison

Date of Interview: 7910406

Documentation: 1 Tape, Index 3 pp.

Abstract: An RCA physicist involved in radar research in
the 1930s and 1940s interviewed in 1976 as part of an RCA
history project, copies of the 2 tapes produced and an index
prepared by Dr. Allison are also contained in the NRL oral
history collection. Wolff discusses his background,
education, contacts with the Army and NRL, personnel at NRL,
the establishment of the Radiation Laboratory, contact with
German engineers in the 1930s which suggested that both
sides knew that the other was working on radar detection,
and his connection with Isidor Rabi.

Repositories: NRL

Individuals mentioned: Rabi, Isidor I.
Zahl, Dr. Harold A.
Taylor, Dr. A. Hoyt
Ruble, ADM W. J.

Institutions: Radiation Laboratory
Victor Talking Machine Company
Bell Laboratories
Radio Corporation of America
U. S. Army Signal Corps

Subjects: Radar
Microwave Radar

Worchesek, CAPT Robert R.

Interview of CAPT Robert R. Worchesek, conducted by
Roger Kempler

Date of Interview: 8208316

Documentation: Transcript, 26 pp

Abstract: CAPT Worchesek discussed the circumstances of his
involvement with Naval personnel research, the people
involved in the reorganization of the Navy's personnel R&D
program, the CO/TD dual executive structure of the Navy
Laboratories, the problems of justifying personnel R&D
relative to hardware R&D, problems of rehabilitation of NOSC

barracks spaces, the Research Liaison Office, close managerial control of NPRDC, prime movers in NPRDC development, its role as coordinator for Human Resources R&D, his major contributions during transition to a single center, his view on CNM management control, and a post-retirement view of the Center.

Repositories: NPRDC, DTNSRDC

Individuals mentioned: Kinnear, RADM George E. R.
Collins, Dr. John J.
Sjoholm, Dr. Allan A.
Bagley, VADM David H.
Ramras, Eugene M.

Institutions: Navy Personnel Research and Development Center

Subjects: Personnel Research

Word, Thomas J.

Interview of Thomas J. Word, conducted by Leroy L. Doig III

Date of Interview: 821128

Other interview date: 821129

Documentation: 4 Tapes

Interview number: S-143

Abstract: Interview primarily concerned with NWC management, organization, and people, focusing on problems.

Repositories: NWC

Institutions: Naval Weapons Center

Cities: China Lake, CA.

Other added entries: Laboratory Management

York, Dr. Herbert

Interview of Dr. Herbert York, conducted by Albert B.
Christman

Date of Interview: 800924

Documentation: 1 Tape, Transcript 40 pp.

Interview number: DNL-T24-80

Abstract: Dr. York discusses the effect of Sputnik on Navy
R&D, his position as Chief Scientist of ARPA, and his
selection to be the first DDR&E. He talks about the reasons
for DDR&E, its relationship with the services, and the
uniformed Navy's success in keeping R&D projects under
control. York describes DDR&D's contacts with high level
government officials, major trends and problems he
encountered as DDR&E, and his management style. He comments
on SECDEF McNamara's effect on centralization of the armed
forces, DDR&D and the general growth of bureaucracy, and why
he left DDR&E. York also details the effect of increased R&D
on the escalation of the arms race and trends in technology.

Repositories: DTNSRDC

Individuals mentioned: Eisenhower, PRES Dwight D.
McNamara, SECDEF Robert S.

Institutions: Director of Defense Research and Engineering
Secretary of the Navy
Assistant Secretary of the Navy (R&D)
Advanced Research Projects Agency

Other added entries: Sputnik

Young, Dr. Leo C.

Interview of Dr. Leo. C. Young, conducted by Stanford
C. Hooper

Date of Interview: nd

Interview Number: 150-151

Abstract: This interview is from the Stanford C. Hooper
papers in the Library of Congress Manuscript Division, it is
a duplication of tapes 150 and 151 of Hooper's series of
tapes on the "History of Radio-Radar-Sonar." Young
reminisces about the discovery and early development of
radar at the Naval Research Laboratory, and a bit about his

background.

Repositories: NRL, LC

Individuals mentioned: Hooper, RADM Stanford C.

Institutions: Naval Research Laboratory

Subjects: Radar
Radio Detection

Youngblood, Curtis

   Interview of Curtis Youngblood, conducted by Albert B. Christman

Date of Interview: 670500

Documentation: Index, Transcript

Interview number: NOTS-75201-S51

Abstract: This interview was originally conducted as background for a biography of RADM William S. Parsons. Mr. Youngblood reminisces about his personal relationship with RADM Parsons at the Naval Proving Ground and during Operation Crossroads. He also talks about the chain of command at NPG; in particular, CAPT Hennick and Parsons' relationships with CAPT Hedrick, ADM Blandy, Dr. Louis T. E. Thompson, and Dr. Ralph Sawyer.

Repositories: NWC, DTNSRDC, NHC

Individuals mentioned: Blandy, ADM George
Bradbury, Dr. Norris E.
Hedrick, CAPT David
Parsons, RADM William S.
Sawyer, Dr. Ralph A.
Thompson, Dr. Louis T. E.

Institutions: Naval Proving Ground
Systems Commands

Cities: Dahlgren, VA.

Zisman, Dr. William A.

Interview of Dr. William A. Zisman, conducted by Steven Markel

Date of Interview: 800724

Documentation: Six Tapes (11 Sides)

Other interview dates: 800715, 800716

Abstract: Dr. Zisman discusses the American scientific community in the 1930's, problems of placement for Jewish scientists, and chemical research from 1937 to 1978. Included are two interviews with associates. Zisman came to NRL in 1933 and made major contributions to the development of synthetic lubricants, including pioneering research leading to the development of Teflon, and establishment of surface chemistry as a critical field of naval research.

Repositories: NRL

Institutions: Naval Research Laboratory

Subjects: Synthetic Lubricants

Other added entries: Chemical Research
Teflon
Surface Chemistry

CONTACT POINTS AT ORAL HISTORY REPOSITORIES

AIP:
American Institute of Physics
335 East 45th Street
New York, New York 10017
(212) 661-9404

ARL:
Applied Research Laboratory
Pennsylvania State University
P. O. Box 30
State College, Pennsylvania 16801
(814) 865-6621
Mr. Charles G. Murphy

COL:
Oral History Research Office
Box 20
Butler Library
Columbia University
New York, New York 10027
(212) 280-2273
Ms. Jeri Nunn

DTNSRDC:
Navy Laboratories Archives
Code 504
David Taylor Naval Ship Research and Development Center
Bethesda, Maryland 20084
(202) 227-1407
AUTOVON 287-1407
Dr. David K. Allison
Ms. C. Elizabeth Nowicke

LC:
Manuscript Collection
Library of Congress
Washington, D.C. 20540
(202) 287-5387

NADC:
Public Affairs Office, Code 701
Naval Air Development Center
Warminster, Pennsylvania 18974
(215) 441-3067
AUTOVON 441-3067

NASM:
Records Management Division
National Air and Space Museum
Smithsonian Institution
Washington, D. C. 20560
(202) 357-13133

NAVAIR:
Code 953
Naval Air Systems Command
Washington, D.C. 20360
(202) 692-7834
AUTOVON 222-7834
Dr. William J. Armstrong

NHC:
Naval Historical Center
Operational Archives Branch
Bulding 57, Washington Navy Yard
Washington, D.C. 20374
(202) 433-3170
AUTOVON 288-3224 (3172)
Dr. Dean Allard
Ms. Martha L. Crawley

NPRDC:
Code 303
Naval Personnel Research and Development Center
San Diego, California 92152
(619) 225-7450
AUTOVON 933-7424
Mr. Robert F. Turney

NRL:
Historian, Code 2604
Naval Research Laboratory
Washington, D.C. 20375
(202) 767-3419
AUTOVON 297-3419
Dr. John A. S. Pitts

NSWC:
Public Affairs Office, Code X02
Naval Surface Weapons Center
Dahlgren, Virginia 22448
(703) 663-8154
AUTOVON 249-8154

NWC:
Code 3411
Naval Weapons Center
China Lake, California
(619) 939-2027
AUTOVON 437-2027
Mr. Leroy L. Doig III

NWCM:
Curator, Naval Historical Collection
U.S. Naval War College
Newport, Rhode Island 02840
(401) 841-2435
AUTOVON 948-2435
Dr. Evelyn Cherpak

MIT:
The Libraries
Institute Archives and Special Collections, Room 14N-118
Massachusetts Institute of Technology
Cambridge, Massachusetts 02139
(617) 253-5688
Ms. Helen W. Samuels

RAD:
The Arthur and Elizabeth Schlesinger Library
Radcliffe College
Ten Garden Street
Cambridge, Massachusetts 02138
(617) 495-8647
Ms. Anne D. Engelhart

USNA:
Special Collections
Nimitz Library
U.S. Naval Academy
Annapolis, Maryland 21402
(301) 267-2220
AUTOVON 281-2220
Ms. Alice Creighton
Ms. Pamela Sherbert

USNI:
U.S. Naval Institute
Preble Hall
Annapolis, Maryland 21402
(301) 268-6110
Ms. Susan Sweeney
Ms. Tomi Johnson

ACRONYMS AND ABBREVIATIONS

ACNO	Assistant Chief of Naval Operations
ADM	Admiral
AEC	Atomic Energy Commission
AEEL	Aeronautical Electronics and Engineering Laboratory
AEW	Airborne Early Warning
AFB	Air Force Base
AIP	American Inst-tite of Physics
AMAL	American Medical Acceleration Laboratory
APL	Applied Physics Laboratory (Johns Hopkins)
ARPA	Advanced Research Projects Agency
ASN	Assistant Secretary of the Navy
ASN(R&D)	Assistant Secretary of the Navy (Research and Development)
ASN(RES)	Assistant Secretary of the Navy (Research Systems & Engineering)
ASP	All Altitude Spin Projectile
ASROC	Antisubmarine Rocket
ASW	Antisubmarine Warfare
ATOWG	Advanced Technical Objectives Working Group
BUAER	Bureau of Aeronautics
BUBUDGET	Bureau of the Budget
BUMED	Bureau of Medicine and Surgery
BUPERS	Bureau of Naval Personnel
BUSHIPS	Bureau of Ships
BUWEPS	Bureau of Naval Weapons
CAPT	Captain
CDR, CMDR	Commander
CLPP	China Lake Pilot Plant
CHNAVMAT	Chief of Naval Material
CNM	Chief of Naval Material
CNO	Chief of Naval Operations
CO	Commanding Officer
COBOL	Common Business Oriented Language
COL	Colonel
COMMO	Commodore
COMNAVAIR	Commander, Naval Air Systems Command
DARPA	Defense Advanced Research Projects Agency
DCNM	Deputy Chief of Naval Material
DCNM(D)	Deputy Chief of Naval Material (Development)
DCNM(L)	Deputy Chief of Naval Material (Laboratories)
DCNO	Deputy Chief of Naval Operations
DDRAT	Director Defense Research and Technology
DDRE	Director of Defense Research and Engineering
DIFAR	Directional Finding and Ranging
DLP	Director of Laboratory Programs
DNA	Defense Nuclear Agency
DNL	Director of Navy Laboratories
DNSARC	Department of the Navy Systems Acquisition Review Council

DOD	Department of Defense
DON	Department of the Navy
DRDT&E	Director, Research, Development, Test and Evaluation
DSARC	Defense Systems Review Council
DTMB	David Taylor Model Basin
DTNSRDC	David W. Taylor Naval Ship Research and Development Center
DUSRAT	Deputy Under Secretary for Research and Technology
EES	U. S. Navy Engineering Experiment Station
EMB	Experimental Model Basin
ENIAC	Electronic Numerical Integrator and Computer
EOSS	Electro-Optical Sensor System
FAA	Federal Aviation Administration
FADM	Fleet Admiral
FBM	Fleet Ballistic Missile
FCRC	Federal Contract Research Center
FOSS	Fiber-Optic Sensor System
FY	Fiscal Year
GAO	General Accounting Office
GEN	General
GUPPY	Greater Underwater Propulsive Power
HIFRAG	High Fragmentation
HQ	Headquarters
IBM	International Business Machines
IG	Inspector General
IGY	International Geophysical Year
JASON	a task force active in the 1970s
JPL	Jet Propulsion Laboratory
LAAV	Light Airborne ASW Vehicle
LAB	Laboratory Advisory Board
LAMPS	Light Airborne Multi-Purpose System
LC	Library of Congress
LOFAR	Low Frequency Analizing and Recording
LORAN	Long Range Navigation
LST	Tank Landing Ship
LTC	Lieutenant Colonel
LTGEN	Lieutenant General
LUS	Laboratory Utilization Study
MAJ	Major
MAT	NAVMAT organizational code prefix
MDL	Mine Defense Laboratory
MEL	Marine Engineering Laboratory
MILCON	Military Construction
MIT	Massachusetts Institute of Technology
MK	Mark
NACA	National Advisory Committee on Aeronautics
NADC	Naval Air Development Center
NAEC	Naval Air Engineering Center
NAMU	Naval Air Modification Unit
NAPC	Naval Air Propulsion Center

NASA	National Aeronautics and Space Administration
NASL	Naval Applied Science Laboratory
NASM	National Air and Space Museum
NATO	North Atlantic Treaty Organization
NAVAIR, NAVAIRSYSCOM	Naval Air Systems Command
NAVMAT	Naval Material Command
NAVORD, NAVORDSYSCOM	Naval Ordnance Systems Command
NAVSEA	Naval Sea Systems Command
NAVSEC	Naval Ship Engineering Center
NAVSTAR	Navy Navigation Satellite
NCEL	Naval Civil Engineering Laboratory
NCSL	Naval Coastal Systems Laboratory
NDRC	National Defense Research Committee
NEL	Naval Electronics Laboratory
NELC	Naval Electronics Laboratory Center
NHC	Naval Historical Center
NIF	Navy Industrial Fund
NMARC	Navy and Marine Corps Acquisition Review Committee
NMC	Naval Material Command
NOL	Naval Ordnance Laboratory
NOL C	Naval Ordnance Laboratory (Corona)
NOL W/O	Naval Ordnance Laboratory (Whiteoak)
NORC	Naval Ordnance Research Calculator
NORDA	Naval Ocean Research and Development Activity
NOSC	Naval Ocean Systems Center
NOTS	Naval Ordnance Test Station
NOTSNIK	NOTS Satellite
NPG	Naval Proving Ground
NPRDC	Navy Personnel Research and Development Center
NRAC	Naval Research Advisory Committee
NRL	Naval Research Laboratory
NSAP	Navy Science Assistance Program
NSF	National Science Foundation
NSRDC	Naval Ship Research and Development Center
NSSNF	Naval Strategic Systems Navigation Facility
NSTEP	Navy Scientist Training Exchange Program
NSWC	Naval Surface Warfare Center
NUC	Naval Undersea Center
NURDC	Naval Undersea Research and Development Center
NUWRES	Naval Underwater Weapons Research and Engineering Station
NUSC	Naval Underwater Systems Center
NUSL	Naval Underwater Sound Laboratory
NWAG	Naval Warfare Advisory Group
NWC	Naval Weapons Center
NWCM	Naval War College Museum
NWL	Naval Weapons Laboratory
OASD	Office of the Assistant Secretary of Defense
ODDR&E	Office of the Director of Defense Research & Engineering

OIC	Officer in Charge
OMB	Office of Management and Budget
ONR	Office of Naval Research
OPNAV	Office of the Chief of Naval Operations
OSD	Office of the Secretary of Defense
OSRD	Office of Scientific Research and Development
PERT	Program Evaluation Review Technique
PRFA	Personnel Research Field Activity
RADM	Rear Admiral
REAC	Research Calculator
RCA	Radio Corporation of America
R&D	Research and Development
RDT&E	Research, Development, Technology and Evaluation
REFLEX	Resources Flexibility
RIF	Reduction in Force
SARAH	Semi-Active Radar Homing
SARS	Selected Acquisition Reporting System
SDRV	Submarine Deep Rescue Vehicle
SECDEF	Secretary of Defense
SECNAV	Secretary of the Navy
SER	Shore Establishment Realignment
SES	Senior Executive Service
SES	Surface Effect Ships
SOFAR	Sound Fixing and Ranging
SOLRAD	Solar Radiation
SUBROC	Submarine Rocket
SWPP	Salt Wells Pilot Plant
SYSCOMS	Systems Commands
T/E	Test and Evaluation
TD	Technical Director
UCLA	University of California, Los Angeles
USA	United States Army
USAF	United States Airforce
USDR&E	Under Secretary of Defense Research and Engineering
USNA	United States Naval Academy
USNI	United States Naval Institute
USNR	United States Navy Reserve
VADM	Vice Admiral
VLAP	Vietnam Laboratory Assistance Program
V/STOL	Vertical Short Take-Off and Landing Aircraft
WAVES	Women Accepted for Voluntary Emergency Service

NAME INDEX

---

[1] An asterisk indicates that the person was interviewed, and the page that the interview begins on.

Bodenburg, John, 22*
Boeing, William, 214
Bohr, Dr. Nils, 119
Bolt, Dr. Richard Henry, 23*
Bondi, Hermann, 79
Bourland, Langford, 103
Bowen, ADM Harold G., 139
Bowen, Dr. Edward G., 23*
Bowen, Dr. Ira S., 25*, 149
Bowen, Harold G., Jr., 25*
Bowen, Ike, 60
Bowen, VADM Harold G., 24*, 25
Bowyer, Dr. C. Stewart, 26*, 39
Bradbury, Dr. Norris E., 26*
Bradbury, Dr. Norris E., 169, 216, 220
Bramble, Dr. Charles C., 27*, 136
Braun, RADM Boynton L., 28*
Braun, Wernher von, 63, 111, 163
Breslow, Arthur, 28*
Brode, Dr. Wallace C., 16, 29*, 142, 201
Brooks, Dr. Harvey, 30*
Brooks, Dr. Lester, 2
Brown, Dr. Frederick W., 97, 200
Brown, Dr. Ira Sprague, 82
Brown, Paul, 58
Brundage, Dr. Everett G., 37, 58, 63
Bryan, Dr. Glenn L., 30*, 58, 154, 177
Bucaro, Joe, 48
Buckley, William H., 138
Burke, ADM Arleigh A., 2*, 31*, 83
Burke, William, 136
Burns, Dr. Robert O., 32*, 183
Burroughs, ADM Sherman E., 32, 34*, 50, 53, 54, 60, 74, 81,
82, 99, 118, 145, 156, 166, 168, 187, 188, 197
Burroughs, Kay (Mrs. Sherman E.), 32
Burroughs, Martha Parsons, 66
Burroughs, Mrs. Robert (former Mrs. William S. Parsons), 33*
Bush, Dr. Vannevar, 16, 29, 149, 202
Byrnes, CAPT James, 35, 50, 160, 167, 168
Byrum, E. T., 35*
Camp, Victor W., 35*
Carmondy, Hazel, 124
Carome, Dr. Edward F., 36*, 48
Carstater, Dr. Eugene D., 37*, 58, 176
Cartwright, Dr. Frank W., 7*, 146
Chaffee, John, 65
Chaplin, Dr. Harvey R., 61
Chase, ADM John Dawson, 180
Christman, Albert B., 37*
Chubb, Dr. Talbot A., 38*, 103
Clarkin, CAPT James J., 176
Clearwater, Walter, 121
Cleeton, Dr. Claud E., 39*, 90, 103

SUBJECT INDEX

INITIAL DISTRIBUTION

Copies		Copies	
2	DUS (R&AT)/A. Berman	4	NRL
			1 Code 1001/T. Coffey
1	DSMC/Ft. Belvoir		1 Code 2600/E. Kirkbride
			1 Code 2604/J. Pitts
1	ICAF		1 Code 2620
1	NDU	2	USNA
			1 Library
1	OSD		1 Dept of History
2	ASN(RES)/J. Probus	1	NAVPGSCOL/Library
8	DNL	1	NAVAIRSYSCOM
	2 G. Morton		1 Code 953/W. Armstrong
	1 Code 05LC/A. Himes		
	3 Code 051/H. Law	2	NAVAIRDEVCEN
	1 Code 052/T. Huang		1 R. Buffum
	1 Code 053/G. Swiggum		1 Code 701
3	CONR	2	NAVPERSRANDCEN
	1 CNR		1 J. Tweedale
	1 Historian		1 Code 303/R. Turney
	1 Library		
		2	NAVWPNCEN
3	NAVHISTCEN		1 B. Hays
	1 Code AR/D. Allard		1 Code 3411/L. Doig
	1 Code AR/M. Crawley		
	1 Library	1	NAVOCEANSYSCEN/R. Hillyer
2	USMA	1	NAVCOASTSYSCEN/C. Dilworth
	1 Dept of History		
	1 Library	2	NAVSWC/Whiteoak
			1 L. Hill
1	USA CMH/DAMH-ZC		1 Code X02
1	USA CMH/J. Bennett	1	NAVSWC/Dalhgren
1	USA MHI	2	NUSC
			1 E. Messere
1	USA DARCOM/DRCDRA/Asst. Deputy for Sci. and Tech./R. Haley		1 Code 0213/D. Hanna
		1	NTEC/W. Lindahl
1	USA CERCOM/R. Cannon	3	NAVWARCOL
			1 Museum/A. Nicolosi
			1 Dept of History/J. Hattendorf
			1 Naval History Collection/ E. Cherpak

Copies		Copies	
1	NNMC/MEDCOM-OOD4/J. Herman	1	Archives Center
1	NAVOBSY/Library/B. Corbin	1	Eisenhower Institute for Historical Research/ F. Pogue
1	HOMC-HD/Library/E. Englander		
1	NAVAVN-History/R. Grossnick	3	SI/NASM
1	NAVFAC/V. Transano		1 Library
			1 A. Needel
12	DTIC		1 D. DeVorkin
1	USAFA/DFH	1	U of California/Regional Oral History Office/Bancroft Lib
1	HO USAF/CHO		
1	USAF/HRC/Albert F. Simpson Historical Research Center	1	Columbia U/Oral History Research Office/Butler Lib
1	DOE/History Office	2	Johns Hopkins U
1	DOL/Historical Office		1 Dept of History/R. Kargon
			1 Applied Physics Laboratory Archives
3	LC		
	1 Sci. Tech Adv.	1	Harvard U/University Archives
	1 National Union List of Manuscript Coll/H. Ostroff	1	Eastern Kentucky U/Dept of History/L. Graybar
	1 Manuscript Division		
		1	U of Illinois/University Archives
4	NARS		
	1 Navy and Old Army Branch (NNMO)	3	U of Maryland
	1 Scientic, Economic, and Natural Resources Branch (NNFN)/S. Thibodeau		1 College of Library and Information Services/ F. Stielow
	1 Motion Picture, Sound, and Video Branch, (NNSM)/ M. Ciarlante		1 Dept of History/R. Friedel
			1 McKeldin Lib
	1 Franklin D. Roosevelt Lib	2	MIT
1	NAS		1 Institute Archives and Special Collections, Room 14N-118/H. Samuels
1	NASA/History Office		1 Program in Science, Technology and Society, Room E51-228B/M. Smith
4	SI/NMAH		
	1 Division of Naval History	1	Western Michigan U/University Archives
	1 Dept of Social and Cultural History		
		1	U of Michigan/Engineering-Transportation Lib

Copies			Copies	Code	Name
1	U of North Carolina/Wilson Lib		100	5211.1	Reports Distribution
1	U of Oregon/Archives		1	522.1	TIC (C)
1	U of Pennsylvania/Dept of History and Sociology of Science		1	522.2	TIC (A)
2	Pennsylvania State U 1 Lib 1 ARL		2	701	P. Buchanan
1	Princeton U/Lib				
1	Radcliffe College/The Arthur and Elizabeth Schlesinger Lib				
1	Temple U/Urban Archives/F. Miller				
1	U of Washington/Library/E. Kukla				
1	American Institute of Physics				
1	United States Naval Institute/ Oral History Office				
1	Hoover Institution on War, Revolution, and Peace				
1	The Laser History Project/ R. Seidel				

CENTER DISTRIBUTION

Copies	Code	Name
1	00	
1	01	A. Powell
1	011	C. Schoman
1	012.3	D. Moran
1	05	R. Gauthey
20	5040	D. Allison
20	5040.1	C. Nowicke

DTNSRDC ISSUES THREE TYPES OF REPORTS

1. DTNSRDC REPORTS, A FORMAL SERIES, CONTAIN INFORMATION OF PERMANENT TECHNICAL VALUE. THEY CARRY A CONSECUTIVE NUMERICAL IDENTIFICATION REGARDLESS OF THEIR CLASSIFICATION OR THE ORIGINATING DEPARTMENT

2. DEPARTMENTAL REPORTS, A SEMIFORMAL SERIES, CONTAIN INFORMATION OF A PRELIMINARY, TEMPORARY, OR PROPRIETARY NATURE OR OF LIMITED INTEREST OR SIGNIFICANCE. THEY CARRY A DEPARTMENTAL ALPHANUMERICAL IDENTIFICATION.

3. TECHNICAL MEMORANDA, AN INFORMAL SERIES, CONTAIN TECHNICAL DOCUMENTATION OF LIMITED USE AND INTEREST. THEY ARE PRIMARILY WORKING PAPERS INTENDED FOR INTERNAL USE. THEY CARRY AN IDENTIFYING NUMBER WHICH INDICATES THEIR TYPE AND THE NUMERICAL CODE OF THE ORIGINATING DEPARTMENT. ANY DISTRIBUTION OUTSIDE DTNSRDC MUST BE APPROVED BY THE HEAD OF THE ORIGINATING DEPARTMENT ON A CASE-BY-CASE BASIS

THE DETERMINATION OF
SOME COMMON ALLOYING ELEMENTS
IN ALUMINUM AND ITS ALLOYS

William Zimmerman, III

Approved by:

Mr. C. M. Bible, Head, Analytical Chemistry Section
Dr. O. T. Marzke, Superintendent, Metallurgy Division

September 30, 1947

NAVAL RESEARCH LABORATORY
COMMODORE H. A. SCHADE, USN, DIRECTOR
WASHINGTON, D.C.

DISTRIBUTION

BuShips	(5)
BuOrd	(1)
BuAer Attn: Code TD-4	(1)
ONR Attn: Code N482	(5)
Cdr., Boston Naval Shipyard	(1)
Cdr., Brooklyn Naval Shipyard	(1)
Cdr., Charleston Naval Shipyard	(1)
Cdr., Mare Island Naval Shipyard	(1)
Cdr., Pearl Harbor Naval Shipyard	(1)
Cdr., Philadelphia Naval Shipyard	(1)
Cdr., Portsmouth Naval Shipyard	(1)
Cdr., Norfolk Naval Shipyard	(1)
Cdr., Terminal Island Naval Shipyard	(1)
Cdr., San Francisco Naval Shipyard	(1)
Dir., USNEL	(2)
Dir., NBS Attn: Colonel Krynitsky	(1)
OCSigo Attn: Ch. Eng. & Tech. Div., SIGTM-S	(1)
CO, SCEL Attn: Dir. of Engineering	(2)
RDB Attn: Library Attn: Navy Secretary	(2) (1)
Science and Technology Project Attn: Mr. J. H. Heald, Ch.	(2)

CONTENTS

PREFACE

This report publishes procedure for aluminum alloy analysis which results from experiences of the Metallurgy Division over a period of several years.

ABSTRACT

A method is proposed for the determination of silicon, copper, silver, lead, titanium, iron, nickel, and zinc in aluminum and its alloys using a single sample weight.

Silicon is dehydrated with perchloric acid; copper, lead, and silver are precipitated as the sulphides, ignited, fused, dissolved and electroplated; an aliquot of the sulphide filtrate is used for the titanium; iron is determined in the balance of the filtrate by titration with ceric sulphate following expulsion of hydrogen sulphide; zinc is precipitated in a formic acid solution with hydrogen sulphide and nickel is determined by precipitation with dimethylglyoxime in the filtrate from the zinc determination.

THE DETERMINATION OF SOME COMMON ALLOYING
ELEMENTS IN ALUMINUM AND ITS ALLOYS

INTRODUCTION

In order to systematize the chemical analysis of aluminum and its alloys and to provide for greater economy of reagents, time, and effort, several different attempts to develop a sequential analytical procedure have been made in this laboratory. Many other sequential procedures have been proposed; the earliest of which were developed by Richards *, Regelsberger † and Moissan ‡. Later methods have been developed by Alcoa § and Balco ** and from a study of the ASTM methods ††, other sequential procedures may be devised. Alcoa has developed a sequence for the determination of copper, silicon, iron and titanium on a single sample weight in commercially pure aluminum. Balco has developed several procedures of limited scope or for special alloys: a) the determination of silicon, copper and iron on a single sample weight of duralumin; b) the determination of antimony, copper and iron in B.A. 35; and c) the determination of copper, manganese, magnesium and nickel following an acid attack on aluminum alloys.

The above methods are limited in scope and cannot be used for general routine laboratory analysis. The ASTM procedure provides for the development of sequential procedures for the determination of silicon, copper, lead, iron, zinc and titanium in a sulphuric acid solution.

The proposed method provides for the determination of the above elements but in a perchloric acid solution and, in addition, provides for the determination of nickel and silver when present. Except for chromium, manganese and magnesium, which, it has been the experience of the author, are best determined on separate samples, the proposed method provides a procedure which permits accurate determinations of all of the common alloying elements of aluminum and its alloys on a single sample weight. This is of particular importance when the amount of sample available is limited.

The dehydration of silica with perchloric acid has been used for many years in this laboratory in iron and steel analyses and the method has proved so efficient that the same medium was tried with aluminum alloys. Although certain precautions must be taken during dehydration, it has proved a very efficient and easy medium with which to work and has been used with aluminum alloys in this laboratory for the past four years.

---

* Richards, J. W., "Aluminium" 2nd Edition, 469-487, (1890)
† Regelsberger, F., "Z. Angew. Chem.," 4, 360-363, 442-446, 473-478 (1891)
‡ Moissan, H., "Compt. Rend." 121, 851-856, (1895)
§ Aluminum Company of America, "Chemical Analysis of Aluminum," (1941)
** British Aluminum Company, Limited, "Analysis of Aluminum and its Alloys," (1941)
†† ASTM, "Methods of Chemical Analysis of Metals," p. 130 ff. (1943).

In the proposed method, copper, lead, and silver are precipitated from the silica filtrate with hydrogen sulphide. Following the expulsion of hydrogen sulphide, an aliquot is taken for the determination of titanium with peroxide and the reduced iron is titrated with ceric sulphate in the balance of the solution. Zinc is precipitated with hydrogen sulphide in a buffered formic acid solution following the titration of the iron and the addition of citric acid. Nickel is finally precipitated with dimethylglyoxime in the filtrate from the zinc determination following expulsion of hydrogen sulphide. Copper, lead and silver are determined electrolytically using platinum gauze electrodes. Copper and silver are stripped from the cathode and the silver is then determined as the chloride.

Chromium, manganese and magnesium are determined on separate samples; chromium and manganese, because they may be determined with no preliminary separations; and magnesium because a caustic attack eliminates the necessity of filtering a large mass of gelatinous aluminum hydroxide.

The following procedure has been in use in this laboratory except for minor changes for the past two years for all routine analysis.

PROCEDURE

Step I a - The Determination of Silicon (Less than 1%)

Weigh out a 2.000 gram sample of millings or drillings to the nearest milligram, place in a 400 ml pyrex beaker, add 30 ml HNO_3 (1-1), place on a medium hot plate until solution is complete (add additional HNO_3 (1-1) to complete solution if necessary). When solution is complete or nearly so, cautiously add 40 ml $HClO_4$ (70-72%) and evaporate to fumes of $HClO_4$. Caution: As the sample dehydrates, there is some danger of spattering which may be minimized by the use of bumping beakers.

After the sample has fumed vigorously for 15-20 minutes, remove from the hot plate and allow to cool slightly. While still hot, remove the cover glass and allow the sample to fume gently in order to remove any Cl_2 formed by the decomposition of the perchloric acid and to prevent the precipitation of AgCl. When cool, dilute to 125-150 ml with hot water, filter through an 11.0-cm #40 Whatman paper, police the beaker thoroughly and transfer the SiO_2 to the paper and wash with warm $HClO_4$ (1-1000) to remove mineral constituents, finally wash paper and precipitate 3-5 times with warm water to remove the last traces of $HClO_4$. Reserve the filtrate (solution A). Place the precipitate and paper in a platinum crucible, ignite carefully to remove carbon and finally at 1000°C. Cool in a dessicator and weigh. Add sufficient H_2SO_4 (1-4) to moisten the impure SiO_2 and add 5-10 ml HF. Evaporate to dryness, heat cautiously to drive off SO_3, finally at 1000°C, then cool and reweigh. $\dfrac{\text{Difference in weight x 46.72}}{\text{sample weight}} = \%\,Si.$

Step I b.- Determination of Silicon (more than 1%)

For silicon content between 1% and 3% use a 2.000-g sample, above 3% use a 1.000-g sample, weighed accurately to the nearest milligram. Place the sample in a platinum dish, add 15 ml water and then slowly add 8-g NaOH pellets (5-6 NaOH for a 1.0-g sample). When the first violent reaction subsides, heat to boiling, then cool somewhat, add 1-2 ml H_2O_2 (30%) dropwise, heat to boiling a second time, repeat the addition of peroxide until no more oxidation takes place, dilute to about 50 ml and pour into a 400-ml pyrex beaker, scrub out the dish thoroughly and wash well, first with water, then with dilute HNO_3, add sufficient HNO_3 to the solution to neutralize the excess NaOH and to dissolve any unattacked metals. Heat to boiling to remove any oxides of nitrogen, cool somewhat, then cautiously add 40 ml $HClO_4$ (35 ml for a 1.000-g sample). Evaporate to fumes of $HClO_4$ and continue as in Ia above, observing the same precautions.

If the ignited SiO_2 appears dark, fuse the impure SiO_2 with a minimum amount of Na_2CO_3, dissolve the melt in hot water, neutralize with HNO_3 (1-1), add 30-35 ml $HClO_4$ and repeat the dehydration, etc. It is best to test the filtrate for other elements to be determined, although they are usually absent.

Step II. - Determination of Silver, Copper and Lead

Heat the filtrate from the silicon determination (solution A) to boiling and saturate with H_2S, allow the precipitated sulphides to settle and filter through an 11.0-cm #42 Whatman paper, wash with H_2SO_4 (1-100) saturated with H_2S. Place the precipitate and paper into a fused-quartz or porcelain crucible and ignite at 550-600°C. Reserve the filtrate (solution B). Fuse the ignited oxides with a minimum amount of $K_2S_2O_7$ at as low a temperature as possible and dissolve the fused melt in 25 ml of water and 5 ml HNO_3. Scrub out the crucible and place the solution in a 250 or 400-ml beaker for electrolysis, dilute sufficiently to cover the electrodes, heat to 40°C, and add 1 ml H_2O_2 (30%). Electrolyze for one-half hour with a current of one ampere, using weighed sand-blasted platinum gauze electrodes. Add additional peroxide as necessary to prevent deposition on the anode. When copper begins to plate out on the cathode, make no more peroxide additions and allow the electrolysis to continue for 15 minutes, then add 4 ml H_2SO_4 and continue electrolysis until deposition is complete as shown by rinsing the sides of the beaker with a jet of distilled water and noting the lack of additional deposition on the freshly immersed platinum. When deposition is complete,, the electrodes are raised, and a beaker of distilled water is substituted for the electrolyte. Remove the electrodes from the electrolysis outfit, dip into fresh-distilled water then into alcohol and dry in the oven at 110°C. Allow the cathode to dry for two to three minutes, but dry the anode with the PbO_2 deposit, for a longer period. (A thirty-minute drying period is recommended but this may be shortened to five minutes for the amount of lead usually found in aluminum alloys.)

After weighing the combined silver and copper plate, the deposit is stripped from the electrode with as little dilute HNO_3 (1-3) as possible. Boil off the oxides of nitrogen and precipitate the silver as the chloride, using 0.1 N HCl. Allow the precipitated AgCl to settle and coagulate overnight, filter through a weighed glass-frit or Gooch crucible, wash with 0.01 N HCl and dry at 150°C. Weigh as AgCl, calculate to Ag and subtract from the combined weight of silver and copper.

Step III. - The Determination of Iron

Transfer the filtrate from the sulphide precipitation (solution B) to a 600-ml beaker and rapidly heat to a hard boil. Boil until a test with lead acetate paper is negative for H_2S (20-30 minutes). Cool in a water bath, transfer to a 200-ml volumetric flask, make up to volume, take a 100- ml aliquot for the determination of titanium. Transfer the balance of the solution to a beaker and titrate with a standard $Ce(SO_4)_2$ solution, equivalent to 2 mg Fe per ml. Use either o-phenanthroline as an indicator, and subtract an indicator blank, or use a poteniometer to determine the end point. Reserve the iron solution for determination of zinc and nickel (Solution C).

Step IV. - The Determination of Titanium

Evaporate the aliquot taken above to about 50 ml and transfer to a 100-ml volumetric flask, filtering if necessary. Add 2 ml H_3PO_4 (1-1) and 2 ml H_2O_2 (30%) and dilute to the mark. Record the transmission with a Klett colorimeter, using a #42 filter and a standard colorimeter test tube. Calculate the percentage of titanium present from a graph made by recording the transmission through standards of known concentration.

Step V. - The Determination of Zinc

To the solution from the iron determination (solution C) add 30 ml of a 20% solution of citric acid, neutralize with NH_4OH using methyl red as an indicator. Add 30 ml formic acid solution (200 ml formic acid, 30 ml ammonium hydroxide, and water to make one liter), heat to boiling, gas with H_2S, filter through an 11.0-cm #42 Whatman paper, wash well with a formic acid wash solution (10 ml of formic acid solution diluted to one liter and saturated with H_2S). Dissolve the precipitated ZnS by placing paper and precipitate in the original beaker and adding 40 ml HCl (1-3), dilute to 150 ml, add 10 ml citric acid solution, neutralize with NH_4OH, add 30 ml formic acid solution, heat, gas, filter as before and ignite in a weighed porcelain crucible at 700-750°C. Weigh as ZnO. Reserve the filtrates.

Step VI. - The Determination of Nickel

Combine the filtrates from the determination of zinc, boil out the H_2S, evaporate somewhat, filter on a #40 paper, add 2-3 ml HNO_3 to oxidize the iron, neutralize the solution, which is now about 400 ml, with NH_4OH, using methly red as an indicator, make just acid with HCl, add 20 ml of an alcoholic 1% solution of dimethylglyoxime (or 20 ml of a 3% water solution of the sodium salt of dimethylglyoxime) for a nickel content up to 0.02 g and add an additional 5 ml for each additional 0.01 g of nickel present. Make the solution just ammoniacal, then add 3-4 drops NH_4OH in excess, coagulate the precipitated nickel dimethylglyoxime at 80°C for one-half hour, allow to cool, and proceed as in either (a) or (b) below.

(a) Filter the nickel precipitate on a weighed glass-frit or Gooch crucible, wash well with cold water, dry at 110°C, cool, and weigh as nickel dimethylglyoxime containing 20.32% nickel.

(b) Filter the nickel precipitate through a #41 Whatman paper, place paper and precipitate back into the beaker, add 15 ml HNO_3 and 10 ml $HClO_4$. Evaporate to fumes of $HClO_4$, cool, dilute to 100 ml, add 5.0 ml 0.3% $AgNO_3$ solution, 20 ml citric acid solution (1 lb citric acid, 1 lb ammonium sulphate, 5 grams ammonium chloride, diluted to three liters), titrate with NH_4OH to a clear solution, add 2 ml 20% KI solution and then titrate to a clear solution with NaCN solution (23 g NaCN, 20 g NaOH, diluted to three liters). Subtract a determined blank by titrating the silver nitrate and potassium iodide with no nickel present. Determine the nickel value of the cyanide by titrating against a sample of known nickel content.

EXPERIMENTAL RESULTS

As an indication of the accuracy and precision of the proposed method, some of the results obtained using Bureau of Standard Samples are given in Table I.

It will be noted that when the percentage of the constituent is very small the results are not particularly accurate, for example, the zinc content of B.S. 85a and the titanium content of both B.S. 85a and B. S. 86B. When great accuracy is desired, it is recommended that separate samples be used for these and similar trace elements which are less than 0.05%.

TABLE I

Results of Analysis of Bureau of Standards Aluminum Alloys

Element	Sample No	Found %	Deviation from Certificate %	Certificate %
Silicon	85a	0.117	+0.003	0.114
		0.113	-0.001	
		0.112	-0.002	
		0.117	+0.003	
		0.110	-0.004	
	86b	0.449	-0.021	0.47
		0.458	-0.012	
		0.476	+0.006	
		0.474	+0.004	
		0.474	+0.004	
Iron	85a	0.206	-0.002	0.208
		0.214	-0.006	
		0.201	-0.007	
		0.222	+0.014	
		0.228	+0.020	
	86b	1.53	0.00	1.53
		1.52	-0.01	
		1.51	-0.02	
		1.54	+0.01	
		1.51	-0.02	
Zinc	85a	0.04	+0.021	0.019
		0.06	+0.041	
		0.02	+0.301	
		0.01	-0.009	
		0.01	-0.009	
	86b	1.52	+0.02	1.50
		1.54	+0.04	
		1.55	+0.05	
		1.53	+0.03	
		1.52	+0.02	

Element	Sample No	Found %	Deviation from Certificate %	Certificate %
Copper	85a	2.47	0.01	2.48
		2.48	0.00	
		2.48	0.00	
		2.49	+0.01	
		2.48	0.00	
	86b	7.84	-0.04	7.87
		7.88	+0.01	
		7.88	+0.01	
		7.87	0.00	
		7.91	+0.04	
Titanium	85a	0.017	+0.001	0.016
		0.018	+0.002	
		0.020	+0.004	
		0.018	+0.002	
		0.016	0.000	
	86b	0.028	-0.004	0.032
		0.030	-0.002	
		0.036	-0.002	
		0.036	-0.004	
		0.037	+0.005	
Nickel	85a	0.411	-0.001	0.41
		0.416	+0.006	
		0.412	+0.002	
		0.412	+0.002	
		0.410	0.000	

NOTES ON THE PROCEDURE

Procedure in Absence of Silver

When silver is not present, the following modifications in the procedure may be made:

Step I a.- Place sample in 400 ml beaker, add 100 ml $HClO_4$ (1-6) then slowly add 15 ml HCl (1-1) for each gram of sample. When reaction stops, add 1-2 ml HNO_3 and then 35 ml $HClO_4$.

Step I b. - Scrub out dish with HCl instead of HNO_3 but add 1-2 ml HNO_3 before the addition of $HClO_4$.

Step II - The precipitated sulphides may best be treated by returning the paper and precipitate to the original beaker, adding 25-30 ml HNO_3, 5 ml H_2SO_4, evaporating to fumes of sulphuric acid, taking up to 200 ml adding 8 ml HNO_3 (1-1) and electrolyzing. For the amount of lead usually present in aluminum alloys this procedure is entirely satisfactory, since the solubility of lead sulphate is apparently greater than the solubility of the electrolyzed lead dioxide.

Determination of Silicon

In the determination of silicon, a two-gram sample is frequently preferable to a smaller weight. However, because of the insolubility of aluminum perchlorate, it is recommended that a one-gram sample be used when practical. As the last traces of water and more volatile acids are removed from the solution a heavy precipitate of aluminum perchlorate is formed, and bumping may occur. In order to eliminate the possibility of bumping, two different methods have been used with equal success in this laboratory. The first is to use bumping beakers, which is extremely satisfactory, provided the equipment is available. The second involves careful evaporation of the solution with the use of glass hooks during the preliminary stages and without glass hooks during the final stages of evaporation. It has been found that by using an electric hot plate on high heat with a single layer of asbestos paper separating the beaker and the hot plate, bumping seldom occurs with a two gram sample.

When the impure silica appears dark, it is usually caused by the presence of metallic silicon or silicides which resist both the sodium hydroxide-peroxide attack and the perchloric acid attack. If a carbonate treatment is not made, the silicon or silicides may resist the HF attack and leave a black residue which may be fused with carbonate but which is insoluble in a fusion with pyrosulphate. In any case the results for silicon will be low. Whereas, by making the carbonate fusion, accurate results may be attained.

In the presence of large amounts of silver, a slight turbidity may develop upon dilution of concentrated $HClO_4$. This seems to have no effect upon the determination since the chloride concentration is too low for the silver chloride to coagulate into large enough particular for retention a #40 paper.

Determination of Silver Copper and Lead

Silver may be precipitated by the addition of 0.1 N HCl directly to the silicon filtrate. In which case, the copper and lead are determined simultaneously.

A rotating electrode apparatus is used for the electrodeposition of copper, lead, and silver; and in the usual case, the stationary electrode is used as the cathode. However, when appreciable amounts of lead are present, it is preferable to reverse the current and plate the lead on the stationary electrode in order to minimize the danger of loss in the lead plate due to flaking.

If both lead and manganese are present, the lead results will tend to be high. Ravner * has shown that this difficulty may be overcome by dissolving the anode plate in dilute nitric acid and replating.

The copper deposit is washed by raising the electrodes and replacing the beaker containing the electrolyte with one containing distilled water without interrupting the flow of current, and then dipping into two separate beakers of alcohol. Previous work done at this laboratory * indicates that this method of washing results in practically no copper loss, and it has the great advantage of not diluting the electrolyte. Although a small amount of the electrolyte is lost in this fashion, it is not sufficient to cause any great error in the results of the succeeding determinations, if any, on the electrolyte. A disadvantage of the copper and silver determination is that it throws any errors in the determination upon the copper results.

Determination of Iron

When permanganate is used to titrate the iron instead of ceric sulphate, the titanium may be determined on the entire sample prior to the determination of zinc and nickel. However, it is advisable to omit the phosphoric acid and set up a special curve for such determinations.

It has been found that if the filtrate from the sulfide precipitation is placed into a 600-ml beaker, then placed on a hot plate which is at a sufficiently high temperature to cause rapid boiling of the solution, it is then unnecessary to maintain a flow of carbon dioxide in order to maintain a non-oxidizing atmosphere. Nor is it necessary to make any special precautions during the cooling of the solution in order to prevent oxidation of the reduced iron despite the presence of perchloric acid. Babson and Johnson † have also shown that, in dilute perchloric acid solutions, hydrogen sulphide gives a quantitative precipitate of copper and lead and also gives a quantitative reduction of the iron.

None of the elements ordinarily present in an aluminum alloy interferes with the determination of iron following the hydrogen sulphide reduction. Lundell and Knowles ‡ have stated that polythionic compounds, which may consume the oxidizing agent, may be formed upon treatment with hydrogen sulphide. No difficulty has been experienced at this laboratory in this respect.

Determination of Titanium

The titanium aliquot, as used in the procedure, gives an effective weight of one gram for the determination. It occasionally happens that this is too large a sample for effective determination of the titanium by the colorimetric method and when this is true,

* Ravner, H., "Ind. and Eng. Chem., Aval. Ed.," 17, 41 (1945)
† Babson, E. K., and Johnson, W. W., "Ind. and Eng. Chem., Aval. Ed." 18, 292-293 (1946)
‡ Lundell, G. E. F., and Knowles, H. B., "J. Am. Chem. Soc.," 43, 1560 (1921)

a smaller aliquot should be used. When vanadium or molybdenum are present in the sample, special separations must be made in order to determine the titanium colorimetrically.

Determination of Nickel and Zinc

In the determinations of nickel and zinc there is some danger of ammonium perchlorate contaminating the precipitate, but, by adjusting the volume to above 300 ml for the zinc determination and to about 400 ml for the nickel determination, all traces of perchlorates are removed by the routine washing procedure and there is no contamination of the precipitate.

* * *

www.ingramcontent.com/pod-product-compliance
Lightning Source LLC
Chambersburg PA
CBHW050409110426
42812CB00006BA/1842